Martin Luther

Martin Luther

A Concise History of his Life & Works

John Schofield

For Charles and Jean

First published 2010

The History Press
The Mill, Brimscombe Port
Stroud, Gloucestershire, GL5 2QG
www.thehistorypress.co.uk

© John Schofield, 2010

The right of John Schofield to be identified as the Author
of this work has been asserted in accordance with the
Copyrights, Designs and Patents Act 1988.

British Library Cataloguing in Publication Data.
A catalogue record for this book is available from the British Library.

ISBN 978 0 7524 5390 3

Typesetting and origination by The History Press
Printed in India, Aegean Offset
Manufacturing managed by Jellyfish Print Solutions Ltd

Contents

List of Illustrations

Preface

*O*f making many books about Luther there seems little end, if I may plagiarise the preacher of old, and until recently it never occurred to me to add to the pile. He has a definitive modern biographer in Martin Brecht, essential reading for serious students of Luther and the Reformation. Shorter books exist as well, the best of which tend to focus on single, specific subjects, like C. Lowell Green's *How Melanchthon Helped Luther Discover the Gospel*, or David Bagchi's *Luther's Earliest Opponents*. There is much, much more on Luther in library stacks, some good but unfortunately not all, because, more than most reformers, Luther has attracted the unwelcome attentions of the over-opinionated, the moralisers and the amateur psycho-analysts.

The problem was summed up when I was asked a simple question – where do I start? The result, because I had copious notes on Luther going back to my student days, is this book. Originally sketched as a simple 'no frills' introduction for students beginning a course on the Reformation at college or university, it later developed into a short biography for a wider readership, but particularly those coming to Luther for the first time. This includes general and lay readers as well as students; indeed anyone who would like a concise but not skimpy history of the principal figure of the Reformation. The material is drawn chiefly from Luther's own writings, and it invites the reader to meet him at his study desk, in the lecture hall, in the pulpit and even at the dinner table.

Regarding terminology, the word 'evangelical' is used in its sixteenth-century sense, meaning Gospel. Terms like 'Gospel' and 'new learning' are used synonymously with the Reformation. Spellings are anglicised and modernised unless stated, and unless there is a pressing reason not to do so.

Acknowledgements

I thank firstly Reverend Ronald Englund, a former pastor of the Lutheran Church of St Anne and St Agnes in London, who, some years ago now, kindly replied to an enquiry of mine concerning Martin Luther, and helped stimulate my interest in him and the Reformation. Secondly, like everyone who has studied Luther, I owe a debt to Jaroslav Pelikan and his colleagues for their labours in producing *Luther's Works* in English. Thanks also to Newcastle University, and particularly Professor Tim Kirk of the School of Historical Studies, for accepting me as a guest member and visiting scholar, thereby allowing me to do the research for this book; and to the staff of Newcastle and Durham University libraries; and to John Cannon, Emeritus Prof. at Newcastle, for kindly reading through the manuscript and for his many helpful ideas; and to Ashgate Publishing for permission to include two short extracts from my earlier monograph *Philip Melanchthon and the English Reformation*; and to Simon Hamlet, Abigail Wood and Christine McMorris and their colleagues at The History Press for bringing this work to completion.

1

The Late Medieval World

*I*t may be useful to begin with an overview of the Western medieval Church in which Martin Luther was born and raised, because before he became its most famous reformer, he had been one of its most loyal and obedient sons.

The Church was the body of Christ on earth, the custodian of divine truth and the means of salvation, commissioned to guide the faithful on the way to heaven. The Church existed to teach the flock of Christ to foster devotion to the saints, the Sacraments, fasting, good works and all pious activities. The faith of the Church was drawn from Scripture, the early Christian Creeds, church councils and traditions, though from place to place variations existed in practice, devoutness and even, though on a limited scale, in doctrine.

Salvation was ministered through the Seven Sacraments: Baptism, the Mass, Penance, Marriage, Confirmation, Ordination and Extreme Unction. Through Baptism the newborn child was spiritually reborn to enter the kingdom of heaven, the family of God. When the child became a young adult and reached the age of understanding, he would be 'confirmed' in full membership of the Church. Marriage needs little explanation. By Ordination men were admitted to the sacred priesthood. Such men had to forego marriage and be celibate; or rather, they had to take a vow of celibacy, but how many actually kept that vow remains an unanswerable question. Penance and the Mass will get a more detailed description below. Extreme Unction, the anointing with oil taken from James 5:14, was applied to those about to depart this life and enter eternity.[1]

The medieval Mass was the Church's re-enactment of the Last Supper and Calvary. The priest recited the Words of Institution used by Jesus at the Last Supper: 'This is my Body ... This is my Blood.' After this, the consecration of the bread and wine, these elements were transformed into the Body and Blood of Christ through the miracle known as transubstantiation. The priest then lifted the sacred Host – the Body of Christ – above his head for the adoration of the faithful. He then 'offered' the sacrifice of the Mass for the salvation of souls, the living and also the departed. The priest spoke the sacred words of the service in Latin; and only he could speak them, because those who offered this holy sacrifice had to be specially consecrated, through the Sacrament of Ordination.

Communion was required annually, usually at Easter, though many, particularly the better off, communed more frequently. Normally the laity received the bread only – this was called communion in 'one kind' as distinct from communion in 'both kinds', where communicants received the wine as well. The reasons why 'one kind' had become normal in late medieval times were more practical than theological, motivated mainly by fears of the consequences of spilling the wine, the blood of the Lord. As well as imagery and artwork on the church walls and the ceilings, Mass services were accompanied by candles, ceremony and sacred music. At Corpus Christi Day the consecrated bread was carried through the streets among adoring crowds.

Forgiveness of sins was ministered by the Church through the Sacrament of Penance. The one who sinned had to confess, receive absolution from the priest and usually perform a 'satisfaction' – this would be a good work, like giving alms or fasting. Confession was a compulsory annual requirement. Sometimes a satisfaction involved making a pilgrimage to a holy site, perhaps a site with a sacred relic, offering the penitent a sort of encounter with the sacred, enabling them to share in the spiritual and contemplative life of monks and nuns in the monasteries. The penitential system consisted of confession, priestly absolution, works of satisfaction, then restoration to a state of grace. Invariably, some penalties remained outstanding at the moment of death, and these had to be atoned for in the fires of Purgatory before the soul could enter heaven.[2]

Purgatory was the unseen place to which most of those who died in the faith of the Church went. Only special saints could avoid it by going straight to heaven. It was a place of temporary but quite severe suffering, of painful purification, necessary to fully cleanse the soul before it could be admitted to enjoy heavenly bliss and rest. Belief in Purgatory was widespread, even though proving its existence from Scripture had long since been a thorny problem for the Church. The New Testament appears to offer a stark option between heaven and hell for those who depart this earthly life; but this was *too* stark for many churchmen, and consequently the belief in a third place – a sort of waiting chamber – had gradually developed. Masses and prayers for the dead, as well as good works in this life, could shorten the time that had to be spent in Purgatory, so wills of the dying requested Masses and prayers aplenty.[3]

The medieval child growing up would be taught the faith of the Church through family prayers, chants, the Lord's Prayer, the Hail Mary, the Creeds and the Ten Commandments. Children also learned about the many saints whose good works were told and retold to inspire the faithful to greater godliness and piety. Thanks to the growth in literacy and the printing press, in the late fifteenth century much of this could be read in catechisms, handbooks and primers. But medieval religion was also a distinctively visual religion, of altars, images, paintings, candles and pilgrimages, as well as the Sacraments and good works. Paintings and images of Christ, Mary and the saints adorned parish churches up and down the lands. Religious plays designed to teach and arouse devotion, mocking vice and praising virtue, and giving instruction in the Creeds were staged frequently, usually with the active support and involvement of the laity. Lay believers participated willingly in the rich liturgical cycle of the Church, with its processions, services and ritual, from Advent, Christmas, Lent, Easter and all the year round, with numerous saints' days and festival days in between.[4]

Mementos of the saints existed everywhere. The Cult of the Saints was not something imposed by dictatorial authorities; it inspired a free and genuine popular devotion among medieval people who loved images and engravings of saints, making pilgrimages to shrines in honour of them, and mentioning them in wills and donations. In parish churches saints stood under the Cross, meditating on Christ's Passion, willing to intercede for the faithful now and until the end of time. Saints were friends and helpers, benefactors and protectors, and manual labour ceased on feast days held to commemorate them. They were also appealed to for help and cure in sickness. Relics — bones and parts of the body that would be raised on the Last Day — were believed to possess healing power. Like the hem of Christ's garment, even the clothes of a saint could benefit. The main functions of the saints, however, were spiritual: to honour God; to help the children of God in their weakness in this life and at the onset of death; and to serve as an example for pious living and salvation. Mary, the Mother of Jesus, was the most adored of all the saints, and she possessed exceptional intercessory powers. The doctrine of the 'Immaculate Conception' — the belief that Mary was born untainted by original sin — was growing in late medieval times (though not formally defined until the nineteenth century).[5]

What was known as the 'treasury of merits' comprised the merits of Christ and the saints in heaven. The effect of this was that a penitent wanting to do good works to prove his contrition could 'draw' on this treasury, and maybe shorten his spell in Purgatory as well. This subject is closely linked to that of indulgences, which, because of its significance on Luther and the birth of the Reformation, will be discussed in more detail in the next chapter.

Overseeing the Western Church was the pope in Rome, the Holy Father and Vicar of Christ on earth. The pope was the successor of the apostle St Peter, and he claimed his spiritual authority from Christ's words to Peter in Matthew

16:18–19: 'And I say unto you, that you are Peter, and upon this Rock I will build my church.' The church liturgy included prayers for the pope, who in theory had no superior, though in practice his power was constrained by the need to win and retain the consent of bishops, church councils and also princes. Rome was a sacred city and a centre for pilgrimages; it was universally believed that St Peter and St Paul were martyred there around the mid AD 60s.

The papacy also had judicial power, though this was less clearly defined, and relations between the pope and Europe's kings were not always predictable. The papacy had largely recovered from the damaging schism of nearly 100 years before (1378–1417), when Western Christendom watched askance as rival popes jostled for power, threatening each other with anathemas and excommunication. During the fifteenth century, however, Europe's kings slowly began asserting themselves, particularly over matters such as papal taxes and ecclesiastical appointments. Meanwhile, Italy was being organised into five main states – Venice, Milan, Florence, Naples and the Papal States of central Italy – with the result that the papacy became one state among the others, and like them it had to protect its independence, compete and advance its influence. More and more St Peter's successors were acting like other intriguing and often warring princes.[6]

Another check on papal power was conciliarism – the idea that the authority of the whole Church, represented by a General Council comprising representatives of the whole of Christendom, was superior to that of the papacy. Naturally the popes did not approve, and ever since the Council of Constance in 1417, Rome had been seeking to reassert her authority. Pius II tried to establish papal primacy in 1460 with the bull *Execrabilis*, forbidding appeals from the pope to a council, but this produced no final papal victory, and discussions and disagreements persisted. French kings could be particularly troublesome for the papacy, habitually threatening to convene an independent council in their tussles with Rome. Conciliarism was strong in France, where some linked it directly with French liberties. Yet even in France the papacy had its supporters. In Europe as a whole in the fifteenth and early sixteenth century, despite all the popes' efforts, neither conciliarists nor papalists gained unchallenged dominion over the other. In practice, however, the papalists had the edge, and for reasons as much practical as moral: France's conciliarism, for example, meant that her enemies were likely to support the pope against her. Morally unsavoury it may have been, but the popes had little alternative to making deals with the princes, whose powers continued to grow, notably over church appointments. Though all English bishops were appointed by the papacy, they were often nominated first by the king in return for a favour from Rome. Consequently, the national church was a recognisable entity by the end of the fifteenth century, though all such churches were part of the common

Western Christian communion, and none entertained serious intentions of breaking away from Rome.[7]

How much the laity knew of the Renaissance papacy is not clear. Maybe it was not very much, and in the case of some of the popes this is probably just as well. By general consent they were notoriously corrupt. Innocent VIII (1484–92) and Alexander VI (1492–1503) shamelessly used bribery and extortion to advance their personal careers before and during their papal reigns. Alexander was also an infamous womaniser, fathering at least nine illegitimate children despite insisting on vows of celibacy from his priests.[8]

The German emperor was probably the only ruler who could have rivalled the pope in power and prestige. Charlemagne, King of the Franks from 768–814, had been crowned Roman Emperor by Pope Leo III in Rome itself. From the twelfth century his successors were known as the Holy Roman Emperors. Initially seeing themselves as the Christian heirs of the Caesars, the emperors had gradually lost interest in Italian affairs, especially when their involvement proved costly and negative. They concentrated instead on establishing their control in Central and Eastern Europe. During the fourteenth and fifteenth centuries, however, the power of the German princes, subjects of the emperor, was growing as well. As early as the diet of Rense in 1338 it was claimed that the emperor owed his authority more to the princes who elected him (the German Electors) than to the pope.[9] The significance of this development in the Reformation will be seen clearly at the end of Chapter 3.

The Western Church did not exist without dangers. From the east the Turkish Islamic power threatened Christendom, especially Hungary and the eastern Mediterranean. More immediate and internal threats were posed by heresy and heretics. A heresy was a belief contrary to an established doctrine of the Church. A heretic was someone who not only believed a false doctrine, but who persisted in it even after being apprehended and offered mercy. Implicitly, therefore, he was once orthodox and had been received into the Church through the Sacrament of Baptism. Heretics who refused to repent were handed over to the secular power, often to suffer death by fire; most medieval believers, at some time in their lives, would have seen an obstinate heretic burned at the stake.

One of the most famous heretics in late medieval Europe was the Bohemian John Huss (*c.* 1372–1415). Huss believed in the supremacy of the Bible, and he called on the clergy to show more Christ-like simplicity in their manner of life; he approved of communion in both kinds, but did not deny transubstantiation. Huss was excommunicated after opposing indulgence sales in his native Bohemia. He was summoned to the Council of Constance in 1414 with a promise of safe conduct, but this promise was not kept, and he was condemned and burned. His execution provoked rebellion and civil war in his native land. The Waldenses were another group that displeased the Church authorities, but more for disobedience than fundamental doctrinal heresies.[10]

The beginnings of the acceptable faith of the Church were the Scriptures and the ancient Creeds, but theology had not stood still since those times. During the fifteenth century there were three main 'schools' or 'ways' of theology: that of Thomas Aquinas (d.1274), Duns Scotus (d.1308) and William of Occam (d.1349). Some rivalry existed between disciples of the different schools, but at many universities adherents of all three coexisted peaceably enough. There was some overlap as well, and it was not always obvious which theologian belonged to which school. The areas of agreement easily eclipsed the differences: all agreed, for example, on the Seven Sacraments, and that salvation was impossible without divine grace. The consensus was that some human involvement and co-operation was required as well, though room was available for discussion about how much. Most theologians rejected the teaching of the fifth-century British monk Pelagius, that natural virtues alone might merit salvation. More typical was the saying of the Occamists that 'God does not deny grace to those who do what is in them'; in other words, we should do the best we can, aided by the grace of God, to love and please Him. Best efforts alone were not enough to obtain salvation, but they were an important step towards it, and received a sort of qualified value known as 'congruent merit'. Full salvation was not to be looked for outside the sacramental ministry of the Church; hence the need for the Sacraments to ensure forgiveness in this world and the next.[11]

Two huge, ancient and somewhat conflicting shadows hung over medieval churchmen and thinkers. The first was the Greek philosopher Aristotle (384–322 BC), a pupil of Plato. In the twelfth century Aristotle's works had been discovered by Western scholars, though in a somewhat elongated manner – they made Latin translations of Arabic translations of the original Greek. Aristotle was a prolific writer, whose works encompassed the sciences, medicine, philosophy, ethics and more. Being a pre-Christian pagan he had written from a rationalist perspective, and his beliefs included the eternity of the world, the mortality of the soul and that man becomes righteous by doing righteous things. Ideas such as these sat uneasily with Christian doctrines of the Creation, eternal life and salvation, and in some places his works were banned. But theologians are inventive beings, and before long some of them were using Aristotle selectively, skilfully adapting him for their own ends. Thomas Aquinas employed Aristotelian theories to prove the existence of God through reasoned arguments, not just as an act of faith. Aquinas also excused, though he did not accept, Aristotle's idea of the eternity of the world, on the grounds that neither reason nor philosophy could prove it true or false, and that the Creation was an article of faith. The dogma of transubstantiation was also based, to a considerable degree, on Aristotelian theories of substance and accidents.[12]

The second large shadow was the great church father, St Augustine (354–430), champion of Christian orthodoxy. His works enjoyed an upsurge of interest in late medieval times, even though his thinking could hardly have been more different from Aristotle's. Augustine's sermons breathe warmth, fervour and tenderness, but on paper his theology could appear chillingly bleak. He took a severe view of the Fall of mankind as told in Genesis 3, when Adam and Eve yielded to the temptation to 'be as gods' and disobeyed the true God by eating the forbidden fruit. The result was original sin, which all of mankind subsequently inherited from their first disobedient parents. According to Augustine, the effect of this was spiritually catastrophic, for it left the human mind incapable of a true knowledge of God and it seriously retarded, though did not destroy completely, man's ability to conduct himself worthily in civil and material things.

Original sin was not something invented by Augustine, of course; the whole Christian Church believed in it, and it seemed self evident that even the best men and women were full of faults as well as virtues. Augustine, however, drew conclusions which not all the Church followed. He taught that because of man's inherent sinfulness, salvation had to depend on divine grace *alone*. Human efforts were wholly unavailing, and this thinking left little room for grades of merit, free will or 'best efforts'. Gradually, Augustine developed his doctrine of the predestination of the elect – a divine decree to select certain ones for salvation before they were even born, perhaps before the foundation of the world, while leaving the rest of humanity to its deserved perdition. One leading critic of the Occamists was Gregory of Rimini (d.1358), an Augustinian scholar. He was not the only one, and a certain tension existed between those who followed Augustine and others influenced by Aristotle and the medieval 'scholastic' theologians. Yet the medieval world was diverse enough to accommodate a variety of Christian thought.[13]

Another late medieval development was the growth of humanism, though in the fifteenth century the word had none of the irreligious connotations it has today. Virtually all Renaissance humanists were Christian; and if there was a tendency in humanism to put man at the centre of the universe, no serious attempt was made to remove God or deny the dogmas of the Church.

Humanism probably began in Italy before spreading to most of Western Europe by 1500. Essentially, it was a love of things old, especially the classical Latin and Greek languages, civilisation, culture and literature. Many classical works had been preserved by medieval monks, but others, particularly Greek manuscripts, were brought into the west by eastern Christians escaping from the Turks. By this route some of the greatest works of ancient Greece came into the hands of admiring westerners; Homer and Plato, for instance, were barely known until the fourteenth and fifteenth centuries. It was believed that humanist studies would cultivate the mind and produce men of learning, virtue and eloquence. The art of rhetoric was an obvious aid to preaching, and Cicero was generally regarded as the greatest of orators. Naturally, humanism impacted on theology as well, because a study of the past entailed a renewed interest in the Church fathers and even the Bible itself in the original Hebrew and Greek languages. Humanists were neither heretics nor proto-Protestants, but many of them doubted and even scoffed at some of the more exaggerated stories of saints, relics and pilgrimages. They could also be critical of the scholastic theologians, who they felt were too speculative, irrelevant and stodgy, prone to wrangling endlessly over trifles. The feeling grew that the glory of the classical past was lost and had to be retrieved.[14]

In theory at least, humanists were closer to the scholastics than they were to Augustine, whose stern, Pauline view of man's intrinsic moral worth (or lack of it) ran somewhat counter to the humanist belief in harnessing man's potential. Humanists could amuse themselves by criticising and even mocking scholastic theology, though they did not fundamentally challenge it; nevertheless, a longing for the past often implies some degree of dissatisfaction with the present, and humanists generally disliked dogma – or at least an obsession with it – preferring instead a more simple, unpretentious Christianity to the convoluted scholastical kind. But humanism had no unique theology of its own.[15]

The papacy had not always approved of the humanist movement. Pope Martin V (1417–31) despised ancient pagan literature. Then came one of the scoops of the century, if not of the entire medieval age, when the 'Donation of Constantine' – a document in which the Emperor Constantine had allegedly committed the government of his western empire to Pope Sylvester I – was exposed as a forgery in 1440 by Lorenzo Valla, a leading humanist. Two other humanist scholars working independently agreed with Valla: Nicholas of Cusa, who later became a German cardinal, and an Englishman, Bishop Pecock. This discovery, however, did little real damage to the medieval faith. The Church did what the Church then and since has been very adept at doing – it took this potentially harmful intellectual trend on board and made good use of it. Pope Nicholas V (1447–55) was a lover of antiquity, arts and books. He decided to create a great library of classical books in Latin and Greek, and he sent envoys all over Europe to search for and bring back ancient manuscripts. This collection eventually grew into the renowned Vatican library. Nicholas also sought to restore Roman buildings in need of repair and renewal, including St Peter's. His humanist ideas were not shared by his successor, Calixtus III (1455–58), who was more concerned with recovering Constantinople from the Turks, but the remaining Renaissance popes were all patrons of art and learning.[16]

Here, then, is the late medieval world in a very brief sketch. It was an age of piety and devotion, trial and tribulation; but it was characterised also by a fascination for the past and a love of learning, at least among the privileged, educated few. The Church was united, but diverse and varied. There were outbreaks of anti-clerical feeling from time to time, and demands for reform here and there. Occasionally kings would flex their muscles and resist the will of the occupant of St Peter's see. Tensions existed between disciples of Aristotle and Augustine, between Augustinians and scholastics, and between scholastics and humanists. Nevertheless, all these diverse elements managed to coexist in this intriguing world, not always with unfeigned brotherly charity perhaps, but all seemingly safely contained under the wings of Mother Church. The Creeds, the Ten Commandments and the Seven Sacraments remained sacrosanct. As the fifteenth century drew to its close, there was no obvious warning sign of an approaching spiritual storm that would batter the Church's foundations.

But, as the Gospel says, the day of the Lord comes 'in such an hour as ye think not ...'

2

Brother Martin

*D*uring his Renaissance pontificate, Pope Sixtus IV (1471–84) greatly expanded the architectural and artistic works of his predecessor Nicholas, the most famous of all being the Sistine Chapel. The great paintings inside, however, were not just art for art's sake. Botticelli's *Punishment of Korah*, a vivid illustration of divine anger against the rebel who defied Moses the man of God, and Perugino's depiction of *Christ giving the keys to St Peter*, seemed commandingly designed to reinforce papal authority. Rather ironic, therefore, that it was during the reign of Sixtus, in November 1483 at Eisleben, that the greatest challenge the papacy had ever faced was born.[1]

From the circumstances of the birth, no one would have guessed that anything remarkable had happened. There were no accompanying signs or wonders. Neither Luther himself nor his father and mother, Hans and Margarete, were even sure of the exact date, though it is generally believed to be the 10th. The child was baptised on 11 November and given the name of the saint of that day – Martin.[2]

Luther later described how his father in his youth had been a 'poor miner'. Elsewhere he called himself the 'son of a peasant'. Obviously Hans Luther had been involved in mining and farming at different stages in his life.[3] Few details of Luther's childhood are known, though that has not prevented the psycho-analysts devising intricate theories to explain the often troubled and perplexing mind of the adult Luther. It is claimed that a brutally strict upbringing left him emotionally damaged. Others talk of an Oedipus complex with his mother. Occasionally Freud is wheeled out to help penetrate Luther's psyche. None of this is of much use in understanding Luther or the Reformation. Even if this sort of psychology has any value at all (which is debateable), far more facts than are available would be needed to make a sensible judgement. The little that is known points to a strict, somewhat

Martin Luther. (*Author's Collection*)

Spartan, but also close and loving home; in other words, it was fairly normal for the times.

Luther always spoke of his parents generously, kindly and even reverentially. When he told guests at the dinner table one day that his mother once whipped him soundly 'for the sake of a mere nut' (no more details are given) he was not whinging or feeling sorry for himself. Most of his friends could relate similar stories. Philip Melanchthon, Luther's chief ally and co-worker, once recalled that his Latin tutor 'applied the rod' every time he made a mistake. Philip was not complaining either: 'this way he made me a linguist … he was a good man.' Such was life in those days.[4]

Luther paid grateful tribute to the memory of his father by recalling the sacrifices he had had to make to finance his son's education. At school in Magdeburg and Eisenach young Martin learned grammar, Latin, rhetoric and logic, as well as the Creed and the Lord's Prayer. He started his university career at Erfurt in 1501, the principal city of the Thuringian basin, where he read, among other things, philosophy, logic and law, and obtained his Master's degree four years later. But the young Luther's soul was troubled by spiritual trials, and soon he began to study the Bible with ever increasing earnestness. Then, one day in June 1505, he visited his parents in Mansfeld. On his way back to Erfurt on Wednesday 2 July – the day of Mary's visitation – Luther was caught in a violent thunderstorm and nearly killed by a bolt of lightning. With a heart full of fear he appealed for help to St Anne, mother of Mary, and vowed to become a monk. Luther likened this experience to St Paul's on the Damascus road. Entreaties from parents and friends failed to dissuade him, for he was convinced that this was his divine calling, necessary for the very salvation of his soul.[5]

Hans Luther was a disappointed man, for he had been desirous of an honourable marriage for his son. Luther would later tell his students how his father 'despised the monks and the sacerdotal and papal masks' and when fellow monks chided him for this irreverence and praised the monastic order, Hans replied that they should have respect for the commandment to honour thy father and mother.[6]

The order of Augustinian Hermits had been established by a papal decree issued by Pope Alexander IV in the thirteenth century. Luther never explained why he chose this order above the others in Erfurt, though he did later liken himself to quicksilver that God had cast among the monks. There is no evidence at this stage that Luther was especially attracted to the theology of St Augustine.[7]

At Erfurt, Luther was introduced to humanism, though this did not significantly affect his future as a reformer of the Church. Luther made use of humanism without ever being devoted to it; but he appreciated learning and the arts, and he was appalled to hear, in 1513, that John Reuchlin, the renowned humanist and Hebrew scholar, might be put on trial by the Inquisition for his love of Jewish literature. Luther welcomed the publication of the Greek New Testament of Desiderius Erasmus, the great Dutch scholar, though the term Erasmian hardly fits Luther even at this stage in his life.[8]

We are now in the pontifical reign of Julius II (1503–13). Raphael was beautifying the new papal apartments, Julius himself laid the foundation stone of the new St Peter's church, originally conceived by Nicholas V, and Julius also commissioned and cajoled Michelangelo to paint the ceiling of the Sistine Chapel. One of the many visitors to Rome, in the winter of 1510, was Brother Martin, as part of a delegation on a matter of church politics. Luther made the visit a pilgrimage, visiting the seven main churches in one day; the itinerary began with St Paul-outside-the-Walls, burial place of St Paul, and then on to St Sebastian on the Appian way, St John Lateran, Holy Cross, St Lawrence-outside-the-Walls, St Mary Major, before climaxing with Mass at St Peter's. He saw the catacombs and accepted, unquestioningly, the pious legends of the saints and martyrs. But he was also shocked by the 'great and shameless godlessness and wickedness there' (this is the later Luther reminiscing). His main aim when he left Germany for Rome was to confess all his sins 'from my youth up and become pious'; instead he returned home sadly disillusioned.[9]

Soon after he was back in Germany he was transferred permanently to Wittenberg, capital of electoral Saxony, where he became preacher of the Wittenberg monastery. In 1512 he earned his Doctor of Theology degree. Elector Frederick the Wise of Saxony, one of the seven electors of the Holy Roman Empire, obligingly paid the graduation expenses. Before the degree was awarded, the candidate had to solemnly swear obedience to the Church and to renounce all heresies. Luther probably began his lecturing at the university in the winter term of 1513/14, on the Psalms and St Paul's epistles to the Romans and Galatians.[10]

As a monk, Brother Martin was almost embarrassingly devout. If he was busy with lectures, he would let his prescribed prayers accumulate and then 'take a Saturday off, or shut myself in for as long as three days without food and drink' until he had worked his way through the backlog of prayers. He told friends that he nearly 'fasted myself to death'. With all solemnity he made his vows to renounce the will, mortify the flesh through fasting, vigils and prayers, and to keep the rules of the order scrupulously. Soon he had learned the Psalter by heart. Regular confession was compulsory for monks, but Brother Martin surpassed all of them in piety. One of his confessions reportedly went on for six hours. Yet, despite all his striving for godliness, his spiritual trials, known as his *Anfechtung*, were becoming ever more acute. He knew that the priest was supposed to be pure before celebrating Mass, but within himself Luther did not

Luther's house at Wittenberg, the Black Cloister. (*Author's Collection*)

feel pure. He longed for the assurance of the forgiveness of sins and righteousness; but that assurance eluded him. The Sacrament and the presence of Christ
on the altar terrified him. At his first Mass, he confessed, 'when I stood before
the altar and was to consecrate, I was so terrified by the words *aeterno vivo vero
Deo* (to thee, the eternal, living and true God) that I thought of running away'.
Luther saw in Christ the face of a stern judge; and when he contemplated the
Crucifixion he beheld not the 'wondrous cross' of a later hymn with its saving
grace and redeeming love, but a terrible portent of divine judgement awaiting
the sinner. 'Christ was generally feared', he would say. 'We fled from Him and
took refuge in the saints … Christ was the executioner, while the saints were
our mediators.' He was vexed by gnawing doubts about his salvation: how
could he be sure that he was really saved; were his good works good enough;
was he predestined to be among the elect or not.[11]

These were his agonies that 'no tongue could adequately express', the sheer
horror of divine wrath. Luther felt 'no flight, no comfort, within or without';
he feared his redemption was impossible. A superior in the order, Johann von
Staupitz, tried to help him see Christ as a suffering, sympathetic Saviour and to
banish morbid fears over election. Luther also sought relief in Mary by reading
the works of Bernard of Clairvaux, and by meditating on an image known
as the 'Stairway of Salvation'. Here God is seated as judge, and before him

Christ shows his wounds; yet God is unyielding. But another is present: Mary is kneeling to Christ, baring the breast that suckled Him. Mary is the refuge for troubled souls, as comforting and gracious as Christ is forbidding.[12]

These, however, were not his only memories of the monastery. For many of his brethren, he would say, it was a 'soft kind of life, free from all the innumerable annoyances of civil government and domestic affairs; yet it was a prison to all good men who did not think simply of their bellies but longed for salvation'. Here may be a clue to understanding the *Anfechtung*, at least in some measure. Luther was trying desperately hard for salvation and he realised he was coming short, while others around him were cheerily untroubled about such things. At Erfurt, while he was fasting and praying mercilessly to make himself pure, he remembered that 'the concubines of priests were held in honour'.[13]

As a monk, Luther had to read the medieval scholastic theologians, but unlike many of his brethren, he diligently read his Bible, and it made his heart aglow. Before lecturing on Scripture he would read, study and meditate long on the selected text. His *Anfechtung* enabled him to empathise, as few others could, with the soul exercises and entreaties of the Psalms. The result was a somewhat gloomy theology, with a heavy emphasis on man's incurable sin and the impossibility of overcoming it by good works, by now very much in the tradition of Augustine. Luther was moving away from the general medieval consensus that human beings can make some contribution, albeit a secondary one, to their salvation. There is much in his works around this time on the so-called 'theology of humility' – the need for humility in accepting God's verdict that all have sinned, and how love should suffer passively in self-surrender to God. There are also glimpses of the later Protestant reformer, though somewhat obscurely expressed, of Christ as the believer's righteousness and salvation. For the time being, however, the emphasis is on sin and the need for humility and repentance; on the prerequisites for grace rather than the gift of grace itself.[14]

Luther was also becoming more critical of the medieval Church and its piety. He castigated the half-heartedness he saw around him, and complained that too much monastic life was inwardly dead, given more to indolence and luxury than to love and suffering. Like some humanists, Luther began to disapprove of excessive devotion or veneration of the saints. He suggested that the secular powers might administer church property. His criticism of clerical laxness, however, was born of a zeal for the purity of the Church, not a rejection of it. Luther wanted nothing to do with separatists like the Bohemians. Nor did he wish for the overthrow of the Cult of the Saints; rather, he sought to direct the hearts of his parishioners more to Christ. He also, though to a lesser extent, spoke out against the greed and pride of rulers and the unjust wars waged throughout Christendom.[15]

By now (1516), Luther had tired of Aristotle and the medieval scholastic theologians with their theories about free will and 'best efforts'. One of them, Gabriel Biel, Luther likened to Pelagius, a charge which provoked a lively reaction from his associates in Erfurt. Luther persuaded Wittenberg colleagues like Andreas Bodenstein von Karlstadt and Nicholas Amsdorf to do as he was doing and lay aside the scholastics and to read Augustine instead. Also about this time, Luther urged a fellow friar to let his soul be 'tired of its own right-eousness' and be 'revived by and trust in the righteousness of Christ'. Here are the first fruits of something that would soon develop in a way that Luther hardly dreamed of at the time. One reason Luther did not further these ideas just yet may be that something more pressing was occupying him – a looming crisis over indulgences.[16]

As discussed in the first chapter, as part of the medieval penitential cycle, anyone who sinned and repented would be received back into full fellowship of the Church after performing acts of penance, sometimes called 'satisfactions', prescribed by the Church. They might also expect some temporal punish-ment for their sins. Examples of satisfactions included giving alms, good works and prayers. If the penance remained incomplete when the penitent died, then a concentrated dose of purification treatment awaited him in Purgatory. An indulgence could reduce, not only the penitential acts prescribed by the Church, but also the temporal punishment and even the pains of Purgatory as well. The pope had authority over indulgences because he dispensed the Church's 'treasury of merit' – the excess merits of Christ and the saints which those doing penance could draw upon if need be. Only the pope could grant a plenary (full) indulgence, though bishops and cardinals could grant more lim-ited ones. Naturally, certain requirements had to be met before an indulgence could be granted: the penitent was expected to be contrite, to say prayers and attend Mass, maybe perform a devotional act like a pilgrimage, or give alms. However, and this was becoming increasingly common, he could also make a payment. Over the years indulgences had become a business and a lucrative source of income; church buildings and crusades were financed by them. But complaints about abuses were growing as well.[17]

In 1515 Pope Leo X issued a plenary indulgence designed to fund the new, extravagant St Peter's basilica in Rome. The previous year, the 24-year-old Albrecht of Brandenburg had been elected Archbishop of Mainz and primate of Germany, largely because of his connections and influence in ruling circles. He was the third occupant of that see, now heavily in debt, in ten years. This appointment was problematic in two ways. Not only was Albrecht officially too young for episcopal office, he was also Archbishop of Magdeburg and administrator of the diocese of Halberstadt, and multiple offices were forbid-den under ecclesiastical law. These difficulties could be overcome by a papal dispensation and a suitable fee – which in this case was 21,000 ducats. The Fuggers banking house in Germany then put up the money and negotiated the deal, under which Albrecht would permit the sale of St Peter's indulgences in his church provinces, and the proceeds would be shared between Rome and Fuggers. This way the pope would get the money for his cathedral and Fuggers would be handsomely repaid for its loan. The expected profit was a princely 52,286 ducats. An exact conversion of ducats into sterling or euros may be impracticable, but some idea of the money involved in contemporary currency is possible from the fact that the annual salary of a country priest in the early sixteenth century was about 25 ducats. Supposing, therefore, that the salary of a modern vicar was £30,000 per annum, then the papal dispensation and the anticipated profit would amount to around 25 and 60 million pounds sterling respectively. A comparable modern building would undoubtedly cost a lot more than this, but in the sixteenth century, not only were labour costs far cheaper, but much less had to be paid on lawyers, accountants, layers of management and various levels of officialdom.[18]

By 1517 the indulgence traffic was thriving, backed up by a sustained campaign of preaching and propaganda. Indulgence preachers, confessors and sub-commissioners were appointed, and the Dominican John Tetzel was made general sub-commissioner. Remission was promised for almost all kinds of sins, and monetary payments were specified for all classes of people from kings to nobles, merchants and townsfolk. All sermons had to preach the indulgence message, and all other indulgences were suspended in favour of this one. Week after week, people were bombarded with promises like 'whoever has an indulgence has salvation', and appeals to 'have mercy on your dead parents' (preachers were promising their congregations that souls in Purgatory could escape their torments when a payment was made). Tetzel carried out his duties zealously and was handsomely paid for doing so.[19]

The whole thing was a racket, but while some were offended, many were persuaded. Because Frederick the Wise, ruler of electoral Saxony, refused to allow the sale of indulgences in his territory, citizens of Wittenberg rushed across to Jüterbog in the territory of the Archbishopric of Magdeburg to get an indulgence letter there, and then returned home expecting Luther to absolve them without bothering to do much penance or improve their lives in any significant way. Luther was not aware until later of the business details negotiated between Albrecht, Fuggers and the papacy, which may have been just as well. For the time being, Luther was more concerned with the theological aspect of indulgences. He objected to them because they cheapened grace and made people fear the punishment for sin, but not the sin itself. Real repentance should be life-long, Luther believed, not something negotiable by a payment. Luther was not yet opposing indulgences on principle, and he still

Frederick the Wise, Elector of Saxony, 1524, after an etching by Albrecht Dürer. (*Author's Collection*)

clung to the general medieval view that they were gifts obtained through the merits of Christ and the saints. But they were of value only to those who were truly contrite in spirit, and this presented Luther with a quandary, because he thought that those who were truly sorry for their sins would neither need nor seek an indulgence, and should be prepared to suffer humbly and penitently. What, therefore, was the point of an indulgence at all? People expected an indulgence to guarantee them automatic entry into heaven, but indulgences neither removed the sinful nature of man nor increased love and virtue.[20]

So here was the dilemma. Luther could not – yet – condemn indulgences outright because he was still a good, pious, conscientious monk. But in this stage of his career he was preoccupied with human sin, God's holiness and the need for suffering and humility in repentance; and indulgences were making penance and salvation scandalously easy. So Luther wrote a devout letter to Albrecht on 31 October 1517. In it he expressed his fears that the people had a wholly wrong understanding of indulgences, and were abusing them and taking penance too casually. He humbly asked Albrecht to rescind the indulgence instructions issued under his name, diplomatically but naively assuming that they had been drawn up and sent out without his knowledge. The letter contained not a word of criticism of the pope, but attached to it were ninety-five theses.[21]

A brief summary of the relevant points of these theses is as follows. Luther still believed in the authority of the pope, though the pope may only remit penalties imposed by him or the penitential canons. The state of souls in Purgatory is uncertain. Luther did not condemn the principle of indulgences, but he distrusted them and sought to limit their power to penalties stipulated during confession. Without true contrition they were worthless, and true contrition would obtain remission of sins without an indulgence. Works of love and mercy were always superior to indulgences. True contrition does not seek instant, painless absolution, but is prepared to suffer and be humbled. Anyone who buys an indulgence when he could have given the money to the poor or done some other charitable deed risks the wrath of God. Luther completely absolved the pope of any abuse of indulgences. When he grants indulgences, the pope really seeks prayer rather than money. If only the pope knew what mischief the indulgence preachers were up to, he would raze St Peter's to the ground rather than fleece the flock of Christ for his extravagant buildings. Those who try to preach indulgences instead of the Gospel are enemies of both Christ and the pope. Indulgences distract from the true Gospel message of the Cross and contrition. Still a loyal monk, Luther was doing all he could to protect the pope personally from charges of corruption and greed.[22]

According to tradition, the theses were posted on the door of the castle and university church in Wittenberg on 31 October 1517, the Feast of All Saints.

This is the commonly accepted date of the birth of the Reformation. Not that it matters a great deal, but there has been some debate about whether this is really accurate.[23] Far more important is the fact that the Ninety-Five Theses were *not* a Protestant document. There is nothing here about justification by faith alone. Nor was any attack on the papacy intended. Luther discusses only the extent of the pope's spiritual authority; he does not question the authority itself. In 1517 Luther might be called a Catholic dissident or dissenter, but he was not yet a Protestant.

Reaction to his letter and his theses varied. Tetzel wished he could see Luther burned, and John Eck, the prominent Ingolstadt theologian, published a rebuttal denouncing Luther as a Bohemian and a heretic. News of the affair soon reached Rome, but the papacy was not greatly concerned at first, and it was felt that the Luther affair should be dealt with through his own Augustinian order. At home, Luther continued to enjoy the patronage of his prince, Elector Frederick the Wise, and the support of colleagues and students. For the time being, the dissident was safe.[24]

3

The Reformation Discovery: Here I Stand

*L*uther's little study room in the old Augustinian monastery in Wittenberg was the place from which, as he put it, he 'stormed the papacy'. It was on the second floor, in a tower-like extension to the main building. By chance, it was not far away from the communal lavatory facilities. This purely coincidental proximity has given rise to one of the most far-fetched stories in Church history, according to which Luther's Reformation discovery came just before or during a welcome and abundant release from a long period of constipation.[1]

Luther's 'Tower experience' is the transition he made from the Catholic dissident to the Protestant reformer. The crucial turning point was Romans 1:17: 'For in the Gospel a righteousness from God is revealed, and righteousness that is by faith.' Until now Luther had understood the righteousness of God as a divine judgement on sin, and no one was more conscious of their sin than Luther. However, 'after meditating day and night' on St Paul's text, Luther's understanding went through a dramatic change. God's righteousness was no longer judgemental: instead it becomes ours through grace, as a gift, received by faith alone, whereby believers are declared righteous and justified in the sight of God; hence the theological term 'justification'. God pardons the sinner not just because He is kind and loving, though He is both; God forgives because He is also entirely righteous to do so. Christ the Saviour has borne the wrath and penalty of a holy God on human sin, so God has an entirely righteous basis to grant forgiveness to all who believe. Righteousness, therefore, is *imputed*, and for Christ's sake; it is not in any sense dependent on works or merits. This forgiveness is received by faith, for the 'just shall live by faith', not by 'observing the works of the Law' (Romans 3:28). If the works of the God-given Law cannot justify, then no works of any kind can, certainly not the pope's indulgences or satisfactions. With his new insight into the grace rather than the stern wrath of God, Luther felt 'I was altogether born again, and had entered paradise itself through open gates'.[2]

According to Luther's personal testimony, this breakthrough occurred sometime during the period 1518–19.[3] Less certain is the exact date, if indeed there was a single, precise date. The main events of this period are these.

Because Rome tried first to deal with Luther through his own order, in April 1518 a debate among the Augustinians took place at Heidelberg. Luther avoided the subject of indulgences, and concentrated on asserting Paul and Augustine over scholasticism in a series of theses presented for discussion. He rejected works as a way of salvation; even the works of Christians are very imperfect. True theology looks to suffering and the Cross, not to works or achievements (this theme has become commonly known as the 'Theology of the Cross'). Free will was also rejected. But Luther was still tied to the theology of humility; and the function of the Law was to lead to the knowledge of sin, which produces humility, by which man obtains divine grace. The emphasis on humility suggests that the Reformation discovery had either not happened yet or was not fully developed. In the closing theses, however, Luther has a passage on how righteousness is attained through faith in Christ, and that works are a result of faith.[4]

In August, Luther received his summons to Rome on suspicion of heresy. In October, he defended himself at Augsburg before the papal legate Cardinal Cajetan. Justification and righteousness were discussed, but this time indulgences and papal authority took up most of the time. There was no agreement and the result was stalemate, with Luther refusing the demand to recant. Shortly after this Luther thought he might appeal to a General Council of the Church.[5]

In March 1519 Luther could say that the 'pure theology of Christ is triumphing over the opinions of men', but he was still writing fairly respectfully about Pope Leo X, and condemning those who 'prostitute the name of the supreme pontiff and take it in vain'.[6]

At the Leipzig debate with John Eck (27 June – 3 July 1519) Luther included a short piece on justification by faith alone without elaborating much (thesis 7), but he was still saying that the 'merit of Christ is the treasure of the church, and that this treasure is enhanced by the merits of the saints' (thesis 10). The chief point at issue was once again papal authority and jurisdiction. Luther's main argument was that papal primacy, as practised and understood in his times, was contrary to Scripture, to the earliest and finest councils of the Church, such as Nicea, and to the first thousand years of Church history. Eck countered with the claim that Christ would never have left his church wallowing in error and deception for the past 400 years. They also debated the relevant Bible texts: Matthew 16:18–19 and John 21:15 ('Upon this rock I will

Charles V, Holy Roman Emperor, after the painting by Titian, engraved by Rubens. (*Author's Collection*)

build my church'). Luther argued that the rock signified either Christ or the faith in Christ that Peter confessed; it was not the foundation of the papacy. (He was not the first to say this, and he could claim support from the Church fathers.) The papacy is a human institution, not a divine one. Christ never made the pope head of the Church universal. Luther cited the Greek Church, which is neither heretical nor schismatic, but nor is it under the dominion of Rome. At this stage, Luther was willing to regard the pope as chief pastor of the Western Church; he was not leading a breakaway movement.[7]

Probably the most crucial work of the period is his sermon on *Two Kinds of Righteousness*. The first kind is the righteousness of Christ which is given, or imputed, to the believer. 'Through faith in Christ, therefore, Christ's righteousness becomes our righteousness, and all that He has becomes ours; rather, He Himself becomes ours.' The second kind is the 'product of the righteousness of the first type, actually its fruit and consequence'; in other words, the good works of the justified believer, like charity and love thy neighbour.[8]

This sermon is the Reformation breakthrough in a nutshell. It was based on Philippians 2:5–6, and Brecht dates it to Palm Sunday, March 1518. However, according to the editor of the Weimar edition of *Luther's Works*, the date was more likely the following year, 1519. Others, like Lowell Green, who have examined the subject closely also prefer early 1519.[9] This difficulty over the exact dating is not terribly important; it seems likely that, rather than a single flash of inspiration, the new theology developed and matured over the period 1518–19. Certainly, by 1520 overtly Protestant works were pouring off the Wittenberg printing presses.

Luther's *Treatise on Good Works* was completed in May 1520.[10] Typically for a man who liked to get to the root of the matter, Luther begins by defining a good work – it is something God has commanded. The highest good work is to believe in Christ (John 6:28–9). Monastic works are not commanded and bring no peace to the soul. 'All these works go on apart from faith; therefore they amount to nothing and are absolutely dead.' Because the just shall live by faith, real good works *follow* faith, and God 'is served by all things that may be done, spoken or thought in faith'. A Christian who works conscientiously at his job and enjoys life with his wife and children is far more pleasing to God than monks and friars with all their affected piety, even though in the monasteries they despise such humble everyday things.

Luther is not teaching perfectionism here or anywhere else. His point is to mark out real good works from fakes. A good work, even when done well, is still a 'venial sin', and a 'righteous man sins in all his good works'.[11] Good works of true Christians are flawed in the sense that along with the good there is invariably some self-seeking as well, so ingrained is the old Adam in all of us. The worst works are those that men have devised, like indulgences or papal satisfactions, by which they presume to make themselves righteous. The *Treatise* then develops into a short, evangelical commentary on the Ten Commandments; the main point is that only by faith can God be truly loved and his name hallowed.

To the Christian Nobility of the German Nation was completed in June and published in August.[12] It was a clarion call to the newly crowned Emperor Charles V and the German princes to curb papal power and begin reforming the Church. On the basis of 1 Peter 2:9 ('Ye are a royal priesthood, a holy nation') Luther argued that all believers were priests; ministers were overseers, selected for their ability and godliness, but possessing no special powers. Rome's 'indelible mark' is a human invention. This doctrine, known also as the 'universal priesthood', was spiritual dynamite because the medieval religion was intrinsically a sacerdotal religion; only the specially consecrated priest, for example, could offer the holy sacrifice of the Mass.

Temporal power, Luther went on, is a divine ordinance, as the apostles Peter and Paul say (Romans 13:1–4; 1 Peter 2:13). Therefore, let the rulers do their duty to punish the wicked and reward the good without fear or favour, 'whether it affects pope, bishops, priests, monks, nuns, or anyone else'. The idea that only the pope may interpret Scripture is a 'fable'. The power of the keys – that foundation of papal authority based on Matthew 16:18 – belonged to the entire Church, not exclusively to the pope, who should be just as subject to church discipline as anyone else. Nor is the calling of a church council in the hands of the pope alone: in Acts 15 the Jerusalem Council was called by the apostles and elders, not by Peter, while the Emperor Constantine, not the bishop of Rome, summoned the Council of Nicea. These were the most Christian councils of all.

Luther then condemns the wealth and worldly ostentation of the papacy, such that 'neither king nor emperor can equal or approach him … he wears a Triple Crown, whereas the highest monarchs wear but one'. And 'of what use to Christendom are those people called cardinals?' They too live in wealth, but they have bled Italy dry and will do the same to Germany. Rome is full of parasites; 'there are more than three thousand papal secretaries alone', plus countless other officials, 'all lying in wait for the endowments and beneficies of Germany as wolves lie in wait for the sheep'. They all think the Germans 'will just keep handing over money to them'. Rulers and princes should no longer hold the clergy in some kind of awe. Germany should stop paying annates as well as indulgences to Rome. Princes should restore church property, beneficies and privileges claimed or sequestered by the 'Romanist See of avarice and robbery'.

Now he gives detailed practical advice. Temporal matters should no longer be referred to Rome. German priests can pronounce absolution. The pope should have no authority over the emperor except to anoint him at his coronation. The kissing of the pope's feet should stop. However, Luther was still not calling for the papacy to be abolished, though he strongly attacked its unchristian pomp and power.

Much of the rest of the work reads like an evangelical petition. Pilgrimages to Rome are useless and it would be best to do away with them, though Luther would not insist on this absolutely. No new religious orders should be founded. Priests should be allowed to marry because compulsory priestly celibacy was contrary to Scripture. Masses for the dead should be abolished or severely reduced in number; 'their only purpose is money-grubbing gluttony and drunkenness'. Luther wanted further restrictions on feast days, canonising of saints and penalties of excommunication. Fasts should be voluntary. Begging should be prohibited because it gives rise only to insincere almsgiving; instead, every city should care for its own poor and charitable gifts should be collected in the church and distributed to them as need be. (A common chest was established in Wittenberg in the early 1520s to support pastors, maintain church buildings and provide for the elderly, the poor and orphans.[13]) The universities should throw Aristotle and canon law out and replace them with Scripture and the study of the sacred languages. Education should be made available for the young, including girls. Finally, Luther appealed to princes to bring about moral improvement. Among the vices Luther disliked were ostentatious dress, gluttony, drunkenness, immorality, brothels, greed and profiteering in commerce, and especially *zynskauf*, the lucrative money lending and charging of interest practised by Fuggers and similar companies.

Such dissent could be overlooked no longer. Already Rome, well briefed by Eck on the Leipzig debate, began to take a sterner line against Luther. The bull of excommunication was prepared, *Exsurge Domine*, taken from Psalm 74:22: 'Arise O Lord, plead thy cause.' It was published on 15 June, along with an order to burn Luther's books. Luther was given sixty days to recant. The bull condemned him for his opinions on penance, original sin, confession, the Sacraments, free will and papal authority as well as indulgences, but, strangely, contained nothing specific on justification by faith. The Emperor Charles V supported the bull, and issued his first mandate for the burning of Luther's books in his Dutch territories. Luther now had the pope and the emperor against him, but the ranks of his supporters were swelling alarmingly. Crucially, Rome failed to persuade Elector Frederick to act against Luther. Erasmus, his hitherto sharp wit blunted by the growing crisis, now took the moderate middle ground, opposing both Luther's aggressive attacks on the Church and the burning of his books. Book-burning ceremonies proliferated but sometimes backfired, meeting with unexpected resistance. The papal nuncio Jerome Aleander received threats on a visit to Mainz. As one anonymous writer aptly

THOMAS
WOLSEY
Cardinall,
Archbishope
of Yorke, and
Chaunceloure
of England.
Died Nou:29
1529.

Non secus vndâ mari paulatim accrescit et alta
Neptuni frontem supereminet; at sua tandem
Vis ruit, et pelago labens deuoluitur imo,
Quam tua te VUOLSEDE tumens evexit honoris
Aura, et sublimen super—extulit ardua regis.
Culmina, sed tandem conuerso CARDINE rerum,
In scopulos, rigidasqs extrusa est gloria syrtes.
Terra olim corpus, tumuit, iam corpore tellus.

Cardinal Wolsey, who ordered the burning of Luther's books. Luther called him a 'slimy sophist'. (*THP Archive*) put it, taking Luther out of the libraries is easy, but removing him from men's hearts without convincingly answering him is less so.[14]

In September, Luther sent an open letter to Pope Leo X, addressing him as 'most blessed father', but condemning the 'godless flatterers' surrounding him. He defended his writings and teachings, and appealed for a fair hearing; but warned that 'I have neither the power nor the will to deny the Word of God'. The Roman Curia was now 'more corrupt than any Babylon or Sodom ever was', but Luther still had hopes for Leo personally, whose character made him 'worthy of being pope in better days' than these.[15]

Along with the open letter, Luther sent Leo his newest work, the *Freedom of a Christian*.[16] It begins with the two 'propositions' on freedom and servitude, adapted from St Paul (1 Corinthians 9:19). 'A Christian is perfectly free, lord of all, subject to none. A Christian is perfectly dutiful, servant of all, subject to all.' Here, employing the sort of arresting contrasts that he loved doing, Luther is exploring the theme of real, inward, spiritual liberty. It does nothing for the soul if the body is well, otherwise the most godless men of all are among the blessed; but physical afflictions do no harm to the soul. Spiritual blessing comes from the Word of God; hence 'man shall not live by bread alone, but by every word that proceeds from the mouth of God'. And the Word 'cannot be received and cherished by any works whatever, but only by faith'. Therefore, the soul is justified by faith alone. So the Christian must abandon all hope in works. No greater honour can be given to anyone than to trust him, and the one who trusts entirely in God's promises of salvation confesses that He is righteous and true, and thus renders Him the 'highest worship'. This is the true hallowing of His name.

Moreover, faith unites the soul with Christ, as a bride with a bridegroom. All that he has is hers. So Christ the Saviour marries his church, 'this poor, wicked harlot', and out of love for her He 'redeems her from all evil and adorns her with all His goodness … and she has that righteousness, in Christ, of which she may boast as her own'.

The apostles say that all believers are 'priests and kings in Christ' (1 Peter 2:9) and that all things work together for the good of those who love God (Romans 8:28). But this power and liberty is spiritual, just as redemption is spiritual. This is the inner, true life. Outwardly, the Christian lives in the world, is part of society and must do all kinds of things, but these civil works do not justify before God. What the believer does, he does willingly, out of gratitude, love and obedience to God. Luther illustrates his meaning by everyday examples: 'Good works do not make a good man, but a good man does good works.' As Christ says: 'A good tree cannot bear evil fruit' (Matthew 7:8). Common observation confirms this: 'a good house or a bad house does not make a good or bad builder; but a good or bad builder makes a good or bad house.' In other words, faith comes first, and good works follow as a consequence.

So the true Christian life becomes one of service, 'each caring for and working for the other'. The Christian's freedom is to serve others and 'devote all our works to the welfare of others'. This is the glory of the Christian life. 'It is lord over sin, death and hell, and yet at the same time it serves, ministers to and benefits all men.' Alas, says Luther, 'in our day this life is unknown … we are taught by the doctrine of men to seek nothing but merits, rewards and the things that are ours'. Luther appeals to all to turn away from this. The true Christian lives by faith and love. 'By faith he is caught up beyond himself into God. By love he descends beneath himself to his neighbour.'

Luther then warns against what would soon be known as 'antinomianism', the idea that justification by faith alone means freedom from all responsibility, duty and works. Not so: 'Our faith in Christ does not free us from works, but from false opinions concerning works.' The Christian takes a middle course between these people and others who are slaves to ceremonials and works as a means of justification.

By now, Luther's controversy with Rome was far more than an attack on abuses or excessive clerical power, and his thrusts went far deeper than those of Huss or any other dissident in times past. The whole Roman system struck him as a false, corrupted Christianity. In the *Babylonian Captivity of the Church*, which first appeared in October 1520, Luther sees the Church in thraldom under the papacy, like the children of Israel captive in Babylon. Here he goes for the jugular of the medieval faith – the Seven Sacraments.[17]

He starts with the Eucharist, and attacks communion in 'one kind' only; denying the cup to the laity was 'tyrannical' and forbidden by the Words of Institution ('drink ye all of it'). Luther quotes St Paul against transubstantiation (1 Corinthians 11:27: 'who eats this bread or drinks this cup'). Luther, however, does believe in a sacramental union of the bread and wine with the body and blood of Christ, rather like a red-hot iron where the fire and iron are so mixed that every part is *both* fire and iron. More grievous is the medieval moral doctrine that the Mass is a sacrifice offered to God by the priest. From the Words of Institution – 'This is my body, this is my blood, given for remission of sins' – the Mass is a *promise* of grace and forgiveness to be received by faith, not a *sacrifice* to be offered to God. A sacrifice is a *work* done by men, so the Roman Mass is a denial of justification by *faith*, and the 'worst of all evils' in the Church, spawning numerous abuses for 'financial gain and filthy lucre for ungodly priests and monks'.

Luther is milder on Baptism, recognising that this is at least rightly administered in the Roman Church. Penance is a subject Luther knew well from his own monastic days, and he rejected the medieval requirement that all sins must be confessed as intolerable and impossible. As the Psalmist said, 'Who can understand his errors? Cleanse thou me from *secret* faults' (Psalm 19:12). The satisfactions that priests imposed for sins are worthless; true satisfaction is a renewal of life. Absolution is the crucial point, because forgiveness of sins comes by faith in the promise of forgiveness, not by endless satisfactions. (Again, this is justification by faith applied to the Sacraments.)

Luther defines a Sacrament as a divine institution offering grace, forgiveness and salvation. Therefore, Confirmation, Marriage, Ordination and Extreme Unction do not qualify as Sacraments. Praiseworthy though they are, no promise of salvation comes with them. Marriage was instituted of God for the present life; it does not offer the grace of eternal life. Ordination is a good church tradition, but it confers no indelible mark on priests, whose calling is to proclaim the Gospel, not to offer the Mass. Scripture allows priests to marry if they wish; this is a matter of Christian liberty. The rite of Unction in the ancient Church was a prayer for the sick, not a Sacrament for the dying (James 5:14–15). Luther closes by restating the primacy of Scripture; and neither the Church, nor popes nor councils may establish articles of faith not contained in Scripture.

On 10 December, sixty days after the bull of excommunication had been received in Wittenberg, Philip Melanchthon posted a notice on the wall of the city church. Another book-burning ceremony was planned, but this one involved books on papal law and scholastic theology. That evening at 9 o'clock, canon law and the scholastics went up in flames. Luther then threw a copy of the papal bull onto the fire, paraphrasing Psalm 21:9 as he did so: 'Because you have confounded the truth of God, today the Lord confounds you: Into the fire with you.'[18]

Luther was now formally a heretic and an excommunicate, and for some time papal nuncios Aleander and Caracciolo had been pressing Charles to place him under the imperial ban. They were opposed by Frederick the Wise, Luther's prince, who interceded for Luther and suggested that his case should be heard independently in the presence of reputable scholars. The emperor, though a loyal Catholic, was aware of the growing public demand for some reform of the Church, and consequently he declined to bow to papal pressure. After considerable political manoeuvring, Charles issued Luther with a summons and a promise of safe conduct to Worms.[19]

The diet of Worms was the first to be convened in Charles's reign. Originally it was intended to address matters concerning the government of the empire, the peace and policing of the realm, economic and foreign policy, and the emperor's forthcoming visit to Rome. The name Luther was not added to the agenda until the controversy surrounding him and his writings had reached the point when it could no longer be ignored. Luther had already appealed to the emperor for a fair hearing, giving his own version of his case.[20]

Erasmus, by Hans Holbein. (*Author's Collection*)

Luther began his journey in April, with Justus Jonas and Amsdorf among his travelling companions. Melanchthon had wanted to go too, but teaching commitments compelled him to stay in Wittenberg. Fired with conviction that he was on a divine mission, Luther resolved to go to Worms 'under Christ's leadership in spite of the gates of hell and the powers of darkness'. On the way, he treated his friends to an evangelical exposition of the book of Joshua, and how the Gospel was destroying the popish (Canaanitish) idolatry. He also preached in the cities he passed through. But the enthusiastic welcomes that greeted him in nearly every place between Wittenberg and Worms failed to lull him into any false confidence, and like Frederick the Wise, he was ever alert to the possibility of martyrdom. Mindful of the fate of John Huss, they wondered whether the promise of safe conduct would stand if, as was certain, Luther refused to recant. So it was more an awareness of danger than arrogance which made Luther liken his entry into Erfurt to Christ's into Jerusalem on Palm Sunday.[21]

On 16 April 1521 the sound of trumpets from Worms Cathedral heralded the arrival of Martin Luther and his entourage. One hundred horsemen escorted him into the city, where 2,000 people lined the streets to greet him. The afternoon following his arrival, and to avoid the crowds, Luther was led through gardens and alleys to the bishop's residence next to the cathedral for his hearing at 4 p.m. There, Luther and the Holy Roman Emperor met for the first time, and Charles allegedly turned to an aid and vowed that 'this monk will not make a heretic out of me'.

Johann von der Eck, an official of the Archbishop of Trier, opened proceedings for the prosecution. (Not the same Eck of the Leipzig debate.) Pointing to a heap of Luther's books lying on a table, Eck asked him to acknowledge that the books were in fact his, and demanded that he recant. Luther had expected a debate about the content of his writings, and was momentarily taken aback. But Dr Jerome Schurff, a Wittenberg lawyer and jurist assigned by Frederick the Wise to advise Luther if need be, was equal to the occasion. Schurff rose to his feet and demanded that the titles of the books be read out. This took some time, enabling Luther to recover his composure. Luther then confirmed that the books were his. As for recantation, because the matter concerned 'faith and the salvation of the soul and the divine Word', he would not wish to speak in haste, so he asked for time to consider. After consultation, Eck censured Luther for not having his answer ready. Nevertheless, a delay of one day was granted, but Luther was reminded that the court expected a recantation, after which the emperor would intercede on his behalf to the pope for a papal pardon.

A number of reasons have been suggested for Luther's request for a delay, varying from a sudden lack of nerve to a calculated ploy designed to outwit his adversaries. It seems that the immediate demand for a recantation, when he was looking forward to a lively debate, threw him off balance.[22] Be that as it may, next day prolonged discussions on affairs of state delayed Luther's hearing until 6 p.m., by which time the hall had to be lit up with torches. Once again Eck demanded a recantation, but by now Luther had had time to prepare himself. Speaking in both German and Latin, he gave an impressive perform-ance. He began by pointing out that the books Eck had assembled were not all on the same subject, so he divided them into three classes. The first, on Christian piety and morality, were so uncontroversial that not even the bull of excommunication had found fault with them, so he could hardly be expected to repudiate these. Regarding the second class – books directed against the papacy – Luther was unrepentant. The pope and his laws, he claimed, were destroying, oppressing and enslaving the Church, especially in Germany; here Luther no doubt realised that he could count on some sympathy in the court, because Rome's interference in German affairs was widely resented. Luther appealed to his hearers: if he recanted, the papacy would grow worse and worse, and then, 'Good God, What sort of tool of evil I would be'. The same applied to the third category of books written against the papacy's supporters, though here Luther acknowledged that he might have written more moder-ately. He then insisted that if he had spoken or written wrongly, his opponents should convict him of his error from Scripture.

Charles and his advisers consulted privately. Then Eck addressed the court again. Luther's classification of his writings, Eck announced, was irrelevant; what the court wanted to hear was a recantation, then the emperor would graciously plead his cause with the pope. If Luther refused, all his books would be condemned and destroyed, even those that contained nothing offensive. Neither the court nor the Church, according to Eck, was interested in Luther's personal understanding of the Scriptures. By using Scripture this way, he was no different from a long line of past heretics like Huss, who had challenged the authority of the Church. Luther should stop pretending that he knew better than the Roman Church. The time had come for a plain, simple answer 'with-out horns or teeth' – would he recant or not. Luther fixed his eyes on Eck, and gave his historic reply:

> Unless I am convinced by the testimony of Scripture or by clear reason – for I do not trust either in the pope or in councils alone, since it is well known that they have often erred and contradicted themselves – I am bound by the Scripture, and my conscience is captive to the Word of God. I cannot and will not retract anything, since it is neither safe nor right to go against conscience. May God help me. Amen.

At once pandemonium broke out. 'Forget your conscience, unhappy man,' Eck protested. 'You could never prove that the councils have been mistaken in matters of faith.' Luther began to reply, but at a signal from the emperor he was bustled out of the hall. Charles angrily declared that he had 'heard enough of such talk' and left. Luther's friends – and he had many – cheered loudly, while his enemies cried 'to the pyre with him'. Once outside, Luther lifted up his arms like a triumphant champion shouting: 'I am through, I am through.'[23]

Later, however, when the excitement had died down a little, Luther was disappointed. He told the artist Lucas Cranach that he had been expecting a scholarly disputation. Instead, in his own account of his hearing: 'Nothing else was done there than this: Are these your books? Yes. Do you want to renounce them or not? No. Then go away!'[24]

The following day, the court assembled once more, this time without Luther. Charles was uncompromising and rejected Luther as a heretic. He could not see how one lone, awkward monk could be right and 1,000 years of Christendom wrong. Charles resolved to fulfil his role as defender and patron of the Catholic faith, and 'stake on this cause my kingdoms, my friends, my body and blood, my life and soul'. Luther was stubborn, and Charles regretted he had not proceeded against him earlier. Nevertheless, Charles did honour the promise of safe conduct. Luther was sent home, but forbidden to preach and agitate along the way.

Charles expected obedience from his subjects and the German princes over his firm stand, and naturally so did the papal nuncios. But the German estates demurred. Some feared popular unrest and even revolution if it appeared that Luther was being dealt with too harshly. On his journey to, and even in Worms, Luther had attracted supporters, sometimes more than the papal representatives enjoyed. To the consternation of the 21-year-old emperor, one enterprising Luther enthusiast managed to breach imperial security and fasten a note on the door of Charles's bedchamber, warning of 'woe to the land whose king is a child' (from Ecclesiastes 10:16). Frederick the Wise was cautiously becoming more favourable to the Reformation, and other princes were sympathetic, especially after Luther's convincing performance in the face of Eck's threats and demands. So the electors requested that one last attempt be made to resolve the Luther affair. Because Luther said he was willing to be 'convinced by Scripture and clear reason', they proposed that he should be heard before a group of scholars and theologians to see whether any agreement could be reached. Rather reluctantly, Charles consented to a delay of three more days before imposing the imperial ban, and a commission was appointed to negotiate further with Luther.

But the talks failed, and Luther left Worms on 26 April. On the way home, at Hersfeld and Eisenach, he disregarded the order forbidding him to preach. Then, on 4 May, he was dramatically 'kidnapped' and taken to Wartburg: actually, this was a pre-arranged plan devised for his own safety, to which Frederick the Wise had consented in principle without knowing all the details. Then Elector Ludwig of the Palatinate, a Luther supporter, left Worms, and two days later Frederick did likewise, officially because he was troubled by gout. The imperial edict of Worms against Luther, dated 8 May, was formally issued at the close of the diet on the 25th. It condemned Luther as an 'obstinate schismatic and manifest heretic … a limb cut off from the church'. Charles would enforce the papal bull against him. Luther was now effectively outlawed: none should support him or give him help; he should be taken prisoner and delivered to the emperor, and likewise his supporters. Printing, reading, buying and selling Luther's books, and also any books against the papacy and the Roman Church, were forbidden. Luther condemned the edict as unjust and unchristian.

Yet in spite of the imperial sentence, Luther lived most of his adult life in relative freedom. The mandate had hardly been issued before Frederick the Wise asked Charles if he might be exempt from it in Saxony, and amazingly, Charles did not refuse. This extraordinary situation had been made possible by political and constitutional pre-Reformation developments in Europe. Whereas England, France and Spain had seen the growth of a strong centralised monarchy, in Germany the trend was the reverse. In 1338 the German electors had defied Pope Clement VII by insisting that the emperor should be chosen by a majority of estates, without the need for papal approval, and this demand was supported by Charles IV in the Golden Bull of 1356. Since then, the emperor had been beholden to the electors in a way that the kings of France, Spain and England no longer were to their nobility. Though law-making and decrees remained the prerogative of the emperor, the electors were practically kings in their own lands, a privilege they were determined to hold on to. So Charles decided not to risk a confrontation with the powerful Frederick the Wise, at least not so early in his reign, and thus he effectively neutralised his own imperial mandate.[25]

4

The Handmaiden of Theology

I am sitting here all day, drunk with leisure.
(Luther from Wartburg to George Spalatin in Wittenberg.)[1]

*T*his was not quite true. He was a busy man and not always in good health, plagued irritatingly by severe constipation. Much of his time he spent writing. He composed church postils, doctrinal works, commentaries on the Psalms and the Magnificat, and polemical tracts. He also began work on possibly his greatest achievement, a German translation of the New Testament. Because he had heard about disturbances among students, artisans and peasants discontented with the princes and the clergy, one line in the Magnificat may have caught his attention: 'He has put down the mighty from their thrones' (Luke 1:52). Luther, however, rejected any idea of revolution; he was convinced that God would, in His own way, remove the mighty and the proud and raise up the afflicted 'without any crash or sound'. Martin Luther was a reformer, not a revolutionary.[2]

Luther had grown a beard to help disguise his identity and he was known as Knight George (*Junker Jörg*). Apart from one hurried secret visit to Wittenberg, and the occasional day out walking, Luther spent nearly a year in Wartburg Castle. He did not particularly enjoy his enforced isolation in 'My Patmos' as he called it (Revelation 1:9). He confessed: 'I yearn again and again for companionship.' Once his hosts took him out hunting hares and partridges as a diversion, but this was a sport Luther did not find at all agreeable; it was 'a worthy occupation indeed for men with nothing to do', but it never appealed to Luther. It reminded him of the devil tearing after innocent souls with his 'ambushes and his dogs' – that is with his monks, bishops and false teachers. With much satisfaction, he described how 'by my efforts we saved a little live rabbit'. Luther rolled the creature up in the sleeve of his cloak, but unfortunately the dogs sniffed it out and finished it off. The rabbit's sad end made Luther 'sick of this kind of hunting'. If men must hunt, Luther wished they would go after wild beasts like wolves and bears.[3]

Luther had left a preaching vacuum in his native Wittenberg. He would have preferred Philip Melanchthon, his closest friend and ally, to take up the task, but Melanchthon was the university's Professor of Philosophy and not greatly inclined to enter the pulpit. Increasingly the office of preaching was taken over by Andreas Bodenstein von Karlstadt, Doctor of Theology and, at least until now, a supporter of Luther. Yet Luther had not given up hope that Melanchthon might be induced to preach even though he was technically a layman. At this stage in his career, Luther would have welcomed lay preaching as a part of church life – 'This would become a custom which would introduce freedom and restore the form and manners of the early church'. Luther did not mind a bit that Philip was 'not anointed or tonsured'.[4]

This latter point may perhaps have been on his mind when he wrote the *Judgement of Martin Luther on Monastic Vows* at Wartburg. Luther rejected vows out of hand. The underlying aim of a vow was to please God by humanly devised works, whereas the Scripture says that the just shall live by faith. Vows were contrary to the Scriptural teaching of justification and also the liberty of the Christian. Vows of chastity were useless and impossible to keep anyway; in the monasteries vows of poverty and chastity were ignored. Nowhere in Scripture is a life-long vow commanded. Occasionally short-term vows are mentioned, usually in the Old Testament. Vows in the New Testament were entirely voluntary, and only relevant to Jewish Christians going through a sort of transition period between the old and new covenants. Gentile Christians were never advised to make vows and, if anything, they were warned away from them.[5]

Meanwhile, Luther was becoming anxious about Karlstadt when he heard of troubles in Wittenberg. Students and townsfolk were interrupting Mass services and chasing priests out of churches. Radical proposals included administering communion in both kinds, removing and destroying church images, allowing freedom for anyone to preach and the immediate closure of taverns and brothels. The Wittenberg city council feared unrest would spread and that it might lead to insurrection. Luther opposed revolution on principle as anti-Christian. The Reformation, he believed, should begin with winning hearts and minds for the Gospel through good preaching, and reforms would then follow in an orderly way. He made a clear distinction between arch-opponents of the Gospel and those he called, without meaning to be patronising, the 'weak'. These were ordinary, pious churchgoers who were not to be blamed for the abuses of the Church, and who, because they might take offence at sweeping reforms suddenly and arbitrarily imposed, should be dealt with patiently, with persuasion rather than coercion. It was not their fault

The Wartburg. Luther called it 'My Patmos'. (*Author's Collection*)

that the pope and his followers had corrupted the Gospel; it was necessary, therefore, to explain and teach them aright, and wait patiently for fruits. Then outward reforms to services could begin and be carried through with the consent of the entire congregation and community. Luther, who had struggled for many years with spiritual trials, could be patient with others.[6]

Probably in the middle of December, Luther wrote his *Sincere admonition … against insurrection and rebellion*, which he sent to his friend George Spalatin, urging him to publish the work as soon as possible. Luther was convinced that divine judgement was about to fall on the papist kingdom, but he was determined to renounce any Christian-led insurrection. Insurrection lacks all power of discernment, for 'when Mr. Mob breaks loose he cannot tell the wicked from the good; he just lays about him at random'. For this reason, Luther would never support rebellion under any circumstances. 'I am and always will be, on the side of those against whom insurrection is directed, no matter how unjust their cause. I am opposed to those who rise in insurrection, no matter how *just* their cause, because there can be no insurrection without hurting the innocent and shedding their blood' (author's emphasis). In times of trouble, the Christian should commit their way to God, not take matters into their own hands. The way to defeat the pope and his bishops is to continue the work already begun, to preach and believe the Gospel – 'better this way than a hundred insurrections'. Rebellion is the devil's work, designed to bring the Gospel into disrepute.[7]

But while this *Admonition* was in transit from Wartburg to Wittenberg, Karlstadt was growing increasingly impatient with the pedestrian pace of change. He did not share Luther's concern about the sensitivities of the weak; if something was wrong, it was wrong, and should be changed. So, on 22 December, Karlstadt announced that he would administer communion in both kinds at the Lord's Supper. He did so, against the wishes of the city council, without priestly vestments, without holding confession first and without making the usual sign of the cross. This sudden departure from tradition, besides causing offence to some, also encouraged his radical supporters to expect more innovations and quickly, and there were further disturbances in churches over the Christmas period.[8]

Matters were exacerbated by the arrival in Wittenberg of a group of men who became known as the 'Zwickau prophets'. At Zwickau there had been much support for Luther while he was at Worms, but these prophets were more of the spirit of Karlstadt. Men like Thomas Müntzer and Nicholas Storch despised Luther's reliance on the written Word of the Bible and the promises in it, and they claimed to have received revelations directly from on high, and visions of the sort early Christians were supposed to have seen. One of them, Marcus Stübner, told Melanchthon that he had seen a vision of St John Chrysostom in Purgatory. Some of them were questioning infant baptism. Melanchthon – the genteel young philosophy professor, accustomed to civilised and orderly debates – was left perplexed and unsure how to deal with these curious visitors, so he asked the elector to recall Luther. At first Frederick was unwilling because, with Luther still under the imperial ban, his early return might provoke demands for his arrest. Melanchthon then wrote to Luther about the problems. Luther advised his young and anxious friend not to be alarmed, but to put these strange, novel spirits to the test. How real were these supposed revelations? How much do they know of the Cross or spiritual trial? Still in Wartburg, and before he had ever met any of them, Luther was already suspicious. Before long he was calling them *schwärmer* (enthusiasts – the German word comes from the bustling activity of bees) or *Rottengeister* (fanatics), sweet-talking false prophets with their spurious revelations.[9]

To Karlstadt's delight, communion in both kinds was well received by evangelical enthusiasts in Wittenberg and the areas round about. Karlstadt now set his sights on more adventurous reforms, including the forced removal of altars and church images. The authorities were shocked at the resulting outbreak of civil unrest and the smashing of church images and property, and they tried to prevent Karlstadt from preaching. Nicholas von Amsdorf, a more moderate man, was appointed to preach instead. Probably at Melanchthon's request, an urgent message was sent to Luther at the end of February asking him to return. Luther knew of the elector's reluctance to invite him back prematurely, but he felt he could wait no longer now that 'Satan has intruded into my fold'. So Luther set off for home.[10]

Three days after his return, on 9 March, he began his *Invocavit* sermons.[11] He appealed to his people: they should not only believe in Christ, but also love one another, 'for without love, faith is nothing, as Paul says' (1 Corinthians 13). It is not enough simply to know the right doctrine, because 'an ass could learn to intone the lessons'. The kingdom of God 'does not consist in talk or words, but in activity, in deeds, works and exercises'. God does not seek mere 'hearers and repeaters of words, but followers and doers'; He also commends patience. Mindful of his own long years of spiritual trials and soul searching, Luther warned his more zealous brethren that they would have to learn this patience. 'Dear brother, if you have been suckled long enough, do not at once bounce off the breast, but let your brother be suckled as you were.' There had been 'too much haste' in Wittenberg of late. He agreed the Mass should be abolished, 'yet Christian love should not employ harshness, nor force the matter'. Preachers should have more thought for the 'weak'; we 'must first win the hearts of the people'. He recalled his own experiences: 'I opposed indulgences and all the papists, but never with force; I simply taught and preached and wrote … then slept and drank beer with my friends Philip and Amsdorf.' This way Luther trusted in the Word of God, which 'broke the papacy more than any king or emperor ever did'.

Church images, Luther admitted, were not essential, and maybe it would be better not to have them at all, but for the sake of pious souls who might be offended by losing them, they should be retained. No fundamental divine principle was at stake. The Law forbidding a graven image applied only to idolatrous worship. Noah, Abraham and Jacob all built altars, while Moses, at God's command, made two cherubim for the tabernacle, and set up the bronze serpent. So images are acceptable so long as they are not worshipped. If they are abused as idols, then they may be destroyed, but only in an orderly manner by the civil authorities, just as godly Hezekiah destroyed the serpent. Mob iconoclasm must be condemned unreservedly. But even in these cases, Luther was urging restraint as it seemed senseless to him to destroy something just because it had been abused and for no other reason. 'Many a man has made a fool of himself with wine and women, but that does not mean we should pour away all the wine and kill all the women.' The need of the hour was for good preaching to convince people of the truth of the new faith. Communion in both kinds, for example, was right and good, but to impose it by force would merely be a new form of legalism.

The sermons made a strong impression and Luther won over his hearers. The enthusiasm for hasty reform dissipated. The limited, but fierce, iconoclasm was stopped, and to this day many Lutheran churches remain as richly adorned with sacred artwork as Roman Catholic churches.

Luther as Knight George, from the painting by Cranach. (*Author's Collection*)

Melanchthon was hugely relieved. 'Everything has been well restored by Dr. Martin', he reported to a friend. Karlstadt was not so happy, but for the time being he yielded. Little more was heard from him in the pulpit, though he continued as dean of the theology faculty at the university.[12]

By means of his personal authority and strength of character, Luther had restored order and calm in Wittenberg. Now, as well as completing his translation of the Bible, he began preaching, seeking to win hearts and minds for the Reformation. He set about the task of persuading people that their salvation was a gift of God to be received by faith, not something that could be earned by going on a pilgrimage, entering a monastery, praying to saints, making a vow or, indeed, any kind of human act or work. The human heart was far too sinful to merit divine grace, so God in His mercy offered remission of sins through faith in Christ the Mediator and Redeemer. Reforms were ushered in gradually. Priestly marriage became progressively more acceptable, communion in both kinds gradually became the norm, private Masses were phased out and an evangelical Mass was introduced, first in Latin and later in German.[13]

In his liturgical reforms, Luther's chief concern was the proclamation of the Gospel. However, although he condemned the 'godless regard for ceremonial', which was smothering true preaching in medieval times, he was not opposed to ceremonial in itself. His declared aim was not to abolish the liturgy, but to 'purify the one that is now in use'. References to the sacrifice of the Mass must go, but 'we shall prove all things and hold fast what is good'. The Introits, the *Kyrie*, the collects, the readings of the epistles and Gospels, with or without candles and incense – for these things are 'free' – and the recital of the Nicene Creed were all accepted. So, crucially, was liturgical music, and Luther worked closely with two musicians of the elector's chapel, Conrad Ruppsch and Johann Walther.[14]

The main difference between Luther's evangelical German Mass and the medieval Mass was this: Luther stressed that the Eucharist was a promise of grace and forgiveness, not a sacrifice to be offered for the living and the departed. Luther commended the new Mass to the congregation and the city authorities, and it was introduced at the end of 1525, though the Latin Mass was not abolished.[15]

At one time, though less so now, it was fashionable to claim that Luther was no great liturgist, but this succeeds only in missing the real point. Luther never set out to create a new liturgy; he set himself the task of reforming, as moderately as possible, the *existing* medieval liturgy. The German Mass, save for the deletion of any notion of a propitiatory sacrifice, did not depart drastically from the traditional order of service, and many other church customs were left intact. Saints were no longer venerated or prayed to, but some saints' days, particularly apostles' days, were retained. Besides Christmas and Easter, Marian festivals of Candlemass, the Annunciation, the Assumption and Mary's Nativity were continued. Images, artwork, candles and crucifixes remained virtually untouched and unharmed. Priests wore vestments as before, and they and the congregation had no scruples about making the sign of the Cross during services, bowing at the name of Jesus or calling Mary the Mother of God. Reform, not revolution, had prevailed; a conservative, measured reformation, consistent with evangelical liberty. The rationale was later succinctly summed up by Melanchthon in his *Apology of the Augsburg Confession*:

> Liberty should be used moderately, lest the weak be offended ... Nothing should be changed in the accustomed rites without good reason. For the sake of harmony, ancient customs that can be kept without sin or without great disadvantage should not be cast aside.[16]

It is worth lingering for a moment on the contrast between Luther's moderation in introducing reform, and his otherwise turbulent nature. It is well known that he could be rough with his opponents. His polemical writings are invariably vigorous, frequently vehement and, at times, ferocious. When roused, Luther is not for the over-sensitive or faint-hearted. He could – and often did – shock even close friends, like the peaceable, refined Melanchthon. The contrast is partly, if not entirely, explained by the fact that Luther generally saved the fireworks for his intellectual equals, prominent religious adversaries or the high and mighty of the world like the popes, bishops and hostile princes, such as Duke George. With 'Hans and Gretha', as he was wont to call his parishioners, he could be a good deal gentler.

Besides composing the melody of the German Sanctus, taken from Isaiah 6, Luther also wrote evangelical hymns, music as well as words, and urged friends to do likewise. About two-thirds of Luther's hymns were written between autumn 1523 and summer the following year. German hymns had been allowed in church since the early Middle Ages, often sung during pilgrimages, processions and special festivals. Luther was keen to encourage congregational singing yet further and include it in the liturgy.[17]

Poetry does not always translate from one language to another as easily as prose. Luther's famous hymn *Ein' feste burg ist unser Gott* is variously rendered as 'A mighty fortress is our God' or 'A safe stronghold our God is still' or 'Our God He is a castle strong', none of which quite captures the rhythm of the German. His best known carol, *Nun komm, der Heiden Heiland*, is usually turned around into 'Saviour of the nations, come', though 'Come, the Heathen's Healing Light' may portray the sense better.[18] However, the following justly praised translations are those given in *Luther's Works*, volume 53, and will hopefully provide some insight into Luther the poet and hymn writer.

'A New Song Here shall be Begun' has been called the first hymn of the Reformation. It was written by Luther to commemorate the death at the stake in 1523 of two of his Dutch supporters, Heinrich Voes and Johann Esch in Brussels, both of the Augustinian order, who refused to recant when pressed to do so by theologians of the University of Louvain.[19] It reads like a folk ballad, almost a story in song:

> The old arch-fiend did them immure
> With terrors did entrap them.
> He bade them God's dear Word abjure,
> With cunning he would trap them:
> From Louvain many sophists came,
> In their curst nets to take them

Luther then mocks the efforts of the enemies:

> Oh! They sang sweet, and they sang sour:
> Oh! They tried every double;
> The boys they stood firm as a tower,
> And mocked the sophists' trouble.
> The ancient foe it filled with hate
> That he was thus defeated
> By two such youngsters – he, so great!
> His wrath grew sevenfold heated,
> He laid his plans to burn them.

The martyrs awaited their fate with patience, and though he was deeply moved at the news of the deaths, Luther turns the hymn into a song of triumph:

> Then gracious God did grant to them
> To pass the true priest's border,
> And offer up themselves to Him,
> And enter Christ's own order.

Fittingly, the hymn celebrating justification by faith – 'Dear Christians Let Us Now Rejoice' – was probably Luther's second.[20] It has an unmistakably auto-biographical feel:

> Forlorn and lost in death I lay,
> A captive to the devil,
> My sin lay heavy night and day,
> For I was born in evil.

Two centuries later the same theme would reappear, magnified, in Charles Wesley's great hymn:

> Long my imprisoned spirit lay,
> Fast bound in sin and nature's night.
> Thine eye diffused a quickening ray,
> I woke, the dungeon flamed with light.

Luther goes on to lament the worthlessness of his works, and how his wretched condition aroused God's pity; and so:

> To His dear Son He said, Go down
> 'Tis time to take compassion.
> Go down, my heart's exalted crown,
> Be the poor man's salvation.

Frequently, Luther adapted Psalms to hymns, as in 'From Trouble Deep I Cry to Thee' (Psalm 130) and 'Ah God from Heaven Look Down' (Psalm 12). The latter was sung to two different melodies. One of these, probably composed by Luther, was later discovered by Mozart in a notebook of one of Bach's pupils, and used in the song 'Two men in Armour' in the *Magic Flute* (Act 2, Finale).[21]

Though still single, Luther adapted Psalm 128 into a praise of marriage:[22]

> So shall thy wife be in thy house
> Like vine and clusters plenteous,
> Thy children sit thy table round
> Like olive plants all fresh and sound.

'Death held Our Lord in Prison' is a hymn Luther wrote based on a traditional piece that subsequently became an Easter folk song. An example of the Gospel proclaimed in music, it has seven verses, the first three and a half narrating the Easter message, while the second three and a half describe the saving benefits of Christ's resurrection for the believer.[23]

Luther freely evangelised some popular medieval motets. Thus 'Saint Mary with us be' became 'God the Father with us be', and in place of a prayer to the saints he included an invocation of the Trinity.[24]

'From Heaven High I Come to You', another of Luther's Christmas hymns, may have been written for his family.[25] He describes, as perhaps only Luther can, the simplicity and also the wonder of the Incarnation:

Take heed then to the token sure,
The crib, the swaddling clothes so poor;
The infant you shall find laid there,
Who all the world doth hold and bear.

Take note, my heart; see there! look low:
What lies then in the manger so?
Whose is the lovely little child?
It is the darling Jesus–child.

Welcome thou art. Thou noble guest,
With sinners who does lie and rest,
And com'st into my misery!
How thankful I must ever be!

Ah Lord! The Maker of us all!
How hast thou grown so poor and small,
That there thou liest on withered grass,
The supper of the ox and ass?

Luther felt no embarrassment writing hymns suitable for young children, because 'If we wish to train children, we must become children with them'; and so the carol goes on:

Dear little Jesus! In my shed,
Make thee a soft, white little bed,
And rest thee in my heart's low shrine,
That so my heart be always thine.

And I so ever gladsome be,
Ready to dance and sing with thee
The lullaby thou lovest best,
With heart exulting in its guest.

'In One True God We All Believe' is a hymnal version of the Creed, though in the second verse, on the Incarnation, he introduces a theme not found in the Creeds:[26]

Born of Mary, Virgin Mother
By the Spirit's operation
He was made our elder brother
That the lost might find salvation.

This is not the only time that Christ becomes our brother in Luther's hymns; it appears again in another Advent hymn, 'From Heaven the Angel Troop Came Near', written in 1543.[27] The angels' message of joy to the shepherds is paraphrased thus:

> And ye may well break out in mirth,
> That God is one with you henceforth;
> For He is born your flesh and blood –
> Your brother is the Eternal Good.
>
> What can death do to you, or sin?
> The true God is to you come in.
> Let hell and Satan raging go –
> The Son of God's your comrade now.

Luther also made a hymn of the Ten Commandments, which few composers would be likely to do nowadays; but for Luther the hymn was the Word in music, not primarily an expression of personal feeling.[28] However, whereas Moses said simply 'You shall not steal' or 'You shall not covet', Luther adds a charitable touch:

> Steal not thy neighbour's goods or gold,
> Nor profit by his sweat and blood.
> Open wide thy kindly hand
> To the poor man in thy land.
>
> Thy neighbour's wife or house to win
> Thou shalt not seek, nor aught within;
> But wish that such his good may be
> As thine own heart would wish for thee.

It is not surprising, therefore, to find him also setting the Lord's Prayer to music in 'Our Father in the Heaven', while his baptismal hymn – 'To Jordan When Our Lord Had Come' – is unapologetically educational:[29]

> Water indeed, not water mere
> In it can do His pleasure,
> His holy Word is also there,
> With Spirit rich, unmeasured.
>
> The eye but water doth behold,
> As from man's hand it floweth;

But inward faith the power untold
Of Jesus Christ's blood knoweth.

Luther's Eucharistic hymns include 'Jesus Christ, Our God and Saviour', possibly based on a verse by John Huss and adapted by Luther in a way that presents the Sacrament as a gift of grace and salvation. 'Let God be Blest', also an adaptation of an older hymn, is used to show that communion in both kinds was practised, though not customarily, before the Reformation.[30]

Luther's last hymn is a German version of an old Vesper hymn, possibly by Ambrose (340–397), a simple confession of faith in the Triune God: 'Thou Who Art Three in Unity.'[31]

Luther's hymns 'killed more souls than his works and sermons'. These are the words of a seventeenth-century Jesuit, Adam Contzen. From that quarter, no higher tribute could be expected.[32]

Luther's liturgical reforms set the pattern and the high standard for centuries in the Church that takes his name, and it was a blessing for the arts in Protestant lands that Luther loved them dearly. Unlike the iconoclasts (and the later Puritans) Luther found images and artwork edifying and desirable, though never compulsory. Crucifixes and images of saints in churches were acceptable, while paintings of Bible scenes and stories for 'the sake of better remembrance and understanding' he encouraged: 'Would to God I could persuade the rich and mighty to permit the whole Bible to be painted on houses, inside and outside, so all can see it'; that would be a true 'Christian work'. Luther would 'gladly see all the arts, especially music, used in the service of Him who gave and made them'.[33]

For music, Luther had a special affection. It was the 'noblest of the arts ... a gift of God next only to theology' with the power to 'give life to sacred texts and put evil spirits to flight'.[34] He could not praise it enough. He marvelled at the wonders of music in nature, still more so in the human voice. 'How can the air projected by a light movement of the tongue and an even lighter movement of the throat produce such an infinite variety and articulation of the voice and of words?' Philosophers cannot understand it. Discussion of music 'transcends the greatest eloquence ... next to the Word of God, music deserves the highest praise'. She is the 'handmaiden of theology ... mistress and governess' of all emotions the heart knows. 'Whether you wish to comfort the sad, to terrify the happy, to encourage the despairing, to humble the proud, to calm the passionate, or to appease those full of hate ... what more effective means than music could you find?' Those unmoved by music are 'stumps of wood and blocks of stone'. Luther was convinced that the devil cannot abide it; he 'takes flight' at the sound of music.[35]

Besides Johann Walther, Luther admired Josquin de Prez, a contemporary church musician. 'God has preached the Gospel through music, through

Philip Melanchthon, after an etching by Albrecht Dürer. (*Author's Collection*)

Josquin. All his compositions flow freely, gently and cheerfully, not forced or cramped by rules; they are like the song of the finch.'[36]

The story of evangelical liturgical music in Germany, which would climax in the genius of Johann Sebastian Bach, is arguably the greatest spiritual and artistic legacy of the Reformation. For all the brilliance of Byrd, Palestrina, Monteverdi, Gabrielli and others, it would be hard to contest the view that the two Lutheran giants, Bach and Handel, were the finest masters of sacred music that the Western world has ever known or is ever likely to know. Philip Spitta, Bach's celebrated biographer, described the works of these two splendid sons of the German nation, and particularly the 'Messiah' and the 'B minor Mass', as the 'artistic *presentment* of the essence of Christianity'[37] (author's italics). And this is the heart and soul of the Lutheran sacred musical heritage, pioneered by Luther himself. Though it may allow room for the believer's response or the Church's response, its core, as Spitta says, is this 'presentment', even the proclamation, of Christianity itself. This music, in liturgy and in hymnody, expresses not just *my* faith, but *the* faith, the objective truth. Hence Luther could, quite naturally and without embarrassment, make hymnal versions of the Creed, the Sacraments and even the Ten Commandments. Nor would he have envied Bach being called the fifth evangelist in some Lutheran circles.

Johann Walther was Luther's friend as well as his musical counsellor. When Walther compiled his *Glory and Praise of the Noble Art of Music*, a poem of over 300 verses on the theology of music garnered from Luther's writings and comments, Luther wrote a poetic 'Preface for All Good Hymnals' as an introduction. In it Luther followed the custom of artists of his time in representing music as a lady, and he has 'Dame Music' unaffectedly singing her praises:[38]

> Of all the joys upon this earth
> None has for men a greater worth
> That what I give with my ringing
> And with voices sweetly singing.

She is a heavenly gift, banishing all sorrows, hate and envy:

> But God in me more pleasure finds
> Than in all joys of earthly minds.
> Through my bright power the devil shirks
> His sinful, murderous, evil works.

She relates how David's lyre soothed Saul's troubled spirit, and how the hand of the Lord came upon Elisha when the harpist was playing (1 Samuel 16:23; 2 Kings 3:15); and then how music is heard in nature:

The best time of the year is mine
When all the birds are singing fine.
Heaven and earth their voices fill
With right good song and tuneful trill.
And queen of all, the nightingale
Men's hearts will merrily regale.

The song of the nightingale, 'so charmingly gay', draws forth Dame Music's praise (really Luther's praise) to the Giver of all good:

But thanks be first to God our Lord,
Who created her by His Word
To be His own beloved songstress
And of *musica* a mistress.
For our dear Lord she sings her song
In praise of Him the whole day long;
To Him I give my melody
And thanks in all eternity.

5

Church and State, Princes and Peasants

Where was your church before Luther? Because Luther spent most of his life attacking the teachings of the Roman Church, this was a favourite question (often used as a taunt) of his opponents.

The Church, Luther replied, is not a single building; neither is it the domain of the papacy. It is the company of those who believe in Christ in all ages and throughout the world. The main visible marks of the Church are the proclamation of the Gospel and the right use of the Sacraments of Baptism and the Eucharist. Luther admitted, however, that true Christians lived in the Roman Church and had done so for centuries: his controversies were with her leaders, the popes, clergy and medieval theologians.[1]

It has been claimed that Luther was the first theologian to make the state as well as the Church a divine institution. Though this claim has been disputed, it contains much truth, for Luther had the highest regard for the office and duty of the civil power.

For his arguments Luther depended on Scripture. On a personal level, he had a low opinion of many of Christendom's political leaders. He caustically noted that 'affairs of state are usually administered by those least capable of the task'. A prince in heaven was a 'rare prize', and very few of them, in Luther's view, were 'not fools or scoundrels'.[2]

He also had blazing rows with some of them. When Henry VIII of England decided to demonstrate his religious orthodoxy by attacking Luther in his *Assertion of the Seven Sacraments*, Luther called him an idiot, a liar, a buffoon and a big sissy – and these are only a selection of the more printable insults. Archduke Ferdinand banned Luther's books in Nuremberg, and when Duke George of Saxony demanded that Luther's New Testament be suppressed, he received the same sort of treatment meted out to King Henry. Luther called him an enemy of the Gospel who 'devours Christ'. When the affronted duke demanded an

Henry VIII, by Hans Holbein. Luther said of Henry: 'That king thinks he's God … he just wants to be pope in his own land.' (*THP Archive*)

apology, Luther replied to the 'ungracious prince and lord'; though, whether out of Christian charity or to rub salt into the wound, he promised he would pray that God might open the prince's eyes to the truth. Luther was unmoved by criticism that he was too harsh; he claimed that he was defending the Gospel, not himself personally, and if the princes did not like his polemic, they should leave him alone. King Henry and the enraged Duke George made formal, but largely ineffective, complaints to Frederick the Wise.

The Luther question was one of the subjects discussed at the diet of Nuremberg, 1522–23. After much political wheeling and dealing, the diet admitted that the edict of Worms was virtually unenforceable. It also tacitly admitted that Luther's critiques of abuses in the Church contained some truth, and proposed a Christian council in Germany to investigate them. Luther welcomed this more conciliatory line and toned down some of his fiery rhetoric, though he did not seriously expect any council to achieve much. He was determined to go ahead with his New Testament no matter what any council decided, for 'the pure Word of God must and shall be unfettered'. When a later diet in 1524 did demand the implementation of the edict of Worms 'as far as possible', Luther resorted to fireworks once more; he condemned the hostility of these 'German beasts' and he ridiculed the claim of opposing princes to be guardians of the faith. He also advised evangelical territories to reject the edict.[3]

But pugnacious though he was to unfriendly princes, he did not renounce his abhorrence of rebellion, and he could not ignore the commands in the New Testament to respect the civil power as an ordinance of God (Romans 13:1–7; 1 Peter 2:13–17). It could not, therefore, be intrinsically evil, and Luther accepted the legitimacy of princes, their right to rule, their role in keeping civil peace and restraining evil. In all civil affairs, rulers were entitled to obedience from their subjects, including the clergy; but the authority of the princes did not allow them to bind consciences or determine articles of faith, so Duke George's opposition to Luther's New Testament was invalid and not to be obeyed. In such cases, 'God must be obeyed rather than men' (Acts 5:29). Luther was developing his idea of the so-called 'two kingdoms' – the spiritual and secular, the right hand and the left hand respectively. The first kingdom was concerned with matters of faith and conscience, and largely the responsibility of the Church and its leaders; the second, the domain of kings and princes, dealt with civil government, law and order, taxes and so on. Church and state could then coexist with mutual respect, each in its own sphere free from intrusion by the other.[4]

In practice, even in Lutheran Saxony, it proved extremely difficult to keep Church and state entirely separate. Luther had little choice but to ask for the elector's help in organising visitations in his territory, and in providing for the upkeep of qualified pastors and their families when contributions from congregations were not plentiful enough.[5]

Luther had no objection to a Christian becoming a civil officer, magistrate or even a prince, which meant that a Christian could find himself in both kingdoms and possibly facing a conflict of interest. A Christian may also, in good conscience, become a soldier. Luther was opposed to aggressive wars of expansionism, and definitely against wars of religion. When, in 1528, Elector John of Saxony and Philip of Hesse were thinking about a pre-emptive war against a Catholic alliance bent on eradicating Lutheran heresy in Germany, Luther opposed the idea and urged peace talks first, and Luther's wish prevailed. But a war to repel an invader or put down a rebellion, or military force to maintain civil peace, Luther was willing to support. Luther likened the bloodshed this would cause to a doctor who has to amputate a limb in order to save the whole body. Such a war is unpleasant and should be avoided if at all possible, but it may be necessary in order to prevent something worse. Proof that a Christian may join the army, he found in Luke 3:14, where John the Baptist did not require converted soldiers to look for employment elsewhere. Luther also accepted that the Schmalkaldic League, the alliance of Lutheran states, would, though as a last resort, be justified in resisting the emperor by armed force if he started a religious war.[6]

Luther's views on princes and the Christian's duty of obedience were soon put to the test in the German Peasants' War.

Since the fourteenth century, Germany and Central Europe had experience of sporadic disturbances among the peasant peoples. The troubles of 1524–25 began in the Black Forest due to a complicated mix of causes. Poverty was one factor, though conditions varied from region to region. Serfdom was a burning issue in Upper Swabia, though not in the Tyrol. Grievances were not just economic; they also included social, political and legal matters relating to community self-government, election of local civil officials and the independence of courts. There was also a degree of anticlericalism. Troubles quickly spread through much of Germany and Austria, though until March 1525 it was more a mass protest movement than a determined rebellion, with demands for social and economic reform rather than a call to arms. Even the word 'peasant' is a little misleading, because some 'peasant' leaders were noblemen, craftsmen, clergy or civil officials.[7]

In March 1525 the peasants of Upper Swabia drew up their Twelve Articles. Anxious to win Luther's support, or at least to make sure they did not alienate him, they renounced violent methods and pledged their faith in the Gospel. They hoped that parishes would be allowed to select their own pastors; they promised they would choose only those who faithfully taught the Word of God, and they would support them, pay the tithe, provide for them and their families and also for the poor. There followed a list of demands for economic and social reform: the abolition of serfdom, greater access to woodland to hunt game for food, relief from burdensome taxation and changes to laws and legal procedures that discriminated against the less well off. The peasants promised that if any demand they had made could be shown to be contrary to the Gospel, they would pursue it no further. They hoped their moderation would commend them to the leaders in Wittenberg, so it was singularly unfortunate that the next month disturbances in Weinsberg got out of control, and a militia supposed to be in alliance with the Upper Swabian peasants lynched Count Ludwig von Helfenstein and other nobles.[8]

The peasants seemed to be hoping that the movement of reform under way in the Church would extend to their material lives. Luther was not against social reform in principle, but he had a deep mistrust of popular agitation and of what we would call pressure groups. Nor was he fully persuaded of the peasants' good intentions. Nevertheless, in his *Admonition to peace*, printed on 6 May, he opened with a salvo against the princes and nobility. 'We have no one on earth to thank for this disastrous rebellion except you princes and lords, and especially you blind bishops and mad priests and monks.' Apart from the papists, the worst enemies of the Gospel were the ruling classes, who also broke all the commandments of love by trampling on the poor. 'You do nothing but cheat and rob the people so that you may lead a life of luxury … The poor people cannot bear it any longer.' Luther denied charges that he and his preaching had caused the troubles: 'I have striven against rebellion, and have energetically encouraged and exhorted people to obey and respect even you wild and dictatorial tyrants.' The fault lay with firebrand preachers like Thomas Müntzer – the 'murder prophets' – exploiting the unrest and clamouring for the overthrow of the existing order. Luther appealed to the princes to show restraint, at least for now: 'Do not start a fight … for you do not know how it will end … try kindness first.' Otherwise a fire will burn that none could put out.

Luther then addressed the peasants, and although he conceded that there was justice in many of their demands, he called to their minds the words of the Gospel that 'all who take the sword will perish by the sword'. No one, and certainly no Christian, 'by his own violence shall arrogate authority to himself'; he must obey the powers that be, as Paul says (Matthew 26:52; Romans 13:1). The peasants cannot start a rebellion and claim to be Christian, because no true Christian can be a rebel. Sedition can never be justified, even if a nation has the misfortune to be governed by wicked rulers; wrongs must be suffered and patiently endured, while calling on God to send help His own way, as Scripture commands (Matthew 5:39–41, 44; Romans 12:19). If the peasants wanted to be rebels, no longer could they call themselves 'Christian'. Luther invited them to learn from his own experiences when the high and mighty of the world set themselves against him: 'Pope and emperor have opposed and raged against me ... but I have never drawn a sword or desired revenge'; yet God has 'preserved my life ... and made my Gospel grow and spread'. Luther prayed that the opposing parties might see sense and not plunge Germany into conflict, else 'God will, as usual in these affairs, use one rascal to punish another'. If the peasants did not listen to him, Luther promised that he would pray, not for them, but against them, and call on God to resist them and frustrate them. He then turned to the princes once more, warning them that divine judgement will come one day on evil rulers, for 'God hates both tyrants and rebels'. He made a final appeal for adversaries to make peace. 'What', he demanded, 'have all these innocent women, children and old people, whom you fools are drawing with you into such danger, ever done to you? Why must you fill the land with blood and robbery, widows and orphans? ... Beware, dear sirs, and be wise ... You still have time to find a better way, by repenting before God, by reaching a friendly agreement, or even by voluntarily suffering for the sake of humanity.' If you will not hearken to me, 'I must let you come to blows; but I am innocent of your souls, your blood or your property'.[9]

Luther's *Admonition* was not well received by either party, and without an effective mediator, unrest soon spread out of control. Castles and churches were plundered, and peasant forces seized control of Erfurt and Salzungen. Luther was alarmed as reports came in, and when he and Melanchthon paid a visit to Eisleben in Thuringia, one of the worst affected areas, to establish a new school, they saw first hand that the reports were true. On a visit to Nordhausen he was heckled by crowds during a sermon. The little sympathy he had felt for the peasants soon melted away.[10]

It was sometime between 6 and 10 May that Luther wrote one of his most controversial tracts, *Against the Robbing and Murdering Hordes of Peasants*. He accused the peasants of breaking their promise to be peaceful; they 'are robbing and raging like mad dogs'. Their Twelve Articles were 'nothing but lies presented under the name of the Gospel'. Luther blamed Müntzer, that 'archdevil ruling at Mühlhausen', for much of the trouble, but even that did not excuse the peasants who had betrayed their pledges and were showing themselves in their true colours. He repeated his hatred of rebellion: it 'is not just simple murder; it is like a great fire which attacks and devastates the entire land ... it makes widows and orphans, and turns everything upside down like the worst disaster'.

Luther's next words have appeared in print many times, and they are frequently quoted out of context. He was not calling for vigilante squads to take the law into their own hands; he was urging all good citizens to support the authorities by all available means. 'Let everyone who can smite, slay and stab, secretly or openly ... nothing can be more poisonous, hurtful or devilish than a rebel.' Such a one has to be put down like a 'mad dog ... if you do not strike him, he will strike you and the whole land with you'. Especially unforgivable is the fact that these rebels 'cloak this terrible and horrible sin with the Gospel, call themselves Christian brethren ... they become the worst blasphemers of God ... under the outward appearance of the Gospel they honour and serve the devil'. Now, unlike the *Admonition*, Luther blasted the peasants' demands for communal ownership of property and goods: 'They want to make the goods of other men common and keep their own for themselves. Fine Christians they are!'This was Luther at his fiercest, but even at this point he saw a ray of hope, and he appealed to those princes who were Christian to make one last effort, and to 'offer the mad peasants an opportunity to come to terms'. If they would not, the prince should act ruthlessly, for 'this is the time of the sword, not the day of grace'.[11]

A decisive battle in the Peasants' War was fought on 14 May near Frankenhausen. Here the combined armies of Duke George, Landgrave Philip of Hesse and the Duke of Braunschweig – 2,500 cavalry and 4,000 infantry – overwhelmed defending peasant forces. One of the casualties was Thomas Müntzer, who was found after the battle hiding in an attic. After interrogation and routine torture, he was executed at the end of May. The uprising was over, and some princes were taking a horrible revenge.[12]

Luther's attitude throughout the troubles has attracted a good deal of controversy. Even an ally like John Rühl, the Mansfeld councillor, told Luther that popular feeling had turned against him, holding him at least partly responsible for the misery of the peasants in the aftermath of the war. The Mayor of Zwickau, another disappointed friend, noted that 'Doctor Martin has fallen into great disfavour with the common people'. The mayor agreed that Luther's *Admonition* was a worthy work, and he blamed Müntzer and others for deceiving the common folk and inciting them to insurrection. If only the princes had had the sense and decency to appoint trustworthy commissioners to negotiate. In the event, alas, Luther had earned an unenviable name for himself as the 'hammer of the poor' with his call for the 'private and public murder' of the peasants. The dejected mayor asked: 'Is the devil, and those who do this, to be our Lord God?' Luther was too rash and impulsive; he was right in principle to criticise rebellion, but he had 'conceded too much to one side ... Martin has not done well ... he has written the truth in condemning rebellion, but the poor have been greatly forgotten'.[13]

Luther was unmoved. When asked whether he would take back or soften his controversial words, he said he would not – 'A rebel is not worth rational argument ... you have to answer people like that with a fist'. He would not listen to lectures on mercy because 'I have taught and written more about mercy than any other man in a thousand years'. God's mercy is for the contrite and the humble, not for men of violence. They deserve to be put to the sword, and a prince who crushes lawless men does a good work and is worthy of all praise because he protects good citizens who live peaceably and honestly. Luther brushed aside suggestions that he was toadying to the princes – he had warned them not to oppress the honest poor and, when necessary, he would do so again. He did, however, stress that his book, *Against the Robbing and Murdering Hordes of Peasants,* was directed solely against those actively taking part in fighting and plundering; and he condemned savage, indiscriminate acts of vengeance against prisoners and others not directly involved.[14]

For Luther, the Peasants' War had been an unhappy and unwanted brush with German politics, and for much of the rest of his life his relations with the peasants were unsurprisingly strained. But of his unconditional opposition to insurrection, and of his words and writings during the conflict, he had no regrets.

Amidst the troubles of 1525 occurred a pleasant, though slightly controversial, interlude. In the summer, Luther, a former monk, outraged the Catholic world by marrying a former nun. Twelve nuns had wanted to leave the Nimbschen convent, and with Luther's knowledge – perhaps even with his help – the Torgau burgher, Leonhard Koppe, spirited them away in his wagon. Luther called Koppe a 'blessed robber'. Three of the nuns went to live with their families, but the others were taken to Wittenberg. 'Yesterday I received nine nuns from their captivity', Luther wrote cheerfully to his friend Wenceslaus Link. The emancipated ladies soon found willing husbands and one of them, Katharine von Bora, landed Luther himself.[15]

The match came as a surprise even to his friends, because until now Luther was not expecting to marry. It appears that Katherine might have taken the initiative; resisting suggestions that she should marry a certain Dr Caspar Glatz, she said she would rather have 'Dr Martinus'. Because he had strongly defended the marriage of priests, Luther quickly convinced himself that he ought to marry as a matter of principle, though later he teased his wife that he was stuck with her because nobody else would have her. It was from these slightly unlikely beginnings that a long, happy and loving marriage was born, of which more will be said in Chapter 11.

6

Controversies: Anabaptists, Erasmus, Zwingli and the Anfechtung

*L*uther's recurring controversies and polemics with Romanist opponents since his appearance before the emperor at Worms can be passed over here, because the issues in dispute are well known from earlier chapters (justification, papal authority, the Mass etc.) Those who need more details are recommended to consult Brecht or David Bagchi's study on the subject.[1] This chapter will concentrate on disputes of a new and different kind.

Anabaptists

The Anabaptist movement began in Switzerland and spread quickly through south and central Germany and Austria.[2] There was no single united group or creed, so beliefs and practices varied. Most, however, did not see eye to eye with Luther on the all-important subjects of the imputed righteousness of Christ and justification by faith alone. Salvation, according to Felix Mantz, one of the Anabaptist founders, belongs to whoever 'believed in Christ, changed his life and did suitably righteous works'.[3] For Luther, good works were a *consequence* of salvation, not in any sense a cause or part of it.

In most Anabaptist congregations anyone, not just the minister, was allowed to speak as he felt led or inspired, though in practice the acknowledged minister generally led the services. They intensely despised infant baptism, calling it a dog's bath and a blasphemy because there was no direct command for it in Scripture, and it seemed obvious that an infant could not believe in any real sense of the word. Revelations and ecstatic experiences were features of some groups. Emotional scenes at baptisms were witnessed too, where members would suddenly fall on the floor and writhe, sweating profusely. Anabaptists tended to stay separate from the rest of society, whom they regarded as godless. They refused on principle to join the civil or military power, and for this they were frequently suspected of sedition because many princes were, or professed to be, Christian. Rarely did they attend weddings of non-members, or social events. Dancing was thought to be immoral, though wine and beer were not forbidden to members. With their emphasis on a pure, holy life, they claimed to be true heirs of the early Church. Some taught that before the second coming, a kingdom of God on earth, purified from evil, would be established. Others among them denied Christian orthodoxies like the deity of Christ and the Trinity.[4]

Anabaptists are most famous for their opposition to infant baptism, and it was to this issue that Luther turned his attention in a letter to two priests living in Catholic territories in 1528.[5] In it Luther angrily disowned a prominent Anabaptist, Balthasar Hubmaier, and his 'blasphemous booklet' on 'rebaptism', and he was especially irritated to hear that Hubmaier had spoken of his closeness to Luther. Luther was, however, opposed to the persecution and execution of Anabaptists for the sake of conscience, usually carried out by burning or drowning: 'we should allow everyone to believe what he wills.' Anabaptists should be put to the sword only if they are seditious.

On the specifics, Luther first rejected the idea that infant baptism should be abolished simply because the Roman Church practised it: true faith is discerning in what it accepts and rejects. He then looked at the text often used by Anabaptists, namely Mark 16:16 – 'He who believes and is baptised shall be saved'; therefore, baptism must follow faith. Not so, says Luther. If you argue this way, then before you baptise anyone you must be sure that they believe, and you cannot be sure. You cannot see into the heart. It is no good relying on someone's confession of faith, because the text says he who *believes*, not he who *confesses*, and a confession may be false.

Second, Anabaptists claim that children do not have faith in the real sense of the word. But how do they know? asks Luther. Did not the child leap in the womb (Luke 1:41)? Luther admits he is unsure *how* children believe, but that is not the point. Jesus commanded us to 'suffer the little children' and bring them to Him. It is idle to pretend there is no command in Scripture to baptise children. There is a command to 'baptise all nations' (Matthew 28:19), and this includes children. There are examples in the book of Acts of households being baptised, and Augustine records that infant baptism dates from the time of the apostles. It does not matter if faith comes after baptism. A girl may be forced to marry a man she does not want, but then she may change her mind and come to love him; but there is no need for a second wedding on that account. Further, if Anabaptists were consistent, then any Christian who falls from grace and repents would need a new baptism.

Then to the crux of the matter: Anabaptists make baptism a human work, a pledge or commitment of their faith. This is a distortion of the true meaning of baptism. Baptism is Christ's institution and carried out according to His Word (Matthew 28:19). Here Luther touches on, though he does not develop, the main difference between the Reformers and the Anabaptists on the Sacrament. For the first, baptism is a means and sign of God's grace to *us*; for the second, it was an act performed *by* us as our pledge or commitment to God. For this reason, Luther frequently lumped Anabaptists and monks together as examples of work-righteousness. Anabaptists turn the Sacrament, this divine ordinance, into a mere 'human trifle'. Then, slightly unusually for Luther, he appealed to the tradition in the Church of baptising children, arguing that this was a worthy tradition received from the apostles and church fathers, not a tradition of the papacy.

Luther's view on infant baptism is best expressed in his letters to Nicholas von Amsdorf and John Löser after the birth of two of his children, Magdalena and Paul. He asked Amsdorf to kindly 'assume a Christian office, to be the spiritual father of the little heathen, and to help her to the Holy Christian faith through the heavenly precious sacrament of baptism'. Four years later he asked Löser to be Paul's godfather at the christening, so that the child might 'come out of the old Adam's nature to rebirth in Christ through the Holy Sacrament of baptism, and become a member of sacred Christendom'.[6]

Erasmus and Free Will

Desiderius Erasmus was the most renowned humanist scholar of the early sixteenth century. Though a sharp critic of abuses and corruption in the medieval Church, he had not become a Reformer. Shortly after Luther's appearance at Worms, Erasmus was urged by supporters and friends, including King Henry VIII, to pit his wit and scholarship against Luther, particularly on the subject of free will. The crux of the matter was whether man's salvation was entirely dependent on an act of divine grace, as Luther said, or whether the human will played some part as well, albeit a minor one. To adapt the lawyer in the Gospels: what should I do, if anything, to inherit eternal life? (Luke 10:25).

Eventually Erasmus yielded to the persuasion of his friends, and the stage was set for a debate between the princes of Renaissance humanism and the Reformation respectively.

Erasmus wrote his *Diatribe* or *Discourse on the Freedom of the Will* in 1524.[7] He knew this had long been a difficult subject for theologians. He also noted the obscurity of certain passages of Scripture, for example, on predestination, as if God does not wish us to enter therein. Too much theological wrangling and disputing is not good. However, there are dangers in Luther's denial of free will. Even if what Luther said was right, why say it at all when it would give licence to numerous ills? If free will counts for nothing, 'what evildoer will take pains to correct his life?' If anyone 'ascribes all things to sheer necessity, what room does he leave either for our prayers or for our endeavours?'

For Erasmus, the difference of opinion on free will was not an issue of the authority of Scripture; on that all were agreed. The issue was the interpretation of Scripture. Against the Reformers 'there is a whole choir of saints who support free choice'. Many passages of Scripture suggested to Erasmus that 'a man can apply himself to the things which lead to eternal salvation, or turn away from them'. Yet Augustine and those who followed him did not read them this way. Erasmus was particularly disturbed by those who argued that 'free choice is of no avail save to sin', and that even when good is done the will 'does nothing more than wax in the hand of the craftsman when it receives the particular shape that pleases him'. People who argued this way were too anxious 'to avoid all reliance on human merit'. Worse still, were those who said that 'free choice is a mere empty name' that avails nothing at all, and that 'it is God who works evil as well as good in us, and all things that happen come about by sheer necessity'.

Erasmus then quotes Scripture texts that he claims support some degree of free will. Examples include Moses to the Israelites: 'I have set before your face the way of life and death. Choose what is good and walk in it.' (Erasmus's rendition of Deuteronomy 30:15–19. Many similar texts are quoted.) Shrewdly, Erasmus claims to find support even from St Paul, for example, to Timothy to 'Labour as a good soldier of Jesus Christ' (2 Timothy 2:3) and 'Let us cast off the works of darkness' (Romans 13:12). In Romans 7:18 – 'I can will what is right, but I cannot do it' – Paul means that he has the power to wish for what is good, and 'this willing good is itself a good work'.

The main texts apparently opposed to free will were the Lord hardening Pharaoh's heart (Exodus 9:12; Romans 9:17) and 'Jacob have I loved but Esau have I hated' (Romans 9:11–13). The first, says Erasmus, arguing linguistically as well as doctrinally, means that Pharaoh's heart was hardened already, despite warnings and appeals, so God simply gave up on him; but this is not the same as making him hardened from the beginning. The case of Jacob and Esau does not apply to their salvation, but of 'temporal misfortune'. (Here Erasmus is a bit vague: he might have done better to say that Jacob, not Esau, was elect to be the father of the twelve patriarchs from whom the Christ would be born.)

Erasmus never denies the need for grace; nevertheless, a teacher 'requires industry in the pupil, even though apart from his teacher the pupil cannot acquire a new language'. Thus Erasmus finds a role for free will while making grace the chief cause. 'God knocks at our soul with His grace, and we willingly embrace it'. The prodigal son of Luke 15 is an example of the 'will of man turning himself towards the impulse of grace'.

Now Erasmus digresses slightly, but in so doing he may explain the real, fundamental difference between him and Luther:

> I will not specially argue with those who refer all things to faith as the fountain and head of all, even though to me faith seems to be born from charity and charity in turn from faith: certainly charity nourishes faith just as oil feeds the light in a lantern; the more strongly we love Him the more freely do we trust Him.

In other words, Erasmus does not believe in justification by faith alone in the same way that Luther does. Nor does he wish us to be 'absorbed in extolling faith' to the extent that we 'overthrow free choice'. Erasmus finishes by rejecting both monks and Lutherans: 'I prefer the view of those who attribute much to free choice, but most to grace.'

Luther delayed his reply, the *Bondage of the Will*, but he assured Erasmus that this was not because he felt daunted by the task. Rather, it was due, he said, to the 'sheer disgust, anger and contempt' that he felt for the 'trash' he had found in the *Diatribe*, which is really no different from the scholastic theologians.

Opening pleasantries over, Luther denied that he had been over-assertive. It is the duty of a Christian to make assertions and confessions. Uncertainty in doctrine is a 'miserable' condition: 'Anathema be the Christian who is not certain and does not grasp what is prescribed for him!' If Scripture is obscure, as Erasmus says some of it is, that is due to our blindness. God's providential ways may be obscure, but God's Word is not, if rightly understood. Christ could not have commissioned men to preach the Gospel otherwise. For Luther, Christianity without doctrine was not really Christianity at all.

Now to divine foreknowledge; and it is 'fundamentally necessary and salutary for a Christian to know ... that God foresees and purposes and does all things by his immutable, eternal and infallible will'. Here is a 'thunderbolt by which free choice is completely prostrated and shattered'. Therefore, everything that happens does so 'necessarily' because the will of God cannot be hindered. Even heathen poets like Virgil had some understanding of this. Here is the Christian's strength and security; the Christian can be certain of the promises of God because they know that God's will is unchangeable. Hence Erasmus is wrong to say that some subjects are better not discussed openly. This is the way of those who wish an easy life, and Luther will have none of it, no matter if the world were to 'be reduced to nothingness'. Controversy is inevitable because 'the world and its god cannot and will not endure the Word of the true God'. The quiet, untroubled life Erasmus prefers would simply play into the hands of the papists.

Now for the question put by Erasmus: if all happens by necessity, who will take pains to correct his life? Luther replies: 'No man will and no man can, for

God cares nothing for your correctors without the Spirit, since they are hypocrites. But the elect and the godly will be corrected by the Holy Spirit, while the rest perish uncorrected.' In other words, it barely matters to Luther what the wicked do. The Gospel will save some, and that is enough. It is essential, he goes on, to abandon all hope of self-help before we can be saved; therefore it is 'for the sake of the elect that these things are published'.

And now to divine necessity and the human will, and Luther's oft-quoted allegory of the will like a beast of burden: 'If God rides it, it wills and goes where God wills … If Satan rides it, it wills and goes where Satan wills.' The will cannot choose between the two riders; 'the riders themselves contend for the possession and control of it'. The lesson: 'free choice without the grace of God is not free at all, but immutably captive and the slave of evil, since it cannot of itself turn to the good.'

Here Luther tried to turn his opponent's argument against him: if Erasmus admits that free will plays only a minor role in salvation, is the will *really* free? If the power of free choice without grace is impotent or so severely restricted, then free choice has no real power at all. Thus the argument for free will answers itself. Free choice applies to God alone; only He can do whatever He pleases. Luther recognises that man has a degree of free choice in earthly things like house and home, but even this is subject to the control of God and other men. What free will do servants have, for example, who must do as they are told all the time?

Luther was unimpressed by the traditional medieval arguments for free will; he read them all when he was in the monastery. If they were truly saintly men, that was due to grace, not their free will. Nor is free will valid simply because the 'church' has taught it, because the purely external Roman Church can fall into error and idolatry just as ancient Israel, the people of God of old, did. The true Church is composed of men like John Huss, burned by the pope. True doctrine is found in Scripture, not on what those claiming to be the Church may say. God has revealed the things of the Gospel through His Spirit, as Paul says (1 Corinthians 2:10). What is free choice worth now? Erasmus is worse than the scholastics when he says that the will can 'apply itself' to good or evil because this makes the Holy Spirit 'superfluous'. Later, however, Luther accused Erasmus of contradicting himself on this point.

The most involved section of the work is the one where Luther answers the texts cited by Erasmus allegedly supporting free will in some degree. Basically, he charges Erasmus with quoting glibly and out of context. The New Testament texts are assurances and exhortations, not invitations to free will. (Here Brecht notes Luther's 'difficulty' with the concept of reward.[8]) On the Old Testament, Deuteronomy for example, Erasmus failed to see that the purpose of the Law was not to give spiritual life, but to convict the soul of its failure to keep the commandments (Romans 3:20). Erasmus has failed to distinguish between the demands of the Law and the promises of the Gospel.

This subject will be covered in more detail in Chapter 8: Luther's lectures on Galatians. Meanwhile, Brecht says that Luther was now going 'contrary to the sense of the passages quoted'.[9] In doing so, Luther was laying himself open to the charge that he was interpreting Scripture according to *his* theology. Nevertheless, he definitely has a point on the matter of context, which Erasmus, despite his extensive learning, does not always allow for. But this is by the by.

When he wrote this work, Luther broadly followed the Augustinian doctrine of predestination (see p.15). What, then, of Scripture texts like this: 'Have I any pleasure at all that the wicked should die? saith the Lord God: and not that he should return from his ways and live'; and: 'For I have no pleasure in the death of him that dieth, saith the Lord God: wherefore, turn yourselves, and live' (Ezekiel 18: 23, 32). The prophet, Luther replied, speaks of the 'preached and offered mercy' of God, not of that 'hidden and fearful will' of God which decreed who would and who would not receive His mercy – this will should not be inquired into, but 'reverently adored'. If God does not desire our death, Luther admitted, the fact that we perish must be charged to our own will. This is true of the 'God who is preached', who wishes all men to be saved (1 Timothy 2:4). Whoever refuses Him is at fault, as Jesus said: 'How often would I have gathered thy children together, and ye would not' (Matthew 23:37). But why God declines to 'take away or change this fault of our will in all persons, when it is not in the power of man to do so, or why He imputes it to man when man cannot be free from it, we should not inquire into, and if you inquire much you would never find out'. So Luther does not soften 'I will harden Pharaoh's heart' as Erasmus has done; it means just what it says. Similarly with Jacob and Esau; all depends on God's election, not free choice. 'The rewards are decreed before the workmen are born and begin working.' *Pace* Erasmus, this does indeed apply to salvation, not just temporal life.

At times, the two men seem to be applying different principles of exegesis to Scripture. For example: 'Without me ye can do nothing', says Jesus in John 15:5. According to Erasmus, 'That man is said to do nothing who does not achieve the end for which he strives, although one who strives has often made progress'. So the word 'nothing' should not be pressed too far, else we could not sin without Christ. Therefore, a door is left open for free will. According to Luther, Christ simply slams free will; end of argument.

Luther accepts that man can co-operate with God, in the sense that Paul co-operates with God in teaching the Corinthians or proclaiming the Gospel. But Paul was a converted man, whereas the point at issue is what we can do of *ourselves* by free will. Before regeneration, man 'does nothing and attempts nothing to prepare himself for this renewal'. Even after this renewal, 'he does nothing and attempts nothing toward remaining' in this grace. So before and after conversion, all is grace, while free choice is nothing.

In the last part of the book, Luther claims all Scripture is on his side. Beginning with Paul, Luther gives a mini commentary on Romans. 'Jews and gentiles alike are all under sin … There is no-one righteous, not even one' (Romans 3:9–10 and many other texts). Here and throughout the epistle is the absolute necessity of grace, because if free will had any power of itself to do or desire good, there would be no need of grace. In Romans 7 (from verse 14) Paul writes of his experience *as a Christian*, not his life *before* his conversion; sin remains in him, but it is not imputed and he struggles against it. Besides Paul, John is also a 'devastator of free choice', as when he says that the 'Light shines in the darkness, and the darkness does not comprehend it' (John 1:5, and several similar texts).

Then the crux of the matter: free choice is nothing less than a denial of grace and of Christ. I want no free choice given to me, says Luther. 'God has taken my salvation out of my hands into His … and has promised to save me not by my own work or exertion but by His grace and mercy.'

Luther rounds off by congratulating Erasmus for perceiving that this subject is the most important of all, far more so than 'trifles' like Purgatory and indulgences. However, he is unimpressed with the theology of Erasmus, who, if he can do no better than this, should 'be content with your own special gift', namely languages and the humanities. In these things, Luther admits he is much indebted to Erasmus. But not on the subject at issue; on that Luther will yield nothing to any man. He closes thus: 'May the Lord, whose cause this is, enlighten you and make you a vessel for honour and glory.'

A somewhat lengthy summary has been given here, partly because Luther acknowledged the importance of the subject, and also because the *Bondage of the Will* has become one of his best known and most frequently printed works. Some have found it bleak and depressing, though this is to focus too much on one side of the coin; the other side is the grace of God that saves not just *despite* man's helpless state, but *because* of it. It should also be noted that Lutheran Orthodoxy, as it later developed, has discreetly modified some of its starker sections.[10] Luther's strongly predestinarian line soon found an unexpected challenger in Philip Melanchthon, who did not like either Luther's theology or his aggressive polemical style, which he feared would do nothing to win over the Erasmians. Philip had been hoping that Luther would grow more moderate with age, but he confided to a friend that he saw no sign of it – rather he is more 'vehement than ever'. Philip soon began championing the doctrine of 'universal grace', really the antithesis of predestination, according to which God's grace is for all mankind, and there is no secret decree that assigns some to blessing and others to perdition. On this subject, the Lutheran Formula of Concord of 1577–80 is closer to Melanchthon than it is to the *Bondage of the Will*, though the Formula confirms, as both Luther and Melanchthon did, that the will of man without grace can do nothing at all towards its own salvation. It is noteworthy that Luther did not oppose Philip, who achieved the distinction of being about the only man ever to disagree with Luther without getting pummelled for it.[11] Erasmus, meanwhile, for all his acknowledged abilities and erudition, was cutting a lonely figure, unhappy with much of what he saw in the medieval Church, but unable to embrace the Reformation either.[12]

Zwingli and the Eucharist

As seen in pp. 37–38, in the *Babylonian Captivity*, Luther rejected the medieval doctrine of transubstantiation on the grounds that it clashed with Scripture ('eat this bread', 'drink this cup': 1 Corinthians 11:26–7). Instead, he believed in a sacramental union of the bread and wine with the body and blood of Christ. Exactly how Christ is present in the elements, Luther preferred to leave undogmatised and undefined, because no mortal mind can fully comprehend divine mysteries such as these. 'We are not commanded to inquire as to how it may come to pass that the bread becomes and is the body of Christ. God's Word is there, that speaks. With that we remain, believing.'[13]

Luther's view was challenged by former allies like Karlstadt and Caspar von Schwenckfeld, who denied the real presence. A more serious opponent soon emerged in Huldrych Zwingli, leader of the Reformation in Zürich. Zwingli's main objections to Luther, with Luther's answers, are as follows.

First, Zwingli argued that the Words of Institution should be interpreted in the light of John 6:63 ('The Spirit gives life; the flesh profits nothing'). Therefore, 'This is my body' means 'this signifies' or 'represents', just as figurative language is frequently used elsewhere in Scripture ('I am the True Vine'; 'I am the Good Shepherd'; and so on). No, retorted Luther. 'This is' means exactly what it says, even in the examples quoted. The 'is' cannot mean 'represents' or 'signifies', else the text should read 'the true vine is Christ', the greater being represented by the lesser; while Christ 'signifies' the true vine is a nonsense. The word 'vine', not the word 'is', has become a new word, no longer its usual one, but perfectly understandable in the normal use of language. Christ really is to His disciples what the vine is to the branches – the source of life and nourishment. The same applies to the Good Shepherd: Christ *is* to the Church what the shepherd is to the sheep – both protector and leader. Luther did not deny that Scripture contained figurative language, but Zwingli had failed to prove that the Words of Institution should be read that way.

HVLDRYCHVS ZVINGLIVS
DVM PATRIÆ QVÆRO PER DOGMATA SANCTA SALVTEM
INGRATO PATRIÆ CÆSVS AB ENSE CADO

OBIIT AÑO DÑI. M.D.XXXI. bcDOB.
ÆTATIS SVÆ XLVIII.

Huldrych Zwingli, after a painting by Hans Asper. (*Author's Collection*)

Second, and again based on John 6 ('my words are spirit and life'), Zwingli claimed that the eating and drinking at communion are spiritual, not literal. Luther replied that John 6 does indeed refer to spiritual eating, but that does not cancel out the Words of Institution.

Third, still on John 6, Zwingli insisted that only true believers (the elect) receive the body of Christ at communion. In Luther's view the unworthy do receive, but only to their judgement, according to 1 Corinthians 11:27,

29. The technical expression for this is the *manducatio impiorum* (the eating of the unworthy).

Fourth, Zwingli laid out what would become the standard Reformed Christology: that according to His human nature, Christ has ascended into heaven, so He may be *spiritually* present in the Sacrament, but not *corporally* present. Luther countered that Christ is omnipotent and everywhere, filling all things, even in His human nature (from Ephesians 1:23 and Colossians 1:19, 2:9). This last point later came to be known as 'ubiquity', and the cause of yet more controversy, most of it after Luther's death. It is, however, misleading to say that Luther's doctrine of the Eucharist was *based* on ubiquity. Luther's convictions regarding the Eucharistic presence were based on the Words of Institution, and he used the ubiquity argument mainly to answer one of Zwingli's objections to that presence.[14]

The Eucharistic controversy was extremely bitter, with Luther more vitriolic than he had been with Erasmus. He warned readers to beware of Zwingli, to 'shun his books like the prince of hell's poison' because he is 'completely perverted and has entirely lost Christ'. Zwingli is 'unChristian and teaches nothing right, and has become seven times worse than when he was a papist'.[15] Zwingli hit back with gusto, and those who enjoy a good scrap will find much to entertain them in these jousts. Others may be aghast to hear that this, of all subjects, should degenerate into a theological brawl. But the men of the sixteenth century did not believe in sweeping their differences under the carpet. Better by far to air them publicly and forthrightly, and, if necessary, disagree.

Nevertheless, Landgrave Philip of Hesse, like other princes in Germany, was worried about the disunity among the reformers, and he set about trying to bring some concord. He had political as well as religious reasons. In summer 1529, the Emperor Charles V and his papal prisoner Pope Clement were reconciled, and in August that year Charles made peace with King Francis of France at Cambrai. Now Charles seemed ready to act against heresy in his German territories, and the last thing the German Protestant rulers needed was internecine evangelical strife. So the landgrave arranged a conference at Marburg in October 1529 between the Wittenbergers and the Swiss. It was the first time that Luther and Zwingli had met face to face. The discussions were generally more good-natured than the previous written exchanges, though at one point Luther bluntly showed his opinion of the Swiss 'spiritual presence' arguments by chalking *Hoc est corpus meum* (This is my Body) on the table. In the end, agreement proved impossible. Determined to salvage something from the conference, Hesse managed to secure an apparent consensus on fourteen other articles of faith, including the Trinity, justification and baptism. So instead of failing to reach agreement on the Eucharist, the conference was able to end with agreement on everything *except* the Eucharist. The parties also promised to halt their aggressive writings, show Christian charity to one another and pray that God would confirm them in the right understanding.[16]

Zwingli and Luther never resolved their differences, and they never met again. Zwingli was killed on the battlefield at Kappel on 15 October 1531, in a religious war which he had supported between Zürich and neighbouring Catholic states. When news reached Luther he called to mind the verse that 'all who take the sword shall perish by the sword' (Matthew 26:52). Luther said he feared for Zwingli's soul, because, besides his errors over the Lord's Supper, he had 'drawn the sword', which the civil power is permitted to do, but no true Christian pastor ever should.[17]

Facsimile signatures of the Marburg Articles. (*Author's Collection*)

Anfechtung

It may be fitting to end this chapter with a controversy that Luther had within himself. His spiritual trials – *Anfechtung* – had not ended with his Reformation discovery, and they would nag and vex him off and on throughout his life. Luther was in no doubt that he was wrestling, not with flesh and blood, but with something more sinister. Time and again in his sermons and writings he talked of striving with the devil, of the need to stand firm in the faith, to resist doubts and a bad conscience. For Luther, the devil was not a reptilian creature with horns and a dragon's tail: the devil could be very religious and an 'excellent theologian'; but his was a false religion and a false theology that denied and detested the saving grace of Christ and persecuted those who proclaimed it.[18]

The exact nature of Luther's problem has puzzled historians. He had a wife and growing family that he cherished, and a vocation he loved – preaching and lecturing on the Word. He had friends he loved and trusted, like Melanchthon, Jonas, Bugenhagen and others. He lived securely under the protection of a supportive elector, who paid him his regular salary. His lot seemed a favourable one compared with, for example, his English ally, Thomas Cromwell, living under the unpredictable and capricious Henry VIII, trying to spread the Gospel throughout the land, but opposed daily by powerful forces in the clergy and at court. One false or thoughtless move could have cost Cromwell his head, and so it turned out in the summer of 1540. Yet there is no evidence that the phlegmatic Cromwell was ever troubled by anything like this *Anfechtung*.

So what exactly was the matter with Luther; and how could the man who championed justification by faith as forthrightly, even as truculently, as he did ever have the slightest doubt about his own salvation? Psycho-analysis is of little use here, so let Luther suggest the answer in his own words. In the late 1530s, lecturing on John's Gospel, he made this candid admission to his hearers:

> In the papacy, we old people were so corrupted that even to-day I find it difficult to believe my own sermons proclaiming that Christ alone is our Saviour; nor can I accept the Light as freely as I would like. The pope's doctrine holds me back and conjures up the opposing view, that I will have to satisfy God's judgement with my good works.[19]

In his sermons, Luther admitted an 'abominable temptation ... deeply ingrained in our nature', namely this:

> I often feel that I would gladly sacrifice all that I have, yes, life and limb, to find at least one work performed by me on which I might stand and which I might

THOMAS CROMWELL.

Lord Privy Seal, Vicar General & Lord Chamberlian. *Created Earl of Essex* 17. *Ap.* 23. *H.* 8. *Beheaded* 28 *Iuly.* 1540.

Thomas Cromwell. In a personal letter, Luther commended Cromwell's 'earnest and determined will regarding the cause of Christ'. (*Courtesy of Ipswich School Archive*) offer to God in the assurance that He would have to acknowledge it and grant me His grace and eternal life for it. I cannot advance to the point – as I should and must – of surrendering myself to Christ unconditionally, without any reliance in, and any overweening estimation of, my works or my worthiness.[20]

Frequently he referred to his past life as a pious monk. Preaching on the words of Christ in John 15:5 – 'Without me ye can do nothing' – Luther recalled that though 'I read mass daily, and so weakened my self with fasting and prayer … what else did I achieve than to plague myself uselessly, ruin my health and waste my time?' Christ passed His damning judgement on it all – it was worth nothing. Luther himself condemned it as 'sin committed in idolatry and unbelief'; it made him 'terrified when I think of it'.[21]

Here, perhaps, may be a clue to the mystery of this strange post-Reformation *Anfechtung*. Luther hates beyond words the years he spent in the monastery, all the more so because he cannot rid himself of the memory of them. He is like a man who has spent a long time in prison or as a hostage, who is now free, but the miserable routine of captivity haunts him still. Or a man who once did something of which he is bitterly ashamed, and can neither forget it nor undo it, even though others have long ago forgiven and forgotten. Luther the Reformer believes the Gospel he proclaims, and is convinced that he is saved by faith alone; but, like St Paul in Romans 7, he finds another law in himself warring against it, the law of the work-righteous monk, and, maddeningly, no matter how hard he tries, he cannot drive it out of his system. (Work-righteousness is a charge reformers levelled at the medieval clergy – the attempt to attain righteousness and salvation by works rather than the gift of saving faith.)

In the monastery, he recalled, with all his fasting and Masses, 'I really crucified the Lord Christ … God forgive me'. What tormented him was not the fear that he had been remiss, like many of his brethren, but the knowledge that he had been far too zealous. 'The most pious monk is the worst scoundrel. He denies that Christ is the Mediator and High priest and turns Him into a judge.'[22]

Shame as well as hatred of his past consumed him, because he knew that if he had been a good son and obeyed his father and mother, he would never have entered a monastery at all. He told his students how he could have gone on to teach at university after his Masters degree: 'but against everyone's will I deserted my parents and relatives, rushed into a monastery and donned a cowl', because he was convinced that this way he was 'showing great allegiance to God'.[23]

Is it possible, therefore, that Luther's sense of shame led him to exaggerate his *Anfechtung*? And that, by banging on ceaselessly about his trials, was he simply making life more difficult for himself than it needed to be? This may seem a frivolous suggestion for a serious subject, but it is one that occurred to some of those close to him. According to his ministerial colleague, John Bugenhagen, God must have often wondered: 'What more can I do with this man? I have given him so many excellent gifts, and yet he despairs of my grace.' This reassuring word cheered Luther up, and at the dinner table one day he told friends that the best cure for spiritual depression was to eat, drink and enjoy company; and 'if you can find help for yourself by thinking of a girl, do so'.[24]

His own irrepressible, raunchy sense of humour also came to his aid. If he could not sleep at night, he once said, and if he felt the devil assailing him with doubts, he would console himself with St Paul's assurance that the Christian is no longer under the Law, but under grace. If that didn't work, and if the devil persisted, Luther would try and 'chase him away with a fart'.[25] The effectiveness of this is not recorded.

7

The Bible, Catechisms and the Augsburg Confession

Die Bibel

*W*hen he returned to Wittenberg from Wartburg, Luther began revising his German New Testament before proceeding with the translation of the whole Bible. It was an astonishing historic work, with imaginative use of language that made a huge impact on the development of literary High German.

The New Testament was finished in 1522; the Pentateuch and historical books in 1523; Job, Psalms and the Books of Solomon the following year. The prophetic books emerged progressively over the next few years and were not all ready until 1532. Two years later, the entire Bible was published with 117 woodcuts, the ideas for many of them coming from Luther himself. The Bible underwent several revisions in Luther's lifetime, one in the last year of his life.[1]

Luther's prefaces to the books of the Bible were designed to help his people towards an evangelical understanding of it.[2] He called the New Testament the book of the Gospel and promises of grace. Gospel (*evangelium*) is a Greek word meaning a good message or good news, and the Gospel is nothing other than the preaching of Christ. See to it, warned Luther, that 'you do not make a Moses out of Christ, or a book of laws and doctrines out of the Gospel' as Jerome and others in the Roman Church have done. The Gospel does not demand works of ours; rather it promises salvation for those who believe.

In early versions of his New Testament the 'best' books, in Luther's view, were John's Gospel and Paul's epistles, especially Romans and 1 Peter – these were the 'true kernel and marrow of all the books … the foremost books'. John's Gospel is 'far, far to be preferred over the other three'. Later editions, however, dropped this passage, for reasons not entirely clear.

The main purpose of the Acts is not to give an example of pious living; rather it teaches the 'chief article' of Christian doctrine, namely justification by faith alone. Luke 'puts side by side both the doctrine about faith and the examples of faith'. Paul was converted, not by any good works of his, because he was threatening to slaughter the Church; but by grace alone.

For Luther, the jewel in the New Testament crown was Romans, St Paul's magisterial treatise on the Christian faith. This was the 'chief part of the New Testament, and truly the purest Gospel', for it deals in great detail with the essentials of Christianity, like the Law, sin, redemption, righteousness and faith. It begins by blasting all work-righteousness, even that of the Law. Justification is by faith alone, and this faith is not some 'human notion'; it is a 'divine work in us which changes us and makes us to be born anew of God'. Nor is faith a mere idle academic theory; 'it is a busy, active, mighty thing ... it does not ask whether good works are to be done, but before the question is asked it has already done them and is constantly doing them'. Again Luther does not teach perfectionism: because righteousness is imputed and not intrinsic, sin remains in the believer, but it does not, or should not 'reign' in him (Romans 6), and consequently there is no condemnation to those in Christ Jesus (Romans 8:1). Whoever knows this epistle will know the whole Bible.

Prefaces of most of the other epistles are very brief summaries and need no comment until we get to Hebrews.

The order of the books in Luther's Bible differs from the Latin Vulgate and our English Bibles. Four books he set apart from the rest – Hebrews, James, Jude and Revelation. 'Thus far', says Luther in his preface to Hebrews, he has dealt with the 'true and certain chief books' of the New Testament. The canonicity of these four books was less certain to Luther, because there had been debate and disagreement over them in the ancient Church.

Luther did not believe that Paul had written Hebrews. (Elsewhere he thought Apollos was the author.)[3] Besides the question of authorship, he found a 'hard knot' in one section which suggests that a Christian who fell from grace could not be restored, an idea inexplicably at odds with the whole tenor of the rest of the New Testament (Hebrews 6:4–6). Luther wondered if 'this is an epistle put together of many pieces'; nevertheless, he agreed it was very fine in parts.

Without wanting to force his personal view on anyone, Luther agreed with those in the ancient Church who did not think that the epistle of James was apostolic. Compared with the gold and silver writings of Paul and John, Luther called James an 'epistle of straw' (the analogy is taken from 1 Corinthians 3:12), mainly because James praises works too much at the expense of faith, and he has nothing about Christ's salvation, death and resurrection. Jude was useful, but not apostolic; it is almost a copy of 2 Peter.

Luther was puzzled by the spectacular and mysterious imagery of Revelation, quite the opposite of the clear, lucid apostolic writings elsewhere. He had no scruples about likening the beast and the scarlet whore to the

Roman Church, but this apart, Luther had little time for the book as a whole – 'I can in no way detect that the Holy Spirit produced it'. In later editions of the Bible he modified his view slightly; nevertheless, like Eusebius and other ancient authorities, he still doubted that the apostle John wrote it. Despite his misgivings, he left it an open question.

It is sometimes claimed that Luther rather cavalierly ranked the books of the Bible in order of importance according to his own opinions or theology. Luther did rank the books of Scripture, but he did so in this sense: just as we would say that Beethoven's ninth symphony is superior to his first, but both were genuinely Beethoven, so Luther said that John's Gospel excelled Mark's, though Mark is just as canonical as John. With Hebrews, James, Jude and Revelation the issue was a different one. Here the question was not how to rank them *within* the canon. Rather, should they be in the canon at all? Luther was not convinced, but this was a personal view and he did not want to make a dogma out of it.

The Old Testament he called the 'ground and proof' of the New, and he urged Christians not to make light of it.[4] 'Here you will find the swaddling clothes and the manger in which Christ lies … Simple and lowly are these swaddling clothes, but dear is the treasure, Christ, who lies in them.'

Genesis is a most evangelical book, full of illustrations of faith and unbelief. In Exodus, God separates the Jewish people for Himself and gives them His Law. The Levitical priesthood is appointed to make atonement before God. Numbers relates the disobedience of the people, or most of them. The main theme of Deuteronomy is faith towards God and the command to love thy neighbour.

The meticulous requirements of the Law are designed to leave no room for reason or free will; God wants His people entirely for Himself, and He will accustom them to follow His Word rather than their own ideas. The main point of the Law, however, is to reveal sin and bring us to Christ, as Paul says. Much of the temporal and ceremonial law is no longer binding, but the Ten Commandments 'cannot be done away'. Christ is the 'man to whom it all applies' spiritually. Thus Aaron, the High Priest at the Great Day of Atonement, is a type of Christ at Calvary, as the epistle to Hebrews explains. The books of the prophets and the histories spread the message of Moses and guard against false prophets.

Job 'stands firm and contends that God torments even the righteous without cause', unless the cause is ultimately the praise of God, as Jesus says to the man born blind (John 9:3). Job's friends don't see this and they 'make a big and lengthy palaver'; they have 'a worldly and human idea of God' as if His ways were no different from the ways and justice of men. Drawing on his own *Anfechtung*, Luther said that Job can be understood only by the righteous who know what it is like when God's grace is hidden.

The Psalms, Luther calls a 'little Bible'. Herein are the prayers, praises and deeds of great saints, and promises of Christ's death and resurrection; here real saints of old speak from their hearts, which is far more wholesome than the innumerable accounts of the lives of saints of the Roman Church. Nothing can truly reveal the 'treasure of the soul' in the way the Psalter does.

Proverbs teaches wisdom and deals with fools and wise men. A wise man is guided by God's Word; a fool pleases himself. Ecclesiastes was probably written, not by Solomon personally, says Luther, but by scholars who took notes of what the king said. The same applies to the Song of Songs. Ecclesiastes slams free will and shows that the counsels of man are vain; therefore, trust in God and, as Jesus says, do not be anxious about the morrow.

To 'Master Know-all' (*Meister Klüglin*) the prophets are 'dead talk', but Luther urges Christians to read them with thanksgiving because they 'proclaim and bear witness to the kingdom of Christ in which we now live'.

Luther divides Isaiah into three parts. The first includes sermons condemning idolatry and foretelling the coming of Christ; the second speaks of the Assyrian kingdom; while the third announces the Babylonian kingdom, the captivity of the Jews and their release under Cyrus. But the three parts are 'completely interwoven', not treated as we might do in chapters or blocks. Luther is unsure whether this is Isaiah's arrangement, or that of those who wrote his prophecies down. The pattern is a model for preachers: the most important thing of all – the preaching of Christ – should always be present even when we may bring in other subjects of interest, such as the Turkish power, the emperor and others.

Jeremiah was called of God to warn the sinful nation of the coming judgement and the Babylonian captivity. He was a 'sad and troubled prophet ... he had a particularly difficult ministry', but he also prophesied of Christ, though not as much as Isaiah (23:5–6; 31:31–4). Ezekiel's opening vision of the Cherubim and the glory of the Lord is a revelation of Christ; it is the 'spiritual chariot of Christ in which He rides here in the world'. Then the prophet tells of the Jews' return to their homeland under Cyrus. The best part of the book is the promise of the new covenant which will replace the Mosaic one. This has been fulfilled in Christ, beginning at Jerusalem, but it will spread into the whole world. The Jews make the mistake of waiting for a Messiah after the old order. Luther admits the difficulty of interpreting Ezekiel's temple (Chapters 40–48), but he recommends reading the medieval theologian Nicholas of Lyra (1270–1340) as a good starting point. Luther rejects literalism and suggests it prefigures the Church.

'St Daniel' is the life of a faithful man in a pagan land. The temporary fall of Nebuchadnezzar and the more definitive judgement on Belshazzar are a consolation for all who suffer under tyrants. The Church should bear patiently with unjust rulers and wait on God to deal with them in His own way. Visions of the future kingdoms appear in later chapters. Daniel's seventy weeks in Chapter 9 is a prophecy of Christ and Calvary and the future resurrection (see especially 9:26–7; 12:2–3). Daniel was a man 'above all prophets', a prophet and prince of the world; and 'among all the children of Abraham, none was so highly exalted'.[5]

Luther gives almost as much care and attention to the Minor Prophets as to the major ones. Hosea, like many true saints, 'had to die as a heretic'. Joel is a 'kindly and gentle man'; he does not rebuke harshly, but 'pleads and laments' and tries to win the people over. Again, Luther sees the main theme of all the prophets as witnesses of the coming Christ.

Luther's gift, we could say genius, as a linguist and translator are justly recognised and have received more full and deserved treatment elsewhere. Not only German words, but sayings and proverbs can be traced to his translation; for example, 'When the heart is full the mouth overflows' (*Wes das Herz voll ist, des geht der Münd über* – Matthew 12:34).[6]

A few other examples may be given here, and where comparisons are made with modern English Bibles, I have taken the liberty of modernising Luther's German.

In the Creation narrative, Adam says of his wife: *Man wird sie Männin heißen, darum daß sie vom Manne genommen ist* (Genesis 2:23: 'She shall be called woman, because she was taken out of man'). As an alternative to *Frau*, Luther has added the German suffix *in* to *Männ*, an inventive adaptation of the Hebrew *isch* (man) and *ischah* (woman).

When the serpent tempts Eve it asks slyly: *Ja, sollte Gott gesagt haben: ihr sollt nicht essen von allen Bäumen im Garten?* (Genesis 3:1). The King James Version (KJV) is similar with: 'Yea, hath God said, Ye shall not eat of every tree of the garden?' But Luther uses *sollen* (to be supposed to) rather than the ordinary past tense, suggesting that the serpent is questioning not only *whether* God said this, but whether He *should* have said it; in other words, he is planting in Eve's mind the idea that the command not to eat is somehow unjust. This way the tempter brings his devious plan to pass. It is a good deal more subtle than the New International Version (NIV): 'Did God really say, You must not eat …?' This is the way we talk about the weather or some piece of humdrum news.

Eve demurs, and Luther's serpent replies: *Ihr werdet mit nicht des tods sterben*; literally: 'You will not die with the death' (Genesis 3:4). Compare William Tyndale: 'The serpent said to the woman, tush, ye shall not die.' Nobody, not even Luther, can match Tyndale's exquisite 'tush'.[7]

As might be expected, Luther's Bible is punchy, vigorous and energetic. God 'has prepared a laugh for me', says Sarah when Isaac is born (Genesis 21:6: *Gott hat mir ein Lachen zugerichtet*). The Sceptre will not depart from Judah until *der*

Held komme (literally the 'hero' in Genesis 49:10). Contrast 'until Shiloh come' (KJV), or the non-committal 'until He comes to whom it belongs' (NIV). At the parting of the Red Sea God *macht einen Schrecken* for the Egyptians ('made a terror', Exodus 14:24). Luther makes the KJV seem a bit pedestrian with 'The Lord troubled the host of the Egyptians', and the NIV downright insipid with 'He threw them into confusion'.

The Lord is my Shepherd, *mir wird nichts mangeln*, says Luther (Psalm 23:1). 'Nothing shall be lacking to me' suggests fullness and plenty, whereas 'I shall not want' implies I shall get by, just. Then, instead of 'I was shapen in iniquity' (KJV) or 'Surely I was sinful at birth' (NIV), which leaves us wondering if something untoward happened at this birth, Luther has *Ich bin aus sündlichen Samen gezeuget* (Psalms 51:5, 'I was born from sinful seed'; or more simply, 'I was born a sinner'). Again Luther is clear and direct; his point is not that the Psalmist did something wrong when or soon after he was born, as the NIV implies, but that he was born with original sin and, in that sense, can do nothing *but* sin.

Merkt doch eins, das mir Gott unrecht getan hat, says Job (19:6). To get the force of this in English we might have to say something like this: 'Now look! [or some minor expletive] God has done me wrong.' It is Job's vigorous, fearless defence of his innocence when he longs for God to stop plaguing him, and when he is wearied by his friends droning on piously but missing the whole point of the drama. The KJV reads grandly, but is a bit cumbersome: 'Know now that God hath overthrown me, and hath compassed me with His net.' The NIV is nearer Luther with 'Then know that God has wronged me'; but 'then know' lacks the power of '*merkt doch eins*'.

Luther combines insight and delicacy with strength and clarity. In our Bibles Isaiah hears a voice saying 'Cry', which can mean just about anything. Luther has *Predige* (Preach), because the message that follows is one of good tidings for Zion (Isaiah 40:6). Incidentally, the word 'preach' in Luther's usage means proclaim the glad news of the Gospel; it does not mean a moral lecture or set of pious strictures.

Also in Luther's Isaiah, the wolf and lamb shall 'graze' together (*weiden*), an agreeable pastoral touch which our versions, with the featureless, all-purpose 'feed', have missed slightly (Isaiah 65:25).

Occasionally, not only the words, but also the rhythm cross the language border, as *Ich weis das mein Erlöser lebet* becomes 'I know that my Redeemer liveth' (KJV, Job 19:25). Luther has the familiar *Wahrlich, wahrlich, ich sage euch* ('Verily, verily I say unto you' in the KJV), which most modern versions for some reason do not like, and prefer a blander 'I tell you the truth' (for example the NIV on John 16:20).

Meine Seile is betrübet bis an den Tod is rendered as 'My soul is exceeding sorrowful, even unto death' (KJV, Matthew 26:38). Whether the 'exceeding' adds to the pathos of Gethsemane is debatable, but the 'even unto death' (*bis an den Tod*) is surely far more powerful than 'My heart is ready to break with grief', as some modern editions have it.

Perhaps Luther is nowhere more stimulating than in John's Gospel. John the Baptist proclaims Jesus as the Lamb of God *welchs der Welt Sünde trägt* (John 1:29: 'who bears the sins of the world'). The word *tragen* – bear, endure, carry – is slightly different from the 'take *away*' of the KJV and NIV, which in German would be *wegnehmen*. Luther's *tragen* conveys the thought that sin remains in the believer, but is not imputed to him because Christ bears it instead. So the Christian can say daily, as Luther did, that 'My sin is not mine'; it is borne by another. Thus the historical act of redemption at Calvary, with its entire efficacy, is made ever present to the believer.[8]

When Jesus approached the tomb of his friend Lazarus, the KJV is restrained but poignant: 'Jesus wept' (John 11:35). Luther is more emotional: *Und Jesus gingen die Augun über*. Again, an exact rendering in English is uncertain because *übergehen* can mean to 'go over' in the sense of defect, which would give: The eyes of Jesus gave way (to weeping). Or possibly: Jesus gave his eyes to weeping. The sense is He could hold back the tears no longer.

Christ's question to the disciples near the end of His valediction is *Jetzt glaubt ihr?* (John 16:31 – literally, 'Now you believe?') The KJV is similar with 'Do you believe now?' Both gently suggest that whatever they may say, the disciples might not *quite* believe everything yet, and a storm is coming that will leave them devastated, a subtlety completely lost in the 'You believe at last!' (NIV).

When the arresting party reach Jesus, and He confesses He is the One they seek, they 'went backward' (KJV) or 'drew back' (NIV). Luther has *wichen sie zurück*, and *zurückweichen* can mean to shrink back, as if cowering (John 18:6). After the scourging, Pilate's cry 'Behold the man' is, in Luther, *Sehet, welch ein Mensch!* Literally, 'See! What a man!' (John 19:5). In both cases, Luther is brilliantly, daringly, interpretative. In the first, Christ is the willing captive, going to the Father of His own accord by the way of the Cross; and not He, but his captors, are the fearful ones. The second highlights His glory in humiliation.

One of Luther's most controversial translations is Romans 3:28, where the original reads: 'For we consider a man to be justified by faith without the works of the law.' Luther puts 'alone' after 'faith' (*das der Mensch gerecht wird ohne des Gesetzes Werke, allein durch den Glauben*). With some *schadenfreude*, Luther heard that the papists were 'making a tremendous fuss' about this 'alone'. Luther was characteristically dismissive – 'none of them knows how to translate or to speak German properly … a papist and an ass are the same thing … we are not going to be their pupils and disciples, but their masters and judges'. For the sake of pious Christian readers, however, Luther offered to explain himself. Linguistically, the 'alone' gets the sense of the text right for German readers; and, for similar reasons, he prefers 'gracious [*holdselige*] Mary' or 'dear [*liebe*] Mary' to 'Mary full of grace'. Theologically, Paul's subject is justification by faith, and he explains that justification is impossible through works, even the divinely given Law of Moses. Consequently, justification must be by faith alone, and 'I will let no papal ass or mule be my judge or critic'.[9]

The power of faith is a favourite theme of Luther's. When our versions of Romans 4:18 say that Abraham 'against hope believed in hope' (KJV) or 'Against all hope, Abraham in hope believed' (NIV), Luther is a bit more forceful, as if he wants to stress the faith that conquers all: *Er hat geglaubt auf Hoffnung, wo nichts zu hoffen war* ('he believed to/in hope where nothing was to hope'; or, as we might say, where the case was hopeless).

When Paul despairs of himself, he cries: *Ich elender Mensch!* ('I, miserable man!' – Romans 7:14). The KJV is wordier with 'O wretched man that I am!', but at least the 'O' injects some feeling into it, unlike 'What a wretched man I am' (NIV).

Who, thanks to grace, will bring a charge against God's elect? (Romans 8:33). 'It is God that justifieth' in the KJV, and the NIV is the same, modernised. Luther has *Gott ist hier, der gerecht macht* ('God is *here*, who makes righteous' – author's italics). So God does not only justify, doctrinally speaking; He is here with us as well. The same appears in the next verse: 'Who is he that condemns? It is Christ Jesus who died and who is raised.' Luther has: *Christus Jesus ist hier, der gestorben ist.* With Luther, Christ has not just died and risen again and gone off somewhere, He is right here, with His Church.

Catechisms

It soon became clear to Luther that while his Bible enjoyed great success and was eagerly read, something simpler would also be needed for many of his countrymen. A visitation in electoral Saxony left him shocked at what he found there. 'Dear God have mercy. What misery I saw.' The ordinary people he found were completely ignorant, and their so-called priests almost as bad; some were so stupid they could not even recite the Lord's Prayer, and lived 'like pigs and brute beasts' rather than Christians.

Luther's Catechisms were not the first attempts to provide elementary Christian instruction to largely uneducated people, but they soon became the best known. They were also made compulsory. Luther realised that no one could or should be compelled to believe, but at least they should be taught. That way his conscience was clear; he had done what he could and no one could plead ignorance.[10]

His Small Catechism was designed for young people, children and those new to the faith. Luther had an especially high regard for the ability to teach

Christianity simply to ordinary people, and this is what he tried to do here. He begins with the Ten Commandments, in a question and answer form. On the first, for example ('you shall have no other gods'), the Catechism reads: 'What does this mean? Answer: we should fear, love and trust in God above all things.' And so on. Luther rarely restricts the meaning of a command to its minimum. 'You shall not kill' means also that 'we should not endanger our neighbour's life, nor cause him any harm, but help and befriend him in every necessity of life'. Similarly, 'you shall not commit adultery' includes living a chaste life, while 'you shall not steal' forbids all dishonest dealing, not just actual theft.

Next comes the Creed, subdivided into three: Creation – 'I believe in God, the Father Almighty, maker of heaven and earth'; Redemption – 'And in Jesus Christ, His only Son'; and Sanctification – 'I believe in the Holy Ghost.'

Continuing the question and answer format, sections follow on the Lord's Prayer, Baptism, Confession and Absolution and the Sacrament of the Altar. After this, Luther gives sample morning and evening prayers and a suitable grace for at the table. Finally, there is a 'Table of Duties' for pastors, parents and children, mainly quotes from the Bible; for example, a bishop 'must be above reproach' (1 Timothy 3:2). At the end, the work is summarised with the words: 'You shall love your neighbour as yourself.'

The Large Catechism, written for pastors and teachers and other more experienced Christians, developed the themes of the Small.

Augsburg Confession

In 1530 Charles V convened the diet of Augsburg in an attempt to settle the religious controversy between the Catholics and the Lutherans in his German territories. He agreed to listen diligently to the Lutherans and he appeared willing to take a more conciliatory attitude than his brother King Ferdinand had taken, deputising for Charles at Speyer the previous year, when the Edict of Worms against Luther and his followers was rigorously upheld. Elector John of Saxony and his divines set off for Augsburg in early April. Luther was still under the imperial ban, so they brought him secretly to Coburg where he grew a beard for disguise, and remained while the others went on to Augsburg. It now fell to Melanchthon, the man who had wanted to devote his life to the humanities and leave theology to others, to lead the Lutheran theological delegation. Philip worked tirelessly in negotiations with leading Romanists, sometimes corresponding with Luther and asking for advice, though occasionally Luther grumbled about not being kept fully informed of developments. Eventually, on 25 June, after much painstaking drafting and redrafting, Melanchthon presented a document that came to be known as the

Augsburg Confession, a statement of the essential Lutheran articles of faith. A deliberately conciliatory work, it was read in German in the Episcopal Palace in the presence of the emperor, the electors, the Roman Catholic and Lutheran divines, and other worthies. After this, the Lutherans appealed to Charles to accept their confession.[11]

While he was at Coburg, Luther heard that his father had died. In his sorrow, Luther took comfort from the Psalms and in the knowledge that Hans had passed away in the evangelical faith.[12]

The Augsburg Confession is a summary of the main aspects of Lutheranism. Most of this has been discussed in earlier chapters, so only a few extra points need to be mentioned here.

Though Luther had always said that the medieval requirement to confess *all* sins was impossible, he retained the custom of private absolution for those who wished it and needed it.[13]

On the subject of the ministry and Church government, Lutheran confessions refer to *one* ministry only, which the Augsburg Confession calls the 'The Office of *the* Ministry' (author's italics). It is, in translation, a little misleading because no legal or official office is meant. 'The ministry' is the proclamation of the Gospel through the Word and Sacrament, exercised in practice by called and ordained pastors (not by anyone who claims he feels led to do so).[14]

Like the later Thirty-Nine Articles of the Elizabethan Settlement, the Lutheran Confession does not specify any form of Church government as binding or having a divine mandate. This sets Luther (and Elizabeth) apart from John Calvin, and still further apart from the future Presbyterians and Episcopalians. Luther had no intrinsic principled objection to the episcopal structure of the Church. At Augsburg he was prepared to accept the ecclesiastical jurisdiction of the bishops provided the pope allowed the Lutherans to keep and preach the Gospel. When he made his offer he could not resist a touch of typically Lutheran bite: 'We will do you bishops no harm', he assured them; 'we are more use than all your scholars and the pope's ... more godly heretics you have never had, nor will ever find.' The Romanists did not accept this offer, so the Lutherans later consecrated bishops of their own.[15]

Luther was also different from later English Puritans on the Sabbath. The apostles, says the Augsburg Confession, *abolished* the Jewish Sabbath; they did not transfer it from Saturday to Sunday. The use of Sunday as the day set apart for church services is entirely a matter of Christian liberty, not a divine law.[16]

Charles gave the Romanists the opportunity to prepare their reply. The Confutation of the Augsburg Confession was presented on 3 August, and Charles demanded that the Lutherans accept it. More detailed negotiations between the two parties followed, but Luther was not in the least surprised when they failed to reach agreement. Finally, in October, the Lutheran delegation left Augsburg and, after a reunion with Luther at Coburg, they began the journey home. Just in case Charles decided to threaten the Lutherans with war, the Lutheran states organised themselves into a defensive league known as the Schmalkaldic League. Luther had the satisfaction of later recalling how, at Augsburg, there were some in the papal party who admitted that the Lutheran faith and writings may be contrary to the traditions of the Roman Church, but not to the Scriptures.[17]

8

The Bible Teacher: The New Testament

Besides his Bible and his Catechisms, no introduction to Luther can ignore his writings, lectures and sermons on Holy Writ, so the next three chapters will invite the reader to be his guest at his study desk, and to listen to him in the classroom and the pulpit.

Because Luther was embarrassed by his early works, which were composed before his Reformation discovery and did not reflect his mature Protestant theology, only those produced since the Tower experience are discussed here.[1]

There have been suggestions that after Luther's death the editors of his works may have added glosses of their own here and there. However, both Pelikan and Brecht agree that the material is substantially Luther's. Pelikan has helpfully indicated sections where he feels some editing might have taken place, and I have avoided these.[2]

Luther preached and lectured throughout his adult life, but it would be extremely difficult to arrange his lectures and sermons entirely chronologically. Even if that were possible, it would mean frequently jumping from one book to another, which would only annoy the reader. The books will, therefore, be covered in the order in which they appear in our Bibles, beginning with the New Testament.

The Magnificat

This short commentary on Mary's 'sacred, chaste and salutary song' was written during his spell at Wartburg. Luther dedicated it to Prince John Frederick of Saxony as being especially fitting for a prince who desired to rule well, because Mary sings about love and fear of the Lord and His ways with those of high and low estate. Luther freely calls Mary the 'Blessed Virgin' and 'Mother of God', but not Mediatrix, because Mary rejoices entirely in God her Saviour. Nor does Mary exalt in her humility as the monks do; she does not glory in her worthiness or unworthiness, but in the divine favour that rests upon her.[3]

Luther had prayed to Mary many times in the monastery, and now he considers how an evangelical may address her, and he suggests this:

> O Blessed Virgin, Mother of God, you were nothing and all despised; yet God in His grace regarded you and worked such great things in you. You were worthy of none of them, but the rich and abundant grace of God was upon you, far above any merit of yours. Hail to you! Blessed are you for ever in finding such a God.

Luther is sure Mary will not 'take it amiss if we call her unworthy of such grace', because she said so herself. What will offend her are the 'vain chatterers' who harp on about her merits; they 'spoil the Magnificat, make the Mother of God a liar, and diminish the grace of God', which Mary, like all truly blessed saints, seeks only to magnify. Luther makes Mary an enemy of work-righteousness: it is the 'Mighty One' who 'has done great things for me'; all glory and merit she ascribes to Him.[4]

Already, in 1521, Luther had begun forming firm views on the role of civil government. He highlights the verse that God 'has brought down rulers from their thrones', meaning that the bad ruler may be cast aside, but not the throne itself. Government is of God, as Paul says (Romans 13:1), and so it will remain for all time.[5]

The Magnificat's chief glory, however, is the theme of mercy, and how God has fulfilled His oath to Abraham, that in his Seed all nations shall be blessed. 'This promise the Mother of God lauds and exalts above all else ... the undeserved promise of divine grace.' Finally: 'May God give us a right understanding of the Magnificat ... May Christ grant this through the intercession and for the sake of His dear Mother Mary! Amen.'[6]

There is no editorial note at this point. The passage reads as though, in 1521, Luther was still willing to grant Mary some limited intercessory role; as if to say *if* Mary would intercede for us, this is what she would wish for.

Sermon on the Mount

Here Luther begins with fists flying. This work has been 'more shamefully distorted' than any other passage in Holy Writ by those 'vulgar pigs and asses' in the papacy and the monasteries. 'Out of this beautiful rose they have sucked and broadcast poison.' Luther's first complaint is the claim that Christ's teaching is merely good counsel for those who seek perfection; in other words, it is work-righteousness at its worst. From the 'crazy heads' of the Anabaptists comes a different kind of nonsense – that a Christian must not own property or take a civil oath. 'Thus the devil blows and brews on both sides.'[7]

With 'Blessed are the poor in spirit' the sermon has a 'fine, sweet and friendly beginning ... Christ does not come like Moses or a teacher of the Law, with demands, threats and terrors, but in a friendly way'. So it continues through the Beatitudes, but Luther stresses the words 'in spirit' or 'spiritually'. Christ speaks of the spiritual kingdom of heaven, not the earthly, secular realm. Monastic poverty is not blessed, while wealth and power is becoming, even necessary, in a prince. The Sermon deals with the 'condition of the heart'. One who is 'poor in spirit' does not set his heart on riches, but prizes the kingdom of heaven above wealth on earth. At this point, the reader half expects Luther to say that spiritual poverty is the absence of work-righteousness, but in fact he does not do so, and he looks instead at the results of faith. 'No one can understand this unless he is already a real Christian. This point and all the rest that follow are purely fruits of faith, which the Holy Spirit Himself must create in the heart.' So a pure heart is one that is purified by the Gospel and is found in people of all walks of life, but rarely, if ever, in monasteries.[8]

'Blessed are the peacemakers' – here Luther inveighs against so-called Christian princes who are nothing but 'bloodhounds' with no other goal than to fight and kill. Luther was not an absolute pacifist, and he realised that a righteous prince may need to go to war to repel an invader or defend his people, but every effort must be made to preserve peace. A just cause is not a good enough reason to go to war; peacemaking should be tried first, even by the injured party. This blessing also includes private citizens who heal quarrels in the family and in society.[9]

The spiritual reading of the Sermon continues. The lustful eye must be plucked out of the heart, not literally out of the body; and then 'I could look at all women, talk with them, laugh and have a good time with them' without committing adultery. 'Yet we should not make the bowstring too taut', and Luther accepts the qualification made by some medieval theologians that 'if an evil thought is involuntary, it is not a mortal sin'. The solution is not to run away from women and society and become a monk, because in a desert or a monastery 'it is no credit to me that I do not commit adultery or that I do not murder or steal'. Luther recognises only two Scriptural grounds for divorce – adultery and desertion (Matthew 19:9; 1 Corinthians 7:13–15).[10]

Because the Sermon is intended for disciples, and Christ is not interfering in the secular order, taking an oath of allegiance to the prince or while on jury service is not forbidden; however, swearing on oath should not be necessary among brethren. Turning the other cheek really means not desiring revenge. Assault and theft must not go unpunished, but that is the responsibility of the magistrate or the prince; individuals should not seek to settle scores themselves. Similarly, a Christian may join the armed forces, become a ruler or a judge, because civil government is ordained of God.[11]

The verses on almsgiving and prayer Luther applies freely to his own times: how there is much praying in the monasteries, but it is all a chore and does not come from the heart. 'Faith quickly gets through telling what it wants', but the monks, who must pray for hours on end, are only too glad to get through 'their babbling'. Prayers should be 'brief, frequent and intense'. On fasting, Luther admits the 'ancient fathers may have meant well', but in the monastery 'I never saw a genuine fast'. Plenty to eat and drink was the norm. They called it fasting to abstain from meat, but they enjoyed the 'finest fish with the most expensive sauces and spices and the strongest wine'. Such fasting should be 'trampled underfoot as a mockery and a reproach to God'. Luther is not opposed to fasting entirely, but it should be voluntary.[12]

Luther identifies the two 'most dangerous and corrupting forces in Christendom: spiritually the false teaching that corrupts faith; physically, the greed that corrupts its fruit'. The Sermon now attacks 'the great idol Mammon'. Again, the evil is not wealth exactly, but the love of it and the craving for it. A city governor who keeps a store of grain and a parish that has a treasury reserved for the poor and needy, are not breaking the commands of the Sermon. But a love of Mammon proves that the heart is far from God and does not trust Him to give us our daily bread, and has no desire for spiritual things. Luther slams the 'rich bellies' – all they care about is 'having their kitchens filled'. Luther loves the illustration of the birds of the heaven that neither sow nor reap. 'Look at the dear little birds'; people put them in cages and give them plenty to eat, but when they are 'free in the air they are happier and fatter' because this is the life they love. They sing their 'Lauds and Matins to their Lord early in the morning', yet none of them know of a single grain laid away in store. 'They sing a lovely, long Benedicite [sic] and leave their cares to our Lord God.' A nightingale is an 'excellent preacher ... happier in the woods than cooped up in a cage'; the birds are our teachers, and how God 'enjoys it when they fly around and sing without a care in the world'. By contrast, what a 'crazy and foolish' creature greedy man is. 'A little finch, which can neither speak nor read, is his theologian and master.' Jesus praises the birds and lilies to shame us and show 'how abominable our unbelief is and to make it look ridiculous'.[13]

'Judge not, that you be not judged' is directed against 'Mr Smart Aleck' (*Meister Klügel*), who thinks he knows it all and is forever passing judgement on someone else. Luther hates the fault-finders and the nit-pickers; 'neither God nor the world likes him, yet he is all over the place'. But this command does not prevent civil government or the magistrate judging cases in court or the legislature, and it does not stop Christians from judging false teaching. Pearls of the Gospel should not be given to swine like the fanatics and schismatics; and here Luther digresses into an attack on princes who have learned to be 'unafraid of the pope', but who have no love for Christian truth, and whose sole desire is to increase their power. (No names are given.) Luther takes heart from the encouragement to pray and that he has entered in through the narrow gate, which is hard only because of the hatred of the devil, the world and the old Adam in us who prefers an easy life. Beyond lies a 'beautiful and wide room', and for those who walk in the faith of Christ, the way will become pleasant and sweet. With the warning to beware false prophets, Luther is just as concerned about the Anabaptists as the papists and monks, because they threaten to undo the work of the Reformation. 'By their fruits ye shall know them' – compare what they say and do with the Word, and 'if we are taken in it is no one's fault but our own'. Luther will 'guarantee that no schismatic spirit will come without making his mark and leaving a stench behind'.[14]

Luther marks the closing words of the Sermon well; the call is to hear, but also to do. For Luther, justification by faith is not some comfortable academic theory. 'The doctrine is a good and a precious thing, but it is not preached for the sake of being heard, but for the sake of action and its application to life.'[15]

The Gospel of St John

For Luther, the Gospel of John was one of the choicest books of the entire Bible. His sermons on it cover Chapters 1–3, 6–8 and 14–16.

Luther marvels at its sublime opening, proclaiming the eternal divinity of Christ the Saviour. It was a 'manifestation of divine grace that Cerenthius assailed this article in the time of the apostles; for this is why John, the foremost apostle still living, wrote his Gospel … it was a true masterstroke'. (Cerenthius was a first-century opponent of John, who denied the Trinity and the divinity of Christ.)[16]

'In the beginning was the Word and the Word was with God and the Word was God': these are 'distinct Persons in a single divine essence'. John 'got the idea from Moses' (Genesis 1:1), but the evangelist's treatment is altogether grander. 'Nothing but faith can comprehend this … it is far too lofty for reason … let anyone who will not believe it let it alone.'[17]

Jews, Turks and heretics laugh at Christians and call us 'stupid geese' for worshipping three gods. Yet 'we did not invent this verse about the eternal divinity of Christ; it was transmitted to us by the special grace of God'. Luther is proud to stand by the Nicene Creed: 'Our dear Lord and Saviour, born of the Virgin Mary, is also the real, true and natural God and Creator together with the Father and the Holy Spirit.' With contemporary radicals like the Anabaptists in mind, Luther warns his people to 'beware of such schismatic spirits' as deny John's Gospel; for if Christ is not God Incarnate we are all doomed, because His death will avail nothing at all, and gone is all hope of eternal life and salvation. 'This is the only saving faith. Let whoever wants another go his own way and see how he fares.'[18]

'He came to His own and His own received Him not', and Luther applies this to his day. Christ has come to His own again, to Western Christendom through the Gospel, yet the 'pope and his faction' do not receive Him. Instead, 'our brethren who bear the Christian name ... persecute, banish and murder us'. What is interesting is this 'our brethren', as if Luther recognises that he and the papists are part of the same Western Latin Christian family, who both confess the Nicene Creed, the Trinity and the Incarnation; yet Rome is now a fiercer persecutor than the Turk, who at least allows some freedom of conscience in his dominions. Luther quotes Christ from elsewhere: 'brother will deliver up brother to death, and a man's foes will be those of his own house' (Matthew 10:21, 36). This Luther sees in his own times.[19]

'The Word became *flesh*', which means that He 'took on the human nature, which was mortal and subject to the terrible wrath and judgement of God because of the sins of the human race'. The Word did not 'flutter about like a spirit, but He dwelt among us ... He took the breast; His mother nursed Him as any child is nursed'; He was true Man from the Virgin Mary, though without sin.[20]

John the Baptist was a great and saintly man with a strict ascetic life, but he does not call the people to 'don a camel's hairy hide and put a leather girdle round their waists'. Unlike the monks, he preaches the Gospel of Christ. St Francis and St Dominic should have done the same instead of founding orders and rules. John had a divinely given understanding of the truth about Christ's eternal divinity before setting eyes on Him; even though John was born first he said, 'He was before me'. John confesses that all saints from Adam till now and the end of the world have received 'grace upon grace' from Christ alone. 'This fountain constantly overflows with sheer grace. Whoever wishes to enjoy Christ's grace – *and no one is excluded* – let him come and receive it from Him. You will never drain this fountain of living water; it will never run dry.' The italics (author's) suggest that Luther, persuaded by Melanchthon, may have left his earlier predestination behind him, and was now won over to universal grace.[21]

Next, the Baptist proclaims Christ as the Lamb of God to take away the sins of the world, unlike the lambs of Moses' Law, which could not take away any sin and were merely types of the true Paschal Lamb: 'The Law lays my sins upon me, but God takes them from me and lays them upon the Lamb.' (There will be more on Law and Gospel below under Galatians.)[22]

Luther harmonises John with the Synoptic Gospels on Christ's baptism; and he sees the Trinity again, in the Father's voice from heaven, the Son as man being baptised and the Holy Spirit descending in the form of a dove. Here 'the celestial choir of all angels is present; they skip and dance for joy'. Yet Anabaptists and fanatics 'speak sneeringly of baptism'; they 'gaze at this sacred act as a cow stares at a new door'.[23]

Luther notes that the cleansing of the temple appears in John 2 at the start of Christ's ministry, but after Palm Sunday in the Synoptics. Most commentators assume that there were two cleansings, but Luther thinks that there was only one, and that John has disregarded the chronological order. But minor problems like this do not bother Luther in the least. There are 'many sharp and shrewd people who are fond of bringing up all sorts of subtle questions', but if one Gospel does not agree with another on a minor point it is of no importance at all: 'just dismiss it from your mind.' What matters is that 'they all agree on this, that Christ died for our sins'.[24]

Nicodemus (Chapter 3) is not like Annas or Ciaphas; outwardly he is a blameless and honourable man, far better than monks and papists. Yet Christ 'lays him low' and tells him he must be born anew, because good works and a fine character will not win him eternal life. Here, once more, is justification by faith alone. Let the monks take heed: 'a cowl covers many a rogue, but it makes no one pious.' The works of man are nothing and are all in vain without new birth through the Holy Spirit and baptism. But Nicodemus cannot understand spiritual new birth. There he sits, 'wrapped in silence, brooding sadly, shaking his head'. So Christ says: 'My dear Nicodemus, why are you so amazed?' (Luther enjoys paraphrasing Scriptural conversations.) 'You cannot tell me where the wind comes and where it goes ... So if you cannot understand earthly things, how can you understand heavenly things?'

Turning back to his audience, Luther carries on the same theme. Who can explain how sound travels, how the movements of the tongue produce speech or how a seed grows into a fruit or tree? We accept these things because we see them; but 'we insist on delving into the extraordinary operations of God' like the Resurrection, Virgin Birth, the Trinity. 'In natural matters we cannot know anything, and yet in matters of faith we want to know everything.' The Law, the Psalms and the Prophets all declare 'that God is wonderful, and that His ways are past finding out'; yet 'we torture ourselves to death trying to explore the nature of God ... we are like patients who long to recover and yet refuse to obey the physician or to take his medicine'. And if reason cannot understand simple things, it will never rise to the heights of heavenly things like new birth or the 'Son of Man who is in heaven' – this is Christ's divinity and humanity, as the Creed says, a subject Luther returns to again and again in John's Gospel. For Luther, this is inseparable from salvation and he connects it directly with the next verse without a break. 'The Son of Man must be lifted up' – that is Mary's Son, Christ the Man. Then 'God so loved the world that he gave His only Son' – that is Christ the Eternal Son (John 3:15–16). It is the same person and the same result: 'whoever believes in Him will not perish but have eternal life.'[25]

This faith, however, is something far more than theoretical knowledge or consent. 'Good works must issue from this faith; otherwise it is not genuine. Faith … cannot remain without good works.' Thus John joins together three truths that can never be parted: the deity and humanity of Christ; faith in Christ the Saviour and Redeemer; and the good works which flow from faith.[26]

Luther does not moralise much in his sermons, but his theology is always practical. Occasionally he attacks immorality, thieving and greed, and he commends a pastor who, one Sunday morning, laid into local bakers for making their loaves too small and fleecing their customers. Luther knew such preaching was not popular and that 'pastors and listeners are soon parted'.[27]

John 6 – Christ the Bread of Life – does not refer to the Eucharist, according to Luther, in which he differs from many commentators. To come to Christ, to feed on Christ and to believe in Christ all mean the same thing.[28] Nor does he take a predestinarian line on verse 43: 'No one can come to me unless the Father who sent me draws him.' The Father draws through His Word and the promise of grace in Christ contained therein.[29] Luther is always driving home the chief theme of the Gospel as he reads it, as in verses 37–40: 'All that the Father gives me will come to me, and whoever comes to me I will not cast out … And this is the will of Him who sent me, that I shall lose none of those He has given me.' Here the evangelist 'weaves the two wills together, making the being of the Father and the Son one – one will, one mind, one wisdom, one work, yes, one Godhead, and one thing'.[30]

At the Feast of Tabernacles (Chapter 7) the Pharisees want to seize Jesus, but are thwarted by Nicodemus, now a disciple though a secret one. The word 'Nicodemite' would later become a derisory term applied to those who keep silent about their faith through timidity or some other reason, but this did not begin with Luther. He sees nothing wrong with a secret disciple, and 'good, pious Nicodemus' is now able to serve the Lord. So it is when enemies threaten the Church, God often 'puts a Nicodemus in their midst … to foil the plots of powerful rulers and angry lordlings'. In the Old Testament, Hushai did the same for David (2 Samuel 17:1–16).[31]

In Christ's valedictory address (John 14–16) Luther sees again the foundations of Christianity: the Trinity, Christ's divinity, justification by faith and the consolation of consciences. Luther takes heart from the weakness and perplexity of Thomas and Philip – so it is with all Christians.

Nowadays (Luther's days), the devil and his bride – 'Dame Witch, crafty reason' – are busy denying the divinity of Christ. They claim that God would not need to say: 'I will ask the Father' (14:16). Very clever, says Luther. But you must look at the passage as a whole, not snatch one verse out of context and twist the meaning. Christ speaks as God and Man in rapid succession: Here He says 'I will pray the Father', but a moment earlier He promised that 'Whatever you ask in my name *I* will do' (author's italics); and so on throughout the discourse.[32]

'My Father is greater than I': Here Luther quotes Hilary and Augustine against the Arians, saying that the Father is greater because the Son proceeds from the Father, not the Father from the Son. 'I shall let this pass', says Luther briefly, not overly impressed. Luther interprets from the context: The Father is greater in the sense that Christ, though God, is on earth in humility, a suffering servant; but this is only for a short time, and soon He will be glorified and ascend into heaven again. 'Christ speaks in this verse of passing from this life into the realms of the Father.'[33]

Only one truly divine could say: 'All that the Father has is mine.' Then Christ adds that the Holy Spirit 'shall take what is mine', so the Holy Spirit Himself is also true God (16:15). Luther is a great Trinitarian.[34]

Luther finds much that he can apply to his own times, for example: 'They will put you out of the synagogues' (16:2). So the pope excommunicates and persecutes real Christians, and the Gospel is driving the devil 'mad and insane'. Nevertheless, Luther draws great strength from the fourth Gospel and particularly these chapters. This is Christ's 'friendly farewell'; here He 'clasps His disciple's hands and bids them good night'.[35]

Romans

The lectures on Romans that have come down to us (*Luther's Works*, volume 25) were delivered during 1515–16, before Luther's Tower experience and also before his Ninety-Five Theses. As Brecht notes, they certainly contain glimpses of Protestant thought, but the 'Catholic Luther' is still in evidence, and he is so wedded to the 'theology of humility' that he can say that 'the only complete righteousness is humility'.[36] For this reason, and because this book is primarily about Luther the Reformer – the finished article – I am going to pass over these lectures. Those who wish to study his long and often tortuous spiritual journey are recommended to read the first volume of Brecht's biography.

After the Reformation breakthrough, Melanchthon wrote a commentary on Romans, and Luther felt that he could never improve on it, so he never tried. This means, ironically, that no treatise on Romans by the fully mature Protestant Luther exists. This deficiency is not as unfortunate as it might seem, because almost everything Luther wrote is, in one sense, a commentary on the epistle he loved more than any other.

Galatians

For a short while, the early, mainly Jewish Church carried on with some of the rituals of the Mosaic Law, like circumcision, though this was intended to be temporary only. When Gentiles were received into the Church the question arose as to whether they too were obliged, if only temporarily, to keep the Law. No, the apostles replied definitively (Acts 15). A little after this, and despite the emphatic decision of the apostles, Paul heard that the church in Galatia, which he had founded, had been induced into following the customs of the Law, including circumcision and the observance of certain festival days. Paul immediately dashed off his short, punchy epistle to the 'foolish Galatians', which covers ground similar to Romans, though it is starker and less expansive.

Its message is the core of the Reformation, namely justification by faith, not through works of any kind, even the works of the Law. Luther had already lectured on Galatians in 1519 and he returned to it in 1531. What follows is taken from the mature Luther's 1531 lectures, published in 1535.

The Mosaic Law is the basis for legal systems in most civilisations. Its main problem is that it can only condemn and never justify. Many may rightly claim that they have never killed anyone or stolen anything, but people who believe they have never coveted anything belonging to someone else are deluding themselves; still less can man love and trust the Lord thy God with *all* their heart, soul and mind. Thus anyone who chooses to live by the Law will end up being condemned by it. Therefore, justification through the Law is impossible; but Christ has redeemed us from the curse of the Law, says Paul, so the Gospel brings the forgiveness and life that the Law cannot do (Galatians 2:15–16; 3:10–14 and elsewhere). Hence Paul's strong warning to the Galatians: if you forsake the Gospel for the Law, you risk losing your salvation (Galatians 5:4).

So here is the difference between the Law and the Gospel, a theme repeated time and again in Luther's works. The Law makes demands and tells us what to do, but it does not give the moral wherewithal to fulfil those demands, which are too exacting for fallen mankind. This way, the Law becomes man's accuser, an indictment of sin and failure to which the human heart has no defence. So the Gospel offers the forgiveness, salvation and eternal life which the Law cannot do. The Gospel makes no demands; we are asked only to receive the blessings offered by faith. Hence justification by faith *alone*, without works of any kind, even the works of the Law.[37]

Linked to this, Luther develops his 'two kinds of righteousness'. One kind is mainly that of the Law, though it also includes traditions and customs handed down from one generation to another. This is useful and commendable in its right place – the secular life – because obviously it is a good thing when people do not commit murder and robbery, and when good laws are made for the benefit of all. But this righteousness cannot bring salvation or a peaceful conscience. Anyone who claims he is justified before God by this kind of righteousness, or by his own works, has effectively denied the Gospel.[38]

But there is another kind of righteousness – that of the Gospel – which is *imputed* to the believer for Christ's sake. The imputed righteousness does not make the believer perfect; perfectionism is impossible in this life. 'A Christian is not someone who has no sin or feels no sin; he is someone to whom, because of his faith in Christ, God does not *impute* his sin' (author's italics). A Christian, therefore, 'is righteous and a sinner at the same time' (*simul iustus et peccator*). They know they are far from spotless, but when they fail or sin they have a mediator, 'and the sin that remains is not imputed, but is forgiven for the sake of Christ'.[39]

Luther sees himself arraigned against Jews, Turks, Anabaptists and Romanists, all of whom, whatever their differences, are work-righteous in religion. The papists are his chief adversaries, because if even the Law, which was divinely ordained, cannot justify, still less can works devised by man, like monasticism, celibacy or the invocation of saints. 'Our Christianity', says Luther, adapting Paul (Galatians 3:17), 'existed four hundred and thirty years before our monastic life ... our sins were expiated by the death of Christ 1,600 years ago, before any monastic order, any penitential canon or any merit ... had been thought up.' Nevertheless, Luther is, as ever, keen to stress that he does not despise godly living. But Paul calls love, joy, peace, patience and kindness (Galatians 5:22) 'fruits of the Spirit', not works; the apostle 'adorns these Christian virtues' with a better title.[40]

This epistle is short – a mere six chapters – but Luther's lectures run to nearly 600 pages. His notes and those of his hearers testify to his earnestness and zeal in the classroom, and the longing that the truth of justification should take root lest it be forgotten, which he feared would happen after he and his generation had passed away. Even in Wittenberg 'some fanatic could stop this blessed progress of the Gospel in a hurry, and in one moment overturn everything we have built up with the hard work of many years'. This teaching of faith in Christ was Luther's one thing needful; 'if it is sound, all the others are sound as well'. His entire theology rested on it, though he still feared that he had failed to do the theme justice. Galatians he called 'My dear epistle ... my Katy von Bora'.[41]

Other Epistles

These can be covered quite briefly. 1 Corinthians 7 is a vigorous defence of the married state. Unlike most commentators, Luther does not agree that Paul was celibate; Luther insists that the apostle was a widower. Marriage is for life except in cases of adultery and desertion. Chapter 15 bases the Resurrection on the authority of Scripture. Luther enjoys stressing that, like all articles of faith, it defies man's reason.[42]

When Paul wishes that women should be silent in church, he is speaking of the public ministry. Luther accepts this without lingering over it. From Paul's warning to Timothy of future apostasy (1 Timothy 4:1–4), Luther turns on papists and Anabaptists alike with their false holiness, celibacy, regulations about eating and so on.[43]

From 1 Peter, an epistle he valued almost as highly as those of Paul, Luther understands the universal priesthood of believers (2:5–10). No Christian priest needs a tonsure. 'If shaving the head and anointing made someone a priest, I could even oil and anoint the hoofs of an ass and make him a priest too.' The word 'priest' should be synonymous with the word 'Christian'. Thus Luther attacked one of the foundations of the medieval Church, according to which the consecration of the priest conferred on him an indelible mark that set him apart from the laity. Luther recognises no such mark. In that sense, any believer could preach and administer the Sacrament. In practice, and for the sake of good order, each congregation has a pastor to do this, who should have a competence in Scripture and the original languages above that which would be expected in most lay people.[44]

Much of this epistle is fairly straightforward, except for the descent into hell (3:19–22). Luther admits this is 'a strange text', more obscure than any he knows. Candidly he confesses that 'I do not know for sure what the apostle means'. He is aware of the view that Christ descended into hell and preached to the unbelieving spirits of Noah's day; 'but I do not understand this, nor can I explain it'. Luther suggests that after His Resurrection Christ preached, through the apostles, to those in the prison of sin and the devil, like those in the times of Noah. But he remains undogmatic: 'Let him to whom a better understanding is revealed, follow it.'[45]

John's epistle has this apostle's familiar style, 'so beautifully and gently does it picture Christ to us'. 'That which was from the beginning, which we have heard, which we have looked upon' – this language, says Luther, 'is altogether childlike; it stammers rather than speaks, and the greatest majesty is combined with the greatest simplicity'.[46] Luther follows the tradition, dating from the Church father Irenaeus, that John wrote his epistle to counter Cerenthius, who denied the divinity of Christ in the latter part of the first century. Luther does not spare the pope either, because he denies the 'power and efficacy' of Christ. 'Although he acknowledges the coming of Christ and keeps the apostolic words', yet with his dogmas on satisfactions, saints and monasticism he has 'removed the kernel, namely that Christ came to save sinners'.

9

The Bible Teacher: The Patriarchs

*B*ecause the Hebrew language was generally less well known than the Greek, the Old Testament presented Luther with a challenge that he warmed to eagerly. His exegetical technique is known technically as the historical-grammatical method. Essentially, this is the way any competent researcher approaches their task, especially when their material is written in a foreign language. The aim is to find out the exact meaning of the text using the best grammatical aids available, and, wherever possible, to understand the historical context in which it was written.

Luther makes good use of the commentaries of the Church fathers, rabbis and medievalists, though he does so critically. Far more important to him is a good book on the Hebrew language, and frequently there are sections discussing grammar and the exact meaning of words or the names of places.

Luther's approach needs to be distinguished from what is nowadays called 'fundamentalism' or strict literalism. These are over-used terms, but normally they mean someone who believes, or is supposed to believe, that every single word in the Bible is literally true. Now Luther believes the Bible as much as anyone; it is the Word of God inspired by the Holy Ghost. But this inspiration does not operate mechanically, like a manager dictating a letter for a secretary to type, and Luther is willing to allow for minor lapses on the part of the writer. Thus, in Genesis 1 Moses 'seems to be forgetting himself' when he misses out the creation of the angels and the fall of Satan. St Matthew makes a 'slight mistake' when he says Jeremiah instead of Zechariah (Matthew 27:8; Zechariah 11:12–13; Jeremiah 19:1–13, 32:6–9). Such trifles do not bother Luther in the slightest, and those who waste time over these things he calls 'worse than mad'. The accounts of the Lord's Supper by Paul and Luke 'please me better' than those in Matthew and Mark, while John's Gospel is his favourite of the four.[1]

Luther began lecturing on Genesis in the mid-1530s and continued with it for most of the rest of his life.

Genesis: Adam to Noah

One of the strangest ideas of modern times is that the 'age of reason' did not begin until the eighteenth century. Another is that until the nineteenth century, everyone thought that the world was a mere few thousand years old, as the Bible says. If this were true, then Luther would have had a nice easy task with Genesis. Yet he begins by saying that no one, even in the Church, has explained the opening chapter satisfactorily. When he came to Genesis, Luther felt he was beginning anew.[2]

Luther knew all about reason, philosophers and 'old world' theories. Based on the atomism of Democritus, Epicurus had taught that the world came into being by a chance combination of atoms. Luther had also read Aristotle and his ideas of the eternity of matter (see p.14). Luther rejects this pagan rationalism, and follows Moses and the Creation of the world 6,000 years ago; but 'of this it is impossible to convince a philosopher, because according to Aristotle no first man or last man can be conceded'. This, however, is the weakness of man's reason, which 'cannot rise to a higher level than to conclude that the world is eternal'. Plato is a bit better because 'he assumes matter and mind to be eternal, but declares that the world had a beginning and was made out of matter'. Even the Church fathers are suspect in Luther's view, because they were a little too much under the influence of Aristotle and Plato. Hillary and Augustine held that the world was created instantaneously, not over six days. Augustine allegorised the six days, and this fondness of allegories increased in the medieval age. So reason and philosophy on the origins of the world and on life itself, far from being a future development, was widespread in the medieval age, and it influenced the ideas even of theologians of the Church.[3]

From all this, Luther broke away. He was determined to stick to the text, which says that God created all things out of nothing. Only in one respect does Luther follow the old Church when he sees the Triune God in Creation: the Hebrew word for God is plural (*elhoeem*). Thus Luther harmonises Genesis with John 1 and the Creed: the Father is Maker of all things, the Son the One by whom all things were made and the Holy Spirit was hovering on the face of the deep.[4]

Luther does not teach blind faith and he welcomes a spirit of enquiry. Nevertheless, he insists on the essential incomprehensibility of the deity which is way beyond man's wit or reason. It is madness to pretend that by reason alone we will learn about the infinite; we must be guided by the Word. Trying to understand God without His Word is like trying to 'ascend to heaven without ladders', and is bound to fail. Hence Arius, when he denied the divinity of Christ, hit on the idea of an 'intermediate being between the Creator and the creature'. Monks are just as bad when they imagine 'a God sitting in heaven who intends to save anyone wearing a cowl'. Monasticism, in Luther's view, was just another example of man's foolish reason at work, stifling faith and true understanding.[5]

When Luther speaks scornfully of reason – and he often does – he means the mind of man presuming to know better than the Word of God in spiritual things, and particularly on subjects like the Creation, salvation and the resurrection. He never despises learning, education, natural intelligence and good sense. He commends the study of useful arts and science, including philosophy, and occasionally he quotes Aristotle and other authorities of his time. This sort of reason Luther warmly commends. Nevertheless, it must recognise its limitations. 'We Christians must be different from pagan philosophers'; we must be honest enough to admit our ignorance, and not deny revealed truth or devise false theories about divine things.[6]

The creation of the sun, moon and stars on the fourth day gives Luther the opportunity to discuss, in a generally friendly way, the views of astronomers of his time. But astrology, a subject that fascinated many Renaissance humanists, Luther rejects. 'I shall never be convinced that astrology should be numbered among the sciences.' It lacks proof; it is based on partial observations only, and 'I do not believe that from such partial observations a science can be established'.[7]

'Let us make man': here God 'summons Himself to a council', a fitting introduction to the uniqueness of human life. Luther despises Epicurus for saying that man exists solely to eat, drink and be merry; this makes man no different from a beast. The 'image of God' is the absence of sin in man – his heart, intellect and will entirely pure, 'an enlightened reason' with a true knowledge of God and without fear of death.[8]

According to a modern theory, Chapters 1 and 2 give competing accounts of the Creation. Luther has anticipated this (or maybe he knew of it already and it is not so modern after all). Chapter 1, says Luther, ends with the creation of man and woman on the sixth day, while Chapter 2 gives the *details* of the sixth day.[9]

The tree of knowledge was created for Adam to show 'worship and reverence toward God ... by not eating from it'. Adam was 'to yield to God the obedience he owed'. Thus it became 'a tree of divine worship'.[10]

Luther knows that the four rivers of Chapter 2 do not have the same source, as the text implies at first glance. (They are assumed to be the Ganges, Nile, Tigris and Euphrates.) But Moses was describing the old world, which is now lost and gone forever, destroyed by the Flood (2 Peter 3:6). Luther warns his students it is impossible to learn about the Edenic world by looking at a map of the present one. Because they forgot this simple lesson, authorities like Origen are full of 'silly allegories'.[11]

Before the Fall, Adam lived in the 'innocence of a child', untainted by sin, but lacking the perfection of a glorified being. He was therefore capable of falling from grace; hence the command not to eat, lest he shall die. Why, then, did God make a creature that fell from grace apparently so easily? Luther recognises the problem, but not enough is revealed in the text to give a proper answer. This is not the only time when Luther is unafraid to say that he wished Moses had given more details.[12]

On the creation of Eve, Luther digresses to speak of reason and faith. Reason, he agrees, must reject this text and follow Aristotle. Because 'nothing comes into existence alive except from a male and a female, then no first human being can be conceded'. Yet where does Aristotle, and reason, go from here? If there was no 'first man or a first woman', only confusion and ignorance remain. 'What does a philosopher know about heaven and the world if he does not know even whence it came and whither it tends?' Luther quotes Aristotle again: 'Man and the sun bring mankind into existence.' Yes, but in that case man and the sun must be infinite, 'for you will never find a human being who is either the beginning or the end'. In other words, philosophy knows nothing and will always know nothing of the 'final and efficient cause' of all things. And what sort of 'wisdom and knowledge' is that, demands Luther?[13]

So Luther turns to Holy Scripture, where 'we find the beginning, which is impossible to find through Aristotle's philosophy'. And why should the Creation be so unbelievable, he asks his students? Nature is full of wonders and incredible things, like childbirth, a small seed growing into a great tree and the motions of the heavenly spheres. Only because these are commonplace do we cease to marvel at them. Yet because the Creation happened only once we cannot take it in, so 'we regard it as a fairy tale'. All this shows 'how awful the fall into original sin was, since the entire human race knows nothing of its origin … such horrible blindness, such a pitiful lack of knowledge'. Yet for Christians, 'it is incalculable wisdom' to know about this 'foolish fairy tale as the world calls it, namely, that the beginning of man's existence was through the Word'.[14]

So this was how God made Eve from the rib of Adam – He spoke and it was done. It is nonsense to imagine that 'like a surgeon He did some cutting'; and Luther ridicules the 'prattle' of some of the commentators he had read, who speculated on whether Adam had one rib too many to begin with, and whether men have more ribs on one side than the other. The way to understand is to believe the Word. Reason cannot explain normal births that happen every day: 'how my mother conceived me, how I was formed in the womb, or how my growth happened – all that I leave to the glory of the Creator.' To

Luther, the account of the creation of Eve is no stranger, nor more unbelievable, than a mother giving birth to her child.[15]

On the Fall (Chapter 3), though Luther follows the narrative faithfully, he is not bothered about what kind of fruit Adam ate, and he brushes aside theories that the fruit was too delicious for Eve to resist. The point is not the eating. The serpent – really Satan – tempts Eve to distrust God, to disbelieve Him and thereby to cut mankind off from Him. 'The source of all sin is unbelief, doubt and abandonment of the Word.' This, not fruit, is the cause of original sin: the distrust and ingratitude shown to God by disregarding His Word, the pride of man that wishes to 'be as gods', to learn the way of life and knowledge independently of God.[16]

Luther does not apportion blame between Adam and Eve – both were guilty. More important is the fact that original sin is the consequence of the Fall. The intellect is darkened, a right knowledge of God is gone and the conscience is no longer at peace. The will and reason have become depraved, now at enmity with God. All are now born 'from unclean seed', from which we inherit 'ignorance of God, smugness, hatred against God, disobedience, impatience and similar grave faults'.[17] The ugly manifestation of this is seen when Adam flees from God. Even Adam's 'discernment and good sense' have vanished – he is afraid because he is naked, yet God made him naked. Adam's trust in God has turned to hatred and resentment as he blames God for 'this woman thou hast given me'. Then Eve blames the serpent and so sin snowballs: first unbelief, then disobedience, then excuses, finally an accusing finger against God. 'This is the last step of sin, to insult God and charge Him with being the cause of sin.' Such is mankind without God and without grace.[18]

God's response is the promise of grace, the Seed of the woman – Christ – who will crush the power of Satan and redeem fallen man from eternal death. This promise Adam believes, and names his wife Eve, mother of the living. The guilty pair will be saved, but they must be banished from Eden. The tree of life is no longer for them. In Eden they would never be safe from the tempter. For salvation and eternal life they must look for the Seed of the woman.[19]

Luther rounds off the Creation and the Fall by defending his trust in the narrative, and rejecting once again the allegorical methods of medieval and some patristic writers. 'It is the historical sense alone which supplies the true and sound doctrine.' Once this is recognised, allegories are permissible 'as an adornment and flowers to embellish or illuminate the account'. But 'bare allegories' alone are just 'empty dreams'.[20]

Now Moses begins the history of the primordial world. Adam knew his wife, and here Luther condemns celibacy and monasticism and praises the married state. At the birth of Cain, Luther translates Eve saying 'I have gotten *the* man of the Lord' (author's italics), as if Eve believed that this was the promised Seed. (Genesis 4:1. The NIV has: 'With the help of the Lord'; KJV: 'I have gotten a man from the Lord.') Eve has faith in the promise, but she is mistaken about the person.[21]

Guided by the New Testament, Luther says it was not Cain's offering that was rejected, but Cain himself. Abel offered 'by faith' in the promise, Cain did not (Matthew 23:35; Hebrews 11:4). Cain and Abel, both sons of believing parents, are types of the false, persecuting church and the true, faithful church. On the murder of Abel, Luther contrasts the compact style of Moses with the classics, and how Cicero or Livy would have narrated the crime: 'in lofty style the fury of the one brother and the fear, the laments, the entreaties, the tears, the suppliant hands of the other.' But such emotions cannot be adequately described, so the terseness of Moses is best: 'he suggests by dots, as it were, what cannot be expressed in words.'[22]

Cain is sentenced to be a wanderer and a fugitive in fear of his life. In vain he builds a city, but he has no security there. The old trick question of Cain's wife is easily answered: Luther notes that Adam and Eve had daughters as well as sons, so Cain married a sister.[23]

Eve's faith is seen again in the birth of Seth (4:25). Now she knows that Abel, not Cain, was the righteous one, and God has given her another son in the place of Abel. Luther wonders why the Roman Church, with 'such a vast swarm of saints', has forgotten Eve.[24]

Unlike modern exegetes, Luther sees design and harmony in the opening chapters of Genesis, even though the details are often sparse. Moses begins with the Creation; then comes the Fall and the promise of Christ, and the enmity that will arise between the Seed of the serpent and that of the woman. This enmity is seen in Cain's murder of Abel. The descendants of Cain are dealt with quickly before the author returns to the Seed of the woman, the birth of Seth and the generation of the godly in Chapter 5.[25]

Yet in Chapter 6, doubtless after many generations, the 'sons of God' – the godly line – depart from the example of their parents, forsake the faith in the promised Seed and intermarry with the Cainites, the ungodly people. The godly race has apostatised and turned to idolatry. This is the greatest wickedness of all, and for this reason the Flood came.[26]

'Giants' and 'men of renown' were the result of this intermarriage; not physical giants, but tyrants, oppressors and scoundrels, just as the 'pope with his cardinals and bishops are today'. Noah, the 'preacher of righteousness' (2 Peter 2:5), was the only faithful man left. So God confirms His covenant with Noah. 'This is the second promise of Christ, and it is taken away from all the other descendents of Adam and bestowed on Noah alone.'[27]

After the disaster of the Flood, Luther has to tackle Noah's tipsiness, and to do so he went in for the exegetical equivalent of method acting – the night before he gave the lecture he deliberately drank too much. Noah's lapse was not a serious one. Shem and Japheth recognise this and act respectfully towards their father, but Ham is self-righteous and contemptuous.[28]

The prophecy that follows – the curse on Ham and the blessing on his brothers – is given extended treatment because its fulfilment is not immediately obvious. Though Ham is cursed to slavery, before long he is building great kingdoms (10:6–20). Nimrod the 'mighty hunter' was a Canaanite (10:9). He seems more prosperous than either Shem or Japheth. Whereas the Canaanites live well, the sons of Shem – Abraham, Isaac and Jacob – live in tents. The Egyptians were descendants of Ham, yet they held Israel in slavery. So it must be, says Luther: the promise is delayed, and the just must live patiently by faith while the ungodly flourish.[29]

Shem is the father of the Jews, and salvation is of the Jews; but Noah prophesied that Japheth may 'live in the tents of Shem'. Luther understands this in the light of Romans 11:11 – in the New Testament Church the Gentiles will be grafted in, and Japheth is the father of these Gentiles. He is not 'of the stock of the people of God, which have the promise of Christ'; nevertheless, he will be 'called by the Gospel'.[30] Luther then notes how some physical Canaanites were saved, like Naaman the Syrian, the widow of Zarephath and others. From this he concludes that the prophecy must be spiritual, not literal. So Shem stands for the believing Jews, the patriarchs, apostles and prophets; Japheth for the believing Gentiles. Ham stands for the unsaved and the unbelieving; and not just the heathen either. Ham also includes Pharisees, papists and Turks. Prosperous and powerful though they may be in this world, Ham's 'slavery' is his godlessness, and the eternal ruin that will eventually overtake him.[31]

Here is an example of the difference between Luther's historical-grammatical method and strict Biblical literalism or 'fundamentalism'. To be consistent, the fundamentalist would have to apply Noah's prophecy literally, somehow. Luther reads the history of Noah's sons and sees that this approach does not work. Using the New Testament as a guide, therefore, he makes it an inspired prophecy of the Gospel. This 'spiritual' interpretation does not clash with the historical-grammatical technique, and Luther has not forgotten the text in front of him. However, Japheth did not literally 'live in the tents of Shem', so unless the prophecy is completely meaningless, it must have a spiritual fulfilment, and that is seen in the Church. This brings to light another aspect of Luther as an interpreter of the Old Testament. Historical books he treats as narrative, and though he may occasionally make an allegory *of* them, he never reduces them to *bare* allegory. Prophetic books or passages very often have a spiritual fulfilment. This will be seen most clearly in Isaiah.

Chapter 10 gives the history of the three sons and their immediate descendants. Those of Japheth settle mainly in the northern lands and Europe; those of Ham in Canaan and the southern lands, including Egypt and Africa. Unlike some men since, who have treated this chapter far more crudely, Luther says nothing about the colour of the skin of the Hamites or Canaanites. Instead of their servitude, he notes their fame and power, their mighty men like Nimrod and the good fortune they enjoyed living in the most agreeable parts of the world. As well as the Jews, Luther includes the Persian, Assyrian and Indian peoples among the descendants of Shem.[32]

Abraham, Isaac and Jacob

The call of Abraham was an act of grace, because his kindred, though descendants of Shem, had lapsed into idolatry (Joshua 24:2). Yet Abraham will be 'physically father of the Son of God' to show Christ is the 'Saviour of sinners'. Abraham in faith leaves all, follows the call and heads out into the unknown, trusting in the divine promise: 'In thy Seed shall all nations of the earth be blessed.' And out of this promise 'flowed all the sermons of the prophets concerning Christ and His kingdom … in these few simple words the Holy Spirit has encompassed the mystery of the Incarnation of the Son of God'. Nor does Luther forget Sarah and Lot, and the servants who loyally accompany them, and how times have changed since then; because 'if these servants and maids had been like ours, they would never have lifted a foot'. The faithful party made up a 'true and holy church, in which Abraham was the high priest'.[33]

Most commentators censure Abraham for his white lies about Sarah being his sister; but not Luther. Abraham did not sin, at least not seriously; he was forced to seek refuge in Egypt because of the famine, and he sought to save his life, not for his own sake, but for the sake of the promise that God had made to him. In any case, God protected Abraham and supported him through all his trials. Luther commends the Egyptian king for quickly returning Sarah to Abraham. Though the text does not actually say this, Luther reckons that after his meeting with Abraham, the King of Egypt 'came to the knowledge of God and of the true religion'. So everything works for good: God protects those who trust him and converts the hearts of those who do not yet know Him.[34] This interpretation is typical Luther: moralising is kept to a minimum, minor faults are readily excused and the Gospel appears wherever it is possible to bring it in.

Abraham is no wandering friar: more than once on his journeying he builds an altar, which means he 'teaches the true religion' and establishes a church. Luther celebrates Abraham's rescue of Lot and his victory over the four kings with a small but dedicated force. 'Where is there in the historical accounts of the heathen to match this courage? The Alexanders, the Hannibals and the Scipios vie among themselves over supremacy in the glory of achievement, but I place Abraham ahead of them all.' Unlike men of the world, Abraham is not ambitious for power; he seeks only to save his kinsman and does not take advantage of his victory to establish a kingdom for himself. Abraham prefers the blessing of Melchizedek, and Luther follows tradition in making Melchizedek the arch patriarch Shem, still alive at this time. He rejects the medieval exegesis that the bread and wine is a type of sacrifice of the Mass: it was just a festive meal and thanksgiving for the victory over the kings. Abraham won't even take his share of the booty that the King of Sodom offers; and what a contrast he makes with 'our centaurs who rightly or wrongly seize for themselves whatever they can'. If Christendom's princes 'add even one village to their domain they demand that their titles and coats of arms are inscribed on it'.[35]

A lengthy discussion follows on how Abraham believed God and it was reckoned to him for righteousness (Genesis 16:6; Romans 4:3). This is the Gospel in the Old Testament. Abraham is justified by faith alone, before either the Law or circumcision was given.[36]

When Sarah offers Abraham her maid, Hagar, Luther does not judge them: 'here were no lustful thoughts.' They were anxious about the promise of the Seed and Sarah knew she was barren; and 'the longer the promise was delayed the more heavily the cross was laid upon them, and the more unbearable the trial became'. Thus Sarah 'relinquishes the glory of motherhood in the utmost humility'.[37]

Luther is generous towards the minor characters in the book. Though they were not in the Messianic line, Hagar and Ishmael, he believes, were saved.[38]

Luther also manages to defend Lot, Abraham's nephew and his daughters, now trapped in Sodom. The destruction of Sodom, like the Flood, moves Luther: 'for it is something awful to feel and experience the wrath of God raging almost beyond measure against the wretched human race.' Luther assumes that the men of Sodom who surrounded Lot's house were the foremost men of the city and not just a rabble; they were married men, but sexual libertines. For men like these the 'ravishing of girls is an every day sport'. They are a proud and tyrannical people (here Luther quotes Ezekiel 16:49–50). Their chief guilt, however, is not immorality but idolatry, forsaking the true God, which will invariably lead to all kinds of evils. Only fifteen years earlier the King of Sodom greeted Abraham (14:17–24) and heard him witness to the true God; yet Sodom was now degenerate and idolatrous.[39]

Like a defence advocate taking on a hopeless case that no one else wants, Luther pleads Lot's cause. He was weak rather than wicked when he offered his daughters to the scoundrels outside; he was at his wit's end and probably would not have actually done what he said. He was desperately trying to protect his guests somehow. The same applies to Lot's incest. 'Lot had lost his very dear wife and his daughters their very lovely mother.' Their home was destroyed, and 'anybody not crushed by such misfortune has a heart harder than adamant'. People in extremity easily become deranged; they say and do things they later regret. Lot's conduct is hardly saintly, but Luther rejects medieval theologians like Lyra who pass a harsh judgement: 'Lyra sat in his monastery and did not see Sodom in flames.' Lot and the girls are sadly misguided; however, they sin 'not because of malice and lust but because of their great disturbance'. (As we would say, the balance of the mind is disturbed.) Luther asks why God allowed such a thing, and admits he does not know. It is a warning to all Christians to take care and pray continually lest they fall. But Luther notes that Ruth the Moabitess is included in the genealogy of Christ (Matthew 1:5).[40]

Back now to Abraham, who is ever on the move, this time going to Negev; and what a different religion this is from that of the monks and papists. These 'moles' in the monasteries can see nothing praiseworthy in the patriarch taking his family with him to visit the people of his times, for they 'admire only their cowls, vigils and fasts', and they get upset when they don't find these things in the Bible. The incident with Abimelech gets similar treatment to the earlier one about the King of Egypt (Chapter 12); Abraham stumbles but not grievously, God preserves him and Abimelech is blessed.[41]

Great rejoicing follows the birth of Isaac; the promise fulfilled at last. Then we have a domestic dispute when Hagar and Ishmael are forced to leave. Luther interprets this in the light of the New Testament (Galatians 4:21–31). Sarah is right; Isaac is not just her son, but the son of the divine promise, whereas Ishmael is not. Abraham is reluctant at first because Ishmael is his son too, by Hagar, and he has a natural feeling for them both. 'In wedlock there is a far severer training in faith, hope, love, patience and prayer than in all the monasteries.' Believers should not worry if such disputes arise, because this happens to the 'most affectionate and the saintliest people'; yet the 'self chosen forms of worship of the monks are nothing but dung'. Eventually Abraham yields, assured that God will protect and bless Ishmael; but the parting, though spiritually necessary, 'is a far heavier burden than when a monk wears a cowl and girds himself with a rope'. It is a sad story, which Luther 'can hardly read with dry eyes', especially when Hagar and Ishmael, mother and son, are wandering alone in the wilderness. The trial is necessary to humble Ishmael, who had derided Isaac, and God preserves them both. As a result, Ishmael lives, and lives well, in Paran, not far from Abraham. The parting was not permanent as Abraham had feared, and Ishmael was later reconciled with Isaac (Genesis 25:9; Numbers 10:12, 13:3, 26).[42]

Abraham's pact with Abimelech, sealed by the gift of a few sheep and cattle, shows the patriarch freely engaging in civil affairs, unlike the pope and his monks. Life must have been so wonderfully simple in those days when 'no wordy documents' had to be drawn up by professional lawyers. The 'artlessness of the ancients' delights Luther; it reminds him how the morals of 'our unfeeling age have deteriorated'.[43]

Luther admits he is struggling with God's terrible command to Abraham to slay Isaac – 'this trial cannot be overcome and is far too great to be understood by us'. The only solution is to 'take refuge in the promise'. Reason says that if Isaac must be killed, the promise is void, and either God has been lying or this command is a trick. But Abraham believes the promise, and that Isaac, born of a woman who was barren, will be raised from the dead by the power of God. Luther, however, is no mere theoretical theologian, and he lingers long over the dreadful sorrow of Abraham, who excels all saints in faith and obedience. 'I could not have been an onlooker, much less the performer and slayer.' It would need a Paul to expound this chapter adequately. Then Luther changes his tone: really God is just 'playing with the patriarch and his son'. As Abraham and Isaac sensed, the whole thing was 'sport and not death'. This is the true lesson to learn, that in the sight of the living God 'death is nothing but a sport and empty little bugaboo'. This the patriarchs understood, this the Christians know; but reason and the heathen are altogether without hope.[44]

Chapter 24, the marriage of Isaac and Rebecca, is a long eulogy of marriage against celibacy and libertinism. 'What is more desirable than a happy and peaceful marriage, where mutual love reigns and there is a most delightful union of the hearts?' This is what Abraham seeks for Isaac. Luther also commends Abraham for marrying Keturah after Sarah passed away. The patriarch wanted to be fruitful and multiply and rightly so, even in old age; he thought his body was as good as dead before Isaac was born, but God gave him added strength and vigour beyond what was normal. He was among the 'angelic husbands'.[45]

Now is the time to 'bury the saintly patriarch Abraham' and move on to Isaac. But Rebecca, Isaac's God-given wife, is barren. Luther speaks much of the need to wait on the Lord in prayer during times of trouble, but this is not just pious waffle and he does not make light of these trials: they are 'far more difficult than the preaching of the Word or other duties in the church'. Mercifully, Isaac does not pray in vain: not only is Rebecca's barrenness taken away, the chiefs of two nations are in her womb. Rebecca remembers the word from God that the elder shall serve the younger, and her affections are drawn towards Jacob; but Isaac admires Esau the hunter, which troubles Luther, especially when Esau shows his true colours in despising his birthright. Luther defends Jacob for inducing his brother to sell it for a dish of pottage: Esau was legally the elder, but Jacob was the child of the promise, the one elect of God.[46]

Luther hugely enjoys the section where Isaac is fondling Rebecca. Here he parodies the reaction of an imaginary, indignant monk: Why does the Holy

Spirit record such 'trifles' and 'stoop to the lowest fooleries of married couples'? Why is there nothing about fasts, vigils, orders and cowls? Because, says Luther, the Holy Spirit is opposed to the 'enemies of marriage' in the papacy and the monasteries. It is an 'extraordinary kindness' of God that He instituted this 'union of one man and one woman', and Luther is delighted that Scripture should take time to record that Isaac 'had fun with his beloved Rebecca'.[47]

The story of Rebecca and Jacob snatching the blessing from Esau has produced much pious disapproval from commentators; but not from Luther. He sets the matter in its context. Rebecca sees that Isaac is about to make a big mistake, and grants to Esau the blessing that God has promised to Jacob: hence the deception. Rebecca is not devious by nature; she has a zeal for the word of God, which Isaac has either forgotten or misunderstood. Rebecca 'relied on the promise'. Whatever the disapproving fathers and the medievalists say, she 'is obeying God … therefore she did not sin'. Rebecca acts with faith and courage, with 'skill, ingenuity and a very beautiful stratagem'; but she does it all 'in accordance with the will of God'. Yet the plan seems to be going badly wrong: though Isaac's sight has failed, he knows the voice is Jacob's voice and he is suspicious. Here, Luther admits, 'I would have let the dish fall, I would have run as though my head were on fire'. But 'Jacob lies magnificently' and Isaac is 'beautifully deceived by the counsel and cunning of Rebecca'. (And it may be advisable for parents not to let their children read this section unsupervised.)[48]

Luther is not, of course, encouraging deceit. He just takes the context into account, and, in his unique and often highly entertaining way, he tries to present the acts of the patriarchal family in the best possible light. He understands that life has its genuine and difficult dilemmas. He also looks below the surface to the heart of the matter. He notes that Esau's claim to be the firstborn son, though apparently factual, is really humbug, because Esau has despised his birthright and sold it for a dish of stew. A superficial reading of the passage suggests that Esau is the one wronged, but in fact his heart is more false than Rebecca's or Jacob's. They do what they do for the sake of the promise of God; Esau claims his birthright only when it suits him.[49]

Luther again praises Rebecca – the 'prudence and shrewdness of the godly woman' – for concealing Esau's murderous intent from the aged Isaac, and prevailing upon him to send Jacob away to find a suitable wife from the family of her brother Laban. Again and again, Luther praises the life of faith of the patriarchs: Jacob is promised the blessing, but the promise is delayed and he has to serve Laban.[50]

But does Luther perhaps exaggerate when he assumes that Jacob set off on his journey 'with many tears and frequent sighs and sobs'; and that it was a 'great misery to go into exile and darkness this way, to depart from father and mother'; and that because of what he and Rebecca had done he is 'tormented and distressed' by fear of Esau, so he trudges on his way 'in great grief and unrest with worries and tears'?[51] None of this is in the text. Jacob is the heir to the blessing, and is setting off to see his mother's family and meet the woman who will be his wife – hardly a depressing thought. Moments of anxiety there may have been, but Luther does not allow for the likelihood that Jacob might relish the prospect of travel, especially with such an agreeable end in view. Luther can speak very movingly about Abraham's feelings when he was ordered to slay Isaac; he is sympathetic to Abraham and Sarah having to wait so long for the promise to be fulfilled, and to Rebecca in her dilemma over the blessing; and he is one of the few exegetes charitable or game enough to stick up for Lot. At times, however, Luther seems rather too ready to read his own *Anfechtung* into the text when it does not really belong there.

Jacob's ladder is interpreted in the light of John 1:50: a renewal of the promise of the Seed who will be God and Man, and the blessing of all nations. Jacob's vow after the vision is one of thanksgiving, quite unlike a monastic vow. He consecrates the place as a church of God, and he promises to give a tenth of all, not because God is in need of anything, but to establish schools and churches and to help the poor and needy.[52]

Jacob meets Rachel and kisses her, and *pace* the monks, 'it is a Christian and godly thing to love a girl and join her to you in marriage'. Jacob is willing to serve for his bride; he is 'no lazy beast like the servants and maids we have today'. Monks may disapprove of Jacob for admiring Rachel's beauty, but God does not. Jacob has been chaste all his life thus far, unlike the 'impure celibacy of the papists in the monasteries, which are now mere brothels'.[53]

Then, despite seven years loyal service, Laban plays a 'dreadful and cruel' trick on Jacob. Luther is amazed at the patriarch's patience and restraint – 'I surely would not have endured it'. Luther wonders what wedding ceremonies were like in ancient times and how it could be that Jacob was so deceived as to mistake Leah for Rachel. But Jacob suspected nothing; he was 'absorbed in love and joy … drunk, not with wine, but with love for Rachel'. Nothing was further from his mind 'than that the old fox would take his bride away'. In the circumstances, Luther justifies Jacob for having two wives – he was too kind a man to ditch Leah. Rachel, however, is the beloved; she is the 'dear girl', the 'lady of the house … she gives herself airs'. Jacob pities Leah, but he does not love her, so poor Leah 'sits sadly in her tent'. God alone has compassion for her; He makes her fruitful and Rachel barren.[54]

Rachel is beautiful, Leah's eyes are tender; because she is barren, Rachel resents Leah and complains to Jacob, who is upset because none of it is his fault. Jacob tends the flocks, someone else is milking cows. Why, asks Luther, does the Holy Spirit record such things, which the 'very saintly pope and the altogether chaste monks and nuns despise … and pride themselves on their celibacy'? Childbirth, looking after sheep, tiffs between husband and wife are beneath them; but God delights in common and lowly things, because He 'wants to be with us, to care for us, and to show that He is our Creator and Ruler'.[55] (Whenever Luther sets the monastic life in contrast with that of the patriarchs, which is quite often, it is plain that he is greatly enjoying himself.)

Motherhood and the longing for children are wonderful, so Rachel does what Sarah did and gives her maid to Jacob; then Leah likewise. Jacob now has two wives and two maidservants. Jacob is no libertine, insists Luther; he does not take the maids by force, and he only accepts them when the wife is barren. (True – see 30:1, 9.) He also works hard for Laban, looking after the flocks and the cattle, and he does not spend all his life making love. (Also true – see 31:38–42.) Jacob is sexually active 'only out of love for offspring'. This last point is Luther's own, with no supporting text. It may sound slightly strange to modern ears, but for centuries, until Luther, almost all Christian commentators were strict celibates, and Luther is forever trying to rebut the idea that there was something unseemly or risqué about the sexual activity of the patriarchs.[56]

Rachel and Leah are 'aflame with the desire to become mothers of the Promised Seed'; they know that to Jacob the 'Saviour of the world was promised'. This is why the sisters are yearning for children and getting envious with each other. Even without the promise, in ancient times fertility was considered a great blessing (Exodus 23:26), and Luther regrets this is no longer so – 'many have an aversion for it, and regard sterility as a special blessing'. Luther says, with disgust, he knows someone who called his wife a 'sow' because she bore him too many children.[57]

Finally Jacob leaves the greedy Laban to return home. True to form, Luther excuses Jacob for fleeing by stealth – he has a command from God to go and Laban has treated him shamefully. Rachel is forgiven for stealing her father's household gods; not only has Laban effectively disowned his daughters and failed to provide for them, he has also turned to idolatry, so whatever happens to him is his own fault. Laban is a self-righteous hypocrite and a worthless man. Jacob's only mistake is to let Laban search the tents for his household gods and put Rachel's life in danger, though Jacob acts innocently, not knowing what Rachel had done. Yet 'God and His angels keep watch when Jacob sleeps'; when Laban rushes into Rachel's tent and sees her sitting on the camel's saddle, God 'turns off his understanding', and he never dreams that his daughter would treat his precious gods so insolently. Rachel acted 'on the spur of the moment', such is a gift in women: 'the first impulse of their nature in sudden dangers is usually excellent and very successful.'[58]

Free at last from Laban, Jacob prepares to meet Esau, advancing towards him with 400 armed men. Luther admits that Jacob's wrestling is one of the most obscure passages in Scripture, but he is determined to make a go of it.

Allegories are instantly rejected. Jacob may not realise it at first, but the man he wrestles with is God, or God's Son, who appears to be Jacob's adversary, preventing him from returning home and seeing the promise fulfilled. But God 'plays with him to discipline and strengthen his faith', just as a godly parent takes an apple away from his son as if in anger, but really in jest. He hopes the child will not run away or sulk, but rather 'embrace his father all the more and beseech him' to give him his apple back. Such 'games' are common in the home, and God is wont to 'play with His saints' this way; it is all a game to Him, though it does not always seem so to us. Yet Jacob prevails. 'Our Lord Jesus Christ tested Jacob not to destroy him but to confirm and strengthen him … that he might conquer and joyfully praise the vision of the Lord.' God then takes away all thoughts of revenge from Esau's heart and the brothers are reconciled. Luther reckons that Esau was saved in the end because he spoke sincerely and candidly to Jacob.[59]

So far, the book has been a story of the grace of God and the great faith and perseverance of the patriarchs. Up to now, the godly clans have acted, on the whole, honourably, and Luther has defended them stoutly. Now the emphasis switches somewhat to the long suffering of God, because some members of the patriarchal family reveal a darker, less pleasing side to them.

Overcome by curiosity, Jacob's daughter Dinah goes to see the girls in the surrounding villages. Luther does not shy away from the story of her rape, and his heart goes out especially to her father Jacob: what has he done to deserve this; where was the divine protection he was promised? 'God and the angels close their eyes and pretend not to see.' Even the 'saintliest men' must suffer terrible trials which no amount of patience can endure. The only certain lesson is that 'we may stop our mouths if similar calamities befall us too'. The anger of her brothers is understandable, but their revenge is 'atrocious and cruel' and cannot be excused. Simeon and Levi are to blame for the slaughter, but not Jacob.[60]

Jacob's sorrows mount. Soon he is mourning the loss of Rachel. Then Reuben, the firstborn, sleeps with Rachel's maid Bilhah, the mother of two of Jacob's sons, a crime which 'even the heathen abominate'. Then 'into hell itself the aged Jacob is hurled by the wickedness and criminality of his sons', who, envious of Joseph because he is his father's favourite, sell him into slavery. Luther calculates that all this happened within a mere three years, leaving Jacob 'in the greatest sorrow, in darkness and the shadow of death'; and it would be twenty-two years before he saw Joseph again in Egypt. These crimes and tragedies are written for the consolation of the Church to show that, despite appearances, God never abandons His people; rather He takes control, as it were, and turns all things, even the worst, for good. The brothers want to ruin Joseph, but, as the Psalmist says, God 'sent a man before them' to Egypt to save Jacob (Psalms 105:17).[61]

Judah, meanwhile, marries a foreigner and commits incest with his daughter-in-law, thinking mistakenly she is a whore. Again Luther asks: why does the Holy Spirit record such shameful things? Partly to tell us who Tamar was, for she appears in Matthew's genealogy of Christ, but also to show the patience of God with his people even when they act dreadfully. The door of mercy is always open. 'What hope would be left for us if Peter had not denied Christ ... and if Moses, Aaron and David had not fallen?'[62]

Now to Joseph in Egypt, and Luther reckons Potiphar is a fortunate man to have such a fine servant, because nowadays most servants are lazy and good for nothing. Luther combines these pithy and homely touches with close attention to detail. 'Moses points out the outstanding wisdom' Joseph showed when he fled from Potiphar's wife, because it is 'difficult for a young man to struggle with a beautiful woman'. Youth is prone to 'rush headlong into love and lust'. Far wiser to flee than to try and reason with a 'smooth tongued lady' like this. Joseph pays the price for his loyal service, and so all Christians must cope patiently with the lies and ingratitude of the world. Once more, it appears that God has deserted him, but again He works it all for good. 'God looks upon our affliction with open eyes; He smiles at us and takes delight in the virtue and victory in our afflictions.' Wrongfully imprisoned, Joseph is not forsaken, for the Lord is with him and Christ 'comes and lights up hell with gracious eyes'.[63]

Meanwhile, Joseph must live by faith and hope. He must also endure the misery of unanswered prayer, because if he prays to be set free to serve Potiphar again, or to return to Jacob, the answer would have to be no. Luther recalls how, in uncertain times, he has often asked in prayer for this or that, only for God to 'laugh' at his wisdom and reply (here is Luther paraphrasing the deity): 'Come now, I know that you are a wise and learned man; but it has never been My custom for Peter, Dr Martin or anyone else to teach, direct, govern and lead Me ... I will do the leading, ruling and directing.' Reason will never understand God, because it is His 'wonderful practice to make all things out of nothing and again to reduce all things to nothing'. Set alongside the divine, man's wisdom 'is truly foolish ... even folly itself'.[64]

Luther, however, never makes light of Joseph's misfortune. He speaks feelingly of the young man, almost as if he were his own son exiled, friendless, unjustly imprisoned, calling in prayer for help but apparently all in vain: 'the hearing follows, to be sure, but the calling lasts too long.' Yet Joseph's prayers are heard, eventually, and again Luther paraphrases the unspoken reply from heaven: 'I am the Lord your God whom you are invoking, whom you are censing ... I smell and take great delight in the burning of that incense; for the incense of your prayer, faith and hope has filled not only My nostrils but also all heaven. I will liberate you in a way beyond what you can understand.' As often, Luther feels free to bring in verses from all over Scripture, not just the text before him, hence 'The word of the Lord proved him true' (Psalms 105:18–20) and 'The sufferings of this little while are not worthy to be compared with the glory to be revealed' (Romans 8:18). So God sends Joseph a 'magnificent and wonderful liberation', far above anything Joseph could have asked for or imagined. 'Ah! Our God is a fine God, if only we could believe it.'[65]

Thus, Joseph is summoned before Pharaoh, who, says Luther, 'becomes a Christian' because he recognises the Spirit of God in a foreign slave. Joseph is raised to the king's right hand, and Luther praises the office of a chief minister of state, a demanding task when carried out well and honourably. Joseph marries the daughter of an Egyptian priest, but Luther is adamant that he did not fall into idolatry and he invokes the Psalms again, that Joseph converted many away from idols to the true God, though probably not the entire nation (Psalms 105:22). Luther wonders why Joseph did not send word to his father – maybe 'God prevented such thoughts' in view of what was to come.[66]

Though, as always, he steers clear of allegorising, Luther sees Joseph as a type of Christ, rejected by his brethren, delivered up to the Gentiles, then exalted among them, and finally leading his brethren to repentance and reconciliation.[67] So when Joseph's brothers come to Egypt to buy food, Joseph plays a 'wonderful kind of game with them'; he feigns harshness in order to humble them, but really he seeks only their good. This is God's way with His people, just as parents may appear angry with erring children. *Pace* the papists, Joseph wants no satisfactions from his brothers, only contrition and restoration to life. Though a guilty conscience plagues them, still they cannot bring themselves to confess the wrong they have done, so the climax is delayed until Judah makes his intercessory prayer, offering his life to save Benjamin.[68]

As ever, Luther stresses the human aspects of the story, as when Joseph is unable to contain himself when he sees Benjamin for the first time. Then Judah so stirs the heart of Joseph with his noble entreaty, and with the memories of his mother and father, that he can hold back no longer, and 'now it comes out like a cloudburst' – *I am Joseph*. Natural love is godly and praiseworthy; only fanatics despise it.[69]

Luther admires Joseph's prudent administration of the country and commends good government. Meanwhile, after a long, eventful life, Jacob sees Joseph again at last, and he blesses the King of Egypt and the Twelve Patriarchs, before 'giving up his spirit in faith and hope in the Christ to come'. When Joseph follows him, the age of the patriarchs draws to a close.[70]

Few in Western Christendom can have devoted more time and sympathetic effort to the study of their lives and works, their faith, virtues and failings as Martin Luther did. He is homely and down to earth, but also scholarly and insightful, invariably thought-provoking, frequently entertaining, often uplifting, at times fanciful, occasionally outrageous, always interesting, never dull. It is a pity the *Anfechtung* is sometimes allowed to intrude, like an unwelcome guest at dinner who sours the atmosphere. It is also a bit unfortunate that Luther was not a little more succinct, because he might have had the time to leave some equally rewarding material on the other great historical characters of the Old Testament – Deborah, Gideon, Jephthah, Samson, Saul, David, Solomon and the kings of Israel up to the captivity and the restoration.

10

The Bible Teacher: Psalms and the Prophets

Psalms

'What is the Psalter but prayer and praise to God?' And for Luther, the chief theme of praise is the Gospel, which he finds over and over again in the Psalms.[1]

In Psalm 2 God laughs at his enemies; this is the divine derision that made a mockery of Pilate, Herod and the chief priests by raising Christ from the dead. The Psalm then proclaims the deity of Christ ('You are my Son, This day I have begotten you') and the Gospel: Zion is given to Christ without His request, but the nations are given Him *at* His request, because the promise of the coming Messiah was given to the Jews. The rod of iron is the Gospel that will dash to pieces all His enemies unless they become wise and yield to the Son. To take refuge in Him means to believe and trust in Him, not in work-righteousness or monasticism. So the Psalm proclaims the 'heavenly religion'.[2]

Psalm 8 is a 'glorious prophecy about Christ', forsaken for a little while (at Calvary) and then crowned with glory and honour. The 'infants and sucklings' are the apostles and the ministers who follow them. To man's reason it seems 'silly and foolish' to send 'poor, simple fishermen' into the world; yet here is a power that 'neither emperor nor king, neither princes nor potentates can resist … the power from the mouths of babes and sucklings slashes through and gains the victory'. The pope cannot stop the Gospel either, even though we do nothing except 'open our mouths and speak the Word … we wield no sword and shoot no guns'.[3]

Psalm 19 – 'The heavens declare the glory of God' – is the Gospel again. The Law of Moses was given only to the Jews, but this voice 'goes out into all the earth'. The prayer at the end – 'cleanse thou me from secret faults' – shows that the 'saints are sinners too, but they are forgiven and absolved'.[4]

The 23rd Psalm gives thanks to God for His Word, which restores the soul and guides in the paths of righteousness. This the Law cannot do; it only makes demands and accuses the soul.[5]

Psalm 45 is a song of 'the kingly bridegroom and His queenly bride', Christ and His Church. This king is the 'most excellent of men', but also true God, whose throne will last forever – His divinity and humanity in the Old Testament again – and His kingdom is spiritual and eternal, not earthly and temporal.[6]

The 'crowd of monks', who chant and pray the penitential 51st Psalm daily, know nothing at all of its real meaning. Here is the truth about repentance, namely contrition and faith in the mercy of God. Hence the Psalm begins – 'Have mercy on me …' The subject is not just David's adultery or any other single act. The Psalm is a master lesson in the root cause of all sin, namely the fallen nature of man, but it also proclaims the grace of God who is ready to forgive and justify. When David confesses he was conceived in iniquity he 'wraps up all of human nature in one bundle'. He asks God to purge, wash and cleanse because he knows the legal sacrifices and the cleansings of the Law cannot purify or 'blot out' transgressions. He knows, too, that the righteousness of the Law does not justify in the sight of God. 'Here there is no difference between the present church of the faithful and the faithful in the Old Testament, except that they believed this sprinkling would come, while we believe that it has been manifested and completed.' All this is the antithesis of everything Luther once heard in the monasteries. 'You young men are lucky', he tells his students.[7]

Psalm 82 is a word to temporal rulers (called 'gods') that God is watching them and will judge them according to their deeds. If their deeds are evil, and if they oppress the poor and the righteous, God will deal with them; but it is not for man or for the Church to take such matters into their own hands, as Paul explains in Romans 13. Luther reserves the right to reprove bad princes from the pulpit provided there is no incitement to sedition or unrest. Obedience to princes does not mean that we must be blind to their wrongs. Princes should also support the Gospel, and punish not only seditious heretics like Anabaptists, but also all openly false teachers. Luther is also prepared to let rulers arbitrate on ecclesiastical disputes, as Constantine did with Athanasius and Arius.[8]

Psalm 90 is 'Moses at his most Mosaic (*Mosissimus Moses*) – a stern minister of death, God's wrath and sin'. In a 'magnificent manner he performs the ministry of the Law'. But at the end he has to appeal to God to 'make us glad according to the days thou hast afflicted us' (verse 15). Here the Law-giver prays for the coming of Christ, without which no redemption is possible.[9]

Psalm 101 is one of 'praise and thanks to God for the secular authorities'. Here Luther defies the tradition, which read into the text the virtues of monasticism; this is a Psalm of a great king, who rules in the fear of God.

Luther recognises that such princes are rare, but he admires good government both as an art in itself and a gift of God, even in the heathen. Roman imperial law is 'heathen wisdom', but it is far superior to canon law, and Luther urges all those who want to become accomplished in civil government to read Homer, Virgil, Demosthenes, Cicero and Livy. Pagan rulers like Augustus are commended as 'noble examples of worldly government'.[10]

Psalm 110 is one of the finest Messianic psalms. It proclaims Christ as David's Son and David's Lord, as the Gospel says (Matthew 22:44). His exaltation proves His deity, even though Arians have tried to 'drill a hole' through this Psalm: God may exalt any mortal man, but never to His right hand.[11]

'The Lord will send the sceptre of thy Kingdom out of Zion' (Luther's translation) – this is the Gospel which began in Jerusalem. Today (Luther's day), and until all enemies are subdued, the Gospel is proclaimed 'in the midst' of enemies, an impossibility in a political kingdom, but true of the spiritual kingdom of Christ. As Son of David, however, Christ has no entitlement to be priest, because David was of the tribe of Judah, not the priestly tribe of Levi. So Christ's priesthood will be different from the one established under the Mosaic Law – Christ will be our eternal priest after the order of Melchizedek (Genesis 14). This theme is developed in Hebrews 7.[12]

'He will drink of the brook in the way' – this is the cup of Calvary. After this 'He shall lift up the head' – this is the resurrection and exaltation. 'This beautiful Psalm, therefore, is the very core and quintessence of the whole Scripture.'[13]

Luther had intended to write a hymn about the Sacrament. 'But the Holy Spirit, the greatest and best Poet, had already composed better and finer hymns, namely the precious Psalms, to thank and praise God. Therefore I gave up my wretched and worthless poetry, and took up this Psalm [111], the Holy Spirit's hymn and poem.' Believing that the Psalm was sung as a commemoration of the Passover, Luther applied it to the Eucharist. He justified this 'borrowing' because Paul applies Isaac and Sarah to the Church (Galatians 4:22–8). He then gives two interpretations: the first from the standpoint of the Israelites; the second for the Church. For the second, though not the first, Luther divides the Psalm into twenty-two verses, as the Hebrew does, with one short verse for each letter of the Hebrew alphabet.[14]

Psalm 117 is the shortest in the Psalter – two little verses – and Luther's commentary on it runs to nearly forty pages, which gave him the chance to cheerfully mock his own wordiness. The praising of God among the Gentiles is, of course, the Gospel age.[15]

Psalm 118 is Luther's favourite. 'I love it so and want to see it enriched and adorned in every language.' He made the words of verse 17 his personal motto – 'I shall not die, but I shall live, and recount the deeds of the Lord'. It is a Psalm of praise for the goodness of God in all things. 'What is a kingdom compared with a healthy body? What is all the money in the world compared with one sunlit day?' Because these gifts are commonplace, no one gives thanks for them. But the greatest gifts are the Word and the Sacraments. Inevitably, the Church is beset by dangers and enemies, but 'in the name of the Lord I cut them off', as the Psalmist says (verse 11). This means 'we Christians crush the heathen through our prayers'.[16]

Later generations of Protestants, like the Roundheads in the English Civil War, would use texts like this as battle cries, but Luther never does. The Christian's struggles and victories are always spiritual, and any vengeance is in God's hands.

The last verse repeats the first – 'Give thanks to the Lord for He is good; for His steadfast love endures forever' – just as we 'often sing a good song over again'. So Luther ends 'this my own beloved Psalm'.[17]

The Prophets: Isaiah

'Two things are necessary to explain the prophet Isaiah', says Luther: knowledge of grammar and the historical background. Thus, the historical-grammatical method is applied to the prophets as well as the historical books like Genesis. As with Noah's prophecy of Ham, this does not demand strict literalism, and it leaves Luther free to give a spiritual interpretation. What guides him is the 'chief and leading theme' of all the prophets, namely the 'coming Christ', as St Peter says (1 Peter 1:10).[18]

Chapter 1 sets the historical context: Isaiah lives in the days of the Kingdom of Judah after the Kingdom of Israel has ended, and he preaches repentance to a sinful and rebellious nation. 'The ox knows its master and the ass his owner's manger … but my people do not understand' – such is 'the wisdom and godliness of men who depart from God', worse than a dumb ass even though 'there is nothing they think they do not know'. Yet a faithful few will always remain; and 'in the latter days the mountain of the house of the Lord shall be established … and many people shall come to it' (Luther's rendition of 2:2–3). Luther applies this and the parallel passage in Micah 4 to the Gospel and the Church.[19]

'Out of *Zion* shall go forth the Law' (author's italics): this is the Gospel beginning at Jerusalem, not the Law given from Sinai. The 'swords into ploughshares' is spiritual: those who receive the Gospel and keep it will not wage war. Luther blames false Christians and the heathen for the bloodshed in the world.[20]

This sets the tone for Luther's treatment of Isaiah. Every prophecy finds its fulfilment in the New Testament kingdom of Christ. Luther does not believe in any literal millennial reign on earth or any kind of millennialism (sometimes called chiliasm). The wolf lying down with the lamb is neither a picture of millennial bliss nor a restored creation, but is one of the reconciliation that the Gospel brings: Saul of Tarsus was a wolf before his conversion, but then he joined the fellowship of the lambs he used to persecute. The child playing on the viper's nest is the Christian playing with the devil and no longer afraid of him. The wilderness rejoicing is the Church flourishing in hitherto heathen lands.[21]

In Chapter 6 Luther empathises with the prophet's confession that 'I am a man of unclean lips'. The Law, under which Isaiah lived and taught, cleanses no one. Something else must take away his guilt and atone for his sin. So the Seraph pronounces him absolved and gives a sign of the live coal; this is the Word and Sacrament foreshadowed. If Luther saw any Trinitarian allusion in the 'Holy, holy holy', he does not mention it here. The prophet's commission is fulfilled in the New Testament.[22]

In Chapter 7 Luther tackles the prophecy that the 'Virgin shall conceive' with a typical combination of earthy good sense and insight (7:14). Modern critics trumpet the fact that the Hebrew word *alma* means 'young woman', not specifically 'virgin'. Luther needs no one to tell him this; he also notes that 'an old woman can be a virgin, but she is not called an *alma*'. To understand the meaning Luther now looks at the context. Because this is a sign given by the Lord, it follows that a special birth is announced. It would hardly be a divinely given sign if a girl, who today is a virgin, later gets married and becomes pregnant: such things happen all the time without signs from on high. So this is no ordinary young woman; she 'has to be both a virgin and with child'. St Matthew explains the rest.[23]

Chapter 9: 'For unto us a Child is born … and the government will be upon His shoulder', and Luther asks what sort of child this can be. Kings of the world are carried by their subjects, but Christ carries His people and bears their burdens. His name is wonderful because it is above all reason and natural wisdom that Christ's righteousness is ours by faith. This is 'the most delightful kingdom … a happy reign in which mercy flourishes'.[24]

In between the chapters on the ancient nations and their downfall, Luther finds favourite Gospel themes. The 'strong city' (26:1) is the Church, against which the gates of hell shall not prevail. 'The righteous nation' is the Church which 'preserves faithful things', the promises of the Gospel. 'Thou shalt keep in perfect peace him whose mind is stayed upon thee' is the same as Romans 5:1: 'Since we are justified by faith we have peace with God.' But Luther is not routinely or unthinkingly Christological, and the king who will reign in righteousness (Chapter 32) is Hezekiah, not Christ; this is a celebration of a godly prince who will survive the assault of the Assyrians. Then in verse 15, 'by a leap the prophet rises up to Christ Himself' and the days to come when the Spirit will be poured out from above. Thus Hezekiah is a type of Christ.[25]

Sennacherib's failed attempt to take Jerusalem (Chapters 36–7) Luther turns into a sermon on the triumph of faith over mighty hostile forces. As the Assyrian taunts Hezekiah and makes tempting offers, Luther draws on his own *Anfechtung* and gives his students some words of homely advice: never debate with the devil, as Eliakim did; do as Hezekiah says and 'do not answer him'. Trust in God, who can deliver from all danger, and call on Him in prayer. Luther never underestimates the challenge, however. 'The faith of the godly ... is not some fixed aptitude in the mind, but it is a spirit that wavers and falls and rises.' Only after a struggle does it triumph and learn that the whole thing was determined long ago. Sennacherib's army is then destroyed utterly; not even 'a thousand Hectors' could save him. Historians and poets would have used a torrent of words to describe the slaughter – 'hail from here, lightning from there, thunder from somewhere else' – but the prophet, like Moses with the destruction of Sodom, needs only a verse or two.[26]

Luther mentions the story that Sennacherib planned to sacrifice his sons to his gods, and when they found this out they killed their father while he was worshipping his idols in the temple – 'this is what the Hebrew writers report, and it may well be true'. He thinks the practice of sacrificing children among the heathen may have begun when 'reason, that most stupid ape', tried to copy, but succeeded only in perverting, the story of Abraham and Isaac.[27]

So Hezekiah is blessed, and fifteen years are added to his life; but Luther is worried that he might have lapsed into smugness when he showed off his treasures to the Babylonian envoys. Pride is a 'great monster ... I have asked God day by day to free me from this. I shall not avoid it so long as I live.' Even this most godly king was not free of it. 'I do not know how to stand up against this sin. Praise puffs us up, hatred exasperates us. Where do we want to go? ... We must despair of ourselves and run to Christ and beg Him to be gracious.'[28]

Luther accepts the division of Isaiah into two books at Chapter 40. From now on the book 'is nothing but prophecy', first of Cyrus and then of Christ; 'and here the prophet is the most joyful of all, fairly dancing with promises'.[29]

'Comfort, comfort, My people' is the Gospel preached to consciences crushed by the Law, because the Law comforts no one. The 'warfare' ('hard service' in the NIV) is ended – the Law has done its work, in the Gospel all iniquity is pardoned and the Christian receives double gifts for all their sins. Luther brushes aside the idea of Jerome and others that this means double punishment.[30]

Luther makes sport of papists and monks when the prophet praises the unfathomable wisdom and counsel of God. 'Who has directed the Spirit of the Lord?' the prophet asks. Those, says Luther, who claim that 'the church has the power to change the Word, so that the sacred Scriptures should get their authority from the faith of the Roman Church'. 'Who has been His counsellor?' Now Luther paraphrases the reply of the monks: 'We are His counsellors. I know that this rule and cowl of mine please Him, because I have chosen them myself.' 'Who taught Him the path of justice?' I did, says the self-righteous monk. But the wisdom of this world is nothing to God; He will blow the proud away while He sustains and helps the weary and fainthearted. Luther now bursts into a doxology reminiscent of St Paul: If I am a sinner, Christ is righteous; if I am poor, Christ is rich; if I am foolish, Christ is wise; if I am a captive, Christ is present to set me free …[31]

Luther sees plenty more Gospel themes in the next few chapters, but the prophet soon digresses to the coming of Cyrus the Great, the Persian king who conquered Babylon and allowed the Jews to return to their homeland and rebuild the temple.[32]

Because the Lord calls Cyrus His 'anointed', just as He did David, Luther reckons Cyrus must have been converted to the true God 'by a great gift of the Holy Spirit'. Luther does not believe the story from Herodotus the historian that Cyrus was killed by a woman. Cyrus was a pagan called of God for the deliverance of His people in captivity, and through him 'the readings and the preaching of the Word were again restored'. All this Cyrus did at his own expense ('not for price or reward' – 45:13). Thus, 'by grace alone all things come to us who merit nothing'.[33]

From Chapter 49 to the end there is virtually 'nothing but Christ' and the Gospel.[34]

Chapter 53 is a meditation on Calvary. 'These words, OUR, US, FOR US [Luther has them in capitals] must be written in letters of gold … He alone is a Christian who believes that Christ labours for us and that He is the Lamb of God slain for our sins.' Without saying explicitly that his opponents are *un*christian, Luther accuses the papists of treating the Cross as little more than a historical fact, while, with their monasteries, satisfactions and work-righteousness, they deny its redeeming power. 'My sin is not mine', the Christian can say, but not the monk. 'The chastisement of our peace was upon Him', and Luther notes the 'wonderful exchange: One man sins, another pays the penalty; one deserves peace, the other has it'. Yet the papists make Christ a Judge rather than a Saviour, and they choose the saints for intercessors. 'And with His stripes we are healed' – here is a 'remarkable plaster'. This is the 'supreme and chief article of our faith, that our sins, placed on Christ, are not ours'.[35]

The remainder of the book, for the most part, is the Gospel message in the Old Testament. Exceptions include Chapter 56, where the prophet urges his people to forsake godlessness and keep the commandments and 'thirst for the Promises afterwards'; then he invites the proselytes and Gentiles to do likewise.[36]

Entertaining polemic frequently enlivens the lectures. 'My thoughts are not your thoughts' slams Erasmus and free will (55:9). The 'dumb dogs who cannot bark' (56:10), who are useless as watchdogs against thieves, are like the bishops, these 'lazy pillow dogs who loll day and night' and gorge themselves and only 'pile up wealth for themselves'. John Huss is an example of a righteous man who perished, but who shall find rest in the last day (57:1). In Chapter 61 – 'The Spirit of the Lord is upon me' – Luther warns against lofty sounding speculations indulged in by monks and scholastics; Christ has come to bring good tidings to the afflicted and bind up the broken-hearted, and simple souls can 'be content with the God Incarnate'.[37]

Closing chapters get a contemporary application, including the trials of faith and the promises and consolations of the Gospel. All must be understood spiritually, and Luther has no time for millennialism or strict literalism. 'The sun shall no more be your light by day' does not mean that the sun will disappear, but that the Church 'will be illuminated and enlightened by Christ'. Occasionally the reader is left unsure whether Luther is ingenious or insightful. The infant who lives but a few days, and the one dying at 100 being a mere youth (65:20) are Hebraisms which 'do not fit well in our language'. So Luther gives it a Law and Gospel meaning. 'Laws and the monastic life beget nothing but pupils, and they remain boys for a hundred years.' The Gospel will do away with all this. Spiritually speaking, 'with all his tonsure and bald head', a monk remains a child all his life.[38]

In the last chapter, Luther notes that some apply the 'Lord coming with fire' and the 'new heavens and earth' to the end of the age. Luther prefers to apply it to the Christian era, the destruction of Jerusalem in AD 70 and the new, everlasting Christian priesthood replacing the Mosaic one.[39]

No commentaries on Jeremiah or Ezekiel have come down to us in translation, though Luther gives an extended preface on Daniel in his Bible (see Chapter 87–88).

Minor Prophets

Luther gives no little time and attention to the so-called 'Minor Prophets', which fill three volumes of the American edition of his works (*LW* 18–20). In general, he takes the same approach as he does to Isaiah: he follows the historical context as closely as he can, while the main theme of the prophet is to warn his people to keep the ways of the Lord and to look ahead to the Gospel and the coming Christ.[40]

The people thought Hosea was a 'fool and a heretic' when he married a woman they imagined was a harlot; but 'this is the nature of the Word, that it deals in apparent foolishness with the very wise'. (Actually, Luther does not think she was a harlot; she was so named because of the spiritual harlotry of the nation.)[41]

Like Hosea, Joel and Micah are especially rich in promises of Christ.[42] Amos was a shepherd of Tekoa, neither a prophet nor a prophet's son; and to show

His contempt of the proud, God raised up this humble man, just as He often chooses the 'foolish and weak things of the world to shame the wise and powerful', as Paul says (1 Corinthians 1:27).[43] Jonah is a story of the power of God that preserves from all dangers, and the efficacy of the Gospel when an entire city converts. It was a great encouragement to Luther, now engaged in controversies with radicals as well as Romanists.[44] Habakkuk 'has not seen the light of day since the apostles'. From this man that 'masterly statement' has been handed down: 'The righteous lives by his faith' (2:4).[45]

Luther begins his lectures on Zechariah by giving thanks to God for the 'many splendid and learned men who have done very intensive research on the Holy Scriptures'. Yet there are also 'frivolous spirits' who claim to know everything, who seek to show off their cleverness by expounding obscure books like Daniel and Revelation. This sort of thing is best kept among scholars in Luther's view, because the ordinary people need the pure and simple teaching of faith in Christ, the Creed and the Commandments. Let others boast, if they wish, of how well they understand the tabernacle of Moses. Luther has had 'about 10 of these exalted prophets before me, and they have always wanted to teach me lofty things'. These meetings motivated Luther to study Zechariah, mainly to show how, even in one of the Bible's most difficult books, the Gospel may easily be found.[46]

Luther does not, as it were, thrust Christ into the text randomly and arbitrarily. Joshua the High Priest, in Chapter 3, is just Joshua, not Christ, because the context demands it (in verse 8 he hears the promise of Christ). However, besides the passages directly quoted in the Gospels, the man with the measuring line in chapter 2 *is* Christ, 'the Master Builder of the [spiritual] New Jerusalem'. The lamp stand of Chapter 4 is the ministry and the various ministers of the Word that teach and feed the Church. The Shepherd's two staves of Chapter 11 – Gentle and Painful (Beauty and Bands in the KJV) – are the Gospel and the Law.[47]

When he gets to the final chapter, Luther makes a confession: 'Here I give up. I am not sure what the prophet is talking about.' He then makes a stab at it: 'The Lord will go forth and fight' is meant spiritually. This is the conquest of the Gospel in which Christ will fight through His Word. It cannot be Judgement Day, because then there will be no fighting and no one to oppose Him. Nor will He stand on the Mount of Olives on the Last Day; but it was there that the Gospel began.[48]

He treats Malachi 4 similarly. Christ rising with 'healing in His wings' cannot be Judgement Day either, so this must be the Gospel as well. The Day of the Lord is great and terrible in the sense of being wonderful; 'it will magnify, give life, justify, save'. And here the Old Testament ends; 'here the prophet stops and waits for the messenger Elijah, who is John the Baptist'.[49]

11

Dinner with the Luthers

The Table Talk is an entertaining collection of Luther's sayings, quips and general observations made at dinner times and other social occasions. Notes were taken down by friends or guests, and after Luther's death, gathered together and printed.[1]

Having listened to Luther in the pulpit and the classroom, the Table Talk offers the chance to meet him at home. But first, a few personal details may be useful.

Witnesses who saw him at the Leipzig debate described him as of medium height, but somewhat emaciated due to years of rigorous fasting, intense soul exercises and hard work. Judging by later portraits, Luther the Reformer must have fasted rather less severely than the Catholic Luther, for in middle age he gained an altogether healthier and more rotund appearance. He was reportedly blessed with a clear, fine ringing voice, which made him an impressive and attractive speaker. He was polite and friendly in manner, and at social gatherings witty and lively. Occasionally he could rebuke sharply, even violently. Others noted his 'dark, sparkling eyes'.[2]

Students who heard him preaching and lecturing in the early 1520s tell us that his voice could be 'gentle in tone, sharp in the enunciation of syllables and words'. He spoke 'with neither a too rapid nor too slow a tempo … with wit and expression, in such logical fashion as if one thought flowed from the previous one'. In the pulpit, says one, Luther was 'kind, mild and good-natured', with a 'pleasant and sonorous' voice that made his parishioners 'marvel at his winsome gift of speech', as he 'drives home his point like nails into the minds of his hearers'.[3]

Much is made by some writers of Luther's coarseness, a point which has some truth. 'We shall relegate the decretals of the pope to the privy', he told his students in one of his lectures. Then – this in a sermon – if you seek eternal

Katy – Catherine Luther – in 1526, from the painting by Cranach. (*Author's Collection*)

life outside Christ 'you are headed for the devil's behind'. Erasmus and Zwingli 'are nothing but wormy nuts that taste like crap'. More examples could be given, but they won't, because this is not to everyone's taste. It upset some of Luther's friends, like the refined Melanchthon, though Philip put up with it as cheerfully as he could. It is, however, a crass exaggeration to imply that Luther was full of such talk. It is quite possible to read 300 or 400 pages of Luther without coming across a single example of this sort of thing.[4]

Luther's health was generally good until his mid-forties. Thereafter he was prone to attacks of dizziness that made him feel faint. He commended the use and study of medicine, but he had no doubt that the chief bringer of plagues and sickness was the devil, and the surest remedy was faith and trust in God to overcome all trials.[5]

He was also troubled with kidney stones. In 1537, during a visit to Schmalkalden, the pain from the stones was severe, while rough and ready medicines only made him worse. Friends feared the end was nigh and arrangements were made to provide for Katy and the children. In agony, he began the slow journey home, hoping to die in his native Saxony. When recovery came quickly one night, Luther had no doubts about who cured him: 'Here the Lord appeared to me.'[6]

These worrisome ailments, however, persisted. Not long after he returned from Schmalkalden he suffered a fainting spell during a church service. In January 1541 an abscess on his neck and a perforated eardrum added to his misfortunes. Bouts of ill health, especially painful stones, dogged him from time to time until his death, frequently interrupting preaching and lecturing and leaving him exhausted.[7]

Fortunately, Luther never lost his sense of humour, and when well he could be an entertaining companion. Married life with Katy he loved dearly. It was all the sweeter because he knew that marital bliss was rare – sometimes husbands are harsh towards their wives, some wives 'domineer everywhere and regard their husbands as servants'.[8] (The modern notion that before the 1960s all women were timid vassals in their own home would have greatly amused Luther.)

Celibacy he despised intensely. He learned in the monastery that men are 'never less chaste than when they were alone and without women' and 'when a girl is denied them, it makes men crazy'. Marriage is a blessed, divine gift. 'There is no sweeter union than that in a good marriage; nor is any death more bitter than that which separates a married couple.'[9]

To friends, Luther would call Katy 'My rib' or 'My Lord Katy'. On his travels he wrote letters home to 'My Lord Katy' – this one signed 'Your obedient servant'. A letter to 'my dearly beloved' ends with 'Greetings, kisses, hugs and regards to all and everyone according to his place'. In expansive mood, another is addressed 'To my kind, dear Lord, Lady Catherine von Bora'.[10]

He opposed parents who forced their children into unwanted marriages, or forbade them marrying someone they loved, for reasons of status. Luther mentioned a certain 'honourable and well-to-do fellow' who wanted to marry a poor girl. She was willing, but her father was not, because he wanted her round the house. 'There are plenty of maidservants', Luther told him. 'Hire one for yourself.' After that Luther performed the marriage service.[11]

Luther could barely understand, let alone endorse, people who married without intending to have children. Nevertheless, children were not the only blessing in marriage, and 'this world has nothing more beautiful than this union of hearts between husband and wife'. Once Luther recalled a verse he had heard from a former landlady: 'To whom it can be given, nothing on earth is dearer than a woman's love.'[12]

A story survives of Luther looking fondly at a portrait of Katy one day. 'I think I'll have a husband added to that painting', he mused, and 'then we can send it to Mantua and ask these papists if they prefer marriage to their celibacy.' (The Romanists were holding a conference at Mantua at the time.) Luther called it the 'greatest blessing of God when love continues to flower in marriage', and this is the beauty of Christian marriage. 'First love is ardent and intoxicating, which dazzles and leads us on; but when the intoxication has been slept off, the connubial love of the godly is genuine, while the ungodly have regrets.' Luther wondered whether Jerome, the Church father who made celibacy such a great virtue, might have been homosexual.[13]

Luther's wife was no shrinking violet. Katy was a spirited lady, neither over-awed by her formidable husband, nor averse to giving her own opinions or putting her foot down. 'If I'm ever to have an obedient wife, I'll have to carve one out of stone', quipped Luther after a little tiff. Another time he told a newly married man to follow the general custom – to be lord in his own house, whenever the wife is not at home.[14]

A rumour once spread round Wittenberg that Katy was telling Luther what he should say in his sermons. It was probably nothing more than a bit of enjoyable gossip; nevertheless, Luther took it seriously enough to insist that while Katy ran the home, he wrote his sermons himself.[15]

Readers may not be shocked to learn that old Luther was not very politically correct. The rule of women in Church and state was not a good idea in his opinion, as Adam found out with Eve; but 'a woman can handle a child better with her little finger than a man can with both fists'. A man looking after a baby is 'like a camel dancing, so clumsily does he do the simplest tasks'.[16]

But raising children and running the home were worthy and blessed vocations in Luther's view; he never despised them. He had a lofty, almost ecstatic view of motherhood. 'Nothing lives without the womb, birth, milk and breasts. All kingdoms, empires, prophets and fathers have their origin from this source.'

Motherhood 'reduces all evils to nothing ... among all the various kinds of death, I consider it the saddest sight when a mother dies with her unborn child'. (These quotes, incidentally, come not from the Table Talk, but from lectures given to young male students.)[17]

After-dinner topics of conversation at the Luthers' included theology, the humanities, politics, social and family life, and, on one occasion, women's breasts. The consensus among the theologians gathered together was that 'large and flabby breasts ... promise much and produce little', whereas 'firm breasts, and even the small ones of tiny women are fruitful and can provide milk for many children'.[18] If some of these pieces read slightly eccentrically, that is because Luther and his colleagues were the first doctors of the Church in centuries to have wives and children, and they were enjoying the experience immensely.

The first child in the Luther household was Hans, born in June 1526. Elizabeth, born in December 1527, died before she became a year old. Magdalena, born in May 1529, was a sweet-natured child who tragically fell grievously ill and died in 1542. The other children were Martin, Paul and Margaret, born in 1531, 1533 and 1534 respectively.[19]

Besides his own family, six children of his now departed sister lived with him. Occasionally relatives came to visit, and sometimes students would stay there. Running the Luther home – Katy's duty – must have been a bit like running a small hotel. Luther was glad to leave Katy in charge of it all, and she had servants to help her.[20]

To his children he was deeply attached. Luther agreed that children had to be disciplined, but he was opposed to excessive harshness, mindful no doubt of experiences at home and school in his own childhood. 'When I'm writing or doing something else, my Hans sings a little tune for me. If he gets too noisy and I scold him a little, he continues to sing but does so more privately, with a certain awe and uneasiness. This is what God wishes: that we be always cheerful, but with reverence.'[21]

There was so much he felt he could learn from children. They are better in the faith than adults, because 'they believe very simply and without any question in a gracious God'. They live happily together 'in faith, without reason'. This engaging simplicity left him humbled. 'Though I am a great doctor, I haven't yet progressed beyond the instruction of children in the Ten Commandments, the Creed and the Lord's Prayer. I still learn and pray these every day with my Hans and my little Lena' (Magdalena).[22]

The death of Magdalena left Luther and Katy naturally distraught. 'It is strange', he reflected, 'to know she is surely at peace and well off there, very well off, and yet to grieve so much.' He consoled himself that 'I have sent a saint to heaven'.[23]

A discussion of the Luther family can hardly be complete without mentioning the much loved dog, Tölpel. Even in a pet Luther admired the work of creation, and he reckoned that his prayers would be answered much quicker if only he could pray to God the way his dog looked at him with its appealing eyes.[24]

Luther was an animal lover. Once he wrote an imaginary *Complaint of the Birds*, in which thrushes and blackbirds sing a lament over the bird-trapping activities of one of his servants, Wolfgang Siberger.[25]

Luther marvels 'how well a little fish multiplies', and how the 'rooster pecks the hen's head, the hen lays a little egg nicely in the nest, sits on it, and soon a young chick peeps out'. Of the wonders of nature, philosophers know nothing at all. Only Moses can explain it – 'God said, and it was so'.[26]

He was no fonder of hunting than he had been at Wartburg. When invited to a hunt by a deputy of the elector one day, Luther replied that 'I give chase to the pope, the cardinals, the bishops, the canons and the monks'.[27]

Luther enjoyed a good meal with wine and beer, and he was a hospitable man. His guests, including students, would ask him for his opinion on almost any subject, and here is a sample of what they heard. Love thy neighbour means love 'as chaste as that as a bridegroom for his bride', so that 'all faults are concealed and covered over, and only the virtues are seen'. Suicides are not necessarily damned; many may be tragically 'overcome by the power of the devil'. Judas could have been forgiven; his real, fatal sin was to despair of grace. Luther seemed understanding to a crime of passion. When a local cobbler caught his wife in the act of adultery, and Katy asked what should happen to the guilty man, Luther replied: 'I would have stabbed him.'[28]

Seventeenth-century English Puritans may not have appreciated Luther calling dancing a 'pleasant pastime'. Provided it was done decorously, he thought it an ideal way for young people of the opposite sex to meet and get to know each other.[29]

According to more than one anecdote, Luther once suggested a mercy killing, as in the case of a 12-year-old boy who lived in what we might call a vegetative state. Occasionally, including at one court case in Germany in 1964, Luther has been cited in support of euthanasia. This, however, is going too far, and for two reasons. First, this was a personal opinion of Luther's in a particular case, not intended as a dogma or general ethical principal. Second, as another has noted, Luther followed the tradition of his day in blaming such deformities on evil spirits. Luther doubted whether the boy mentioned above even had a soul at all, a view that would hardly count for much in a medical or ethical debate on euthanasia today.[30]

Luther had a reputation for generosity to the point of being careless with money. 'I spend far more than I get from my stipend', he admitted. Luther also hated solitude, which may have been partly due to bad memories of his time alone in Wartburg, 'imprisoned in my Patmos'.[31]

Merriment he commends warmly, and an engaging rhyme has been attributed to him:

He who loves not women, wine and song
Remains a fool his whole life long.

It may have been based on something said at table one day, related thus in the Table Talk: 'How would you outdo a German, dear Cordatus, except by making him drunk – especially a German who doesn't love music and women?'[32]

Naturally, conversation often touched on the arts, humanities and theology. Luther did not agree with Plato about the pre-existence of the soul. God made man, the whole man, body and soul; so 'when a child is born today the soul is created together with the body'. Though aware that others might disagree, Luther thought the soul 'is created out of the matter of the semen … it must be born out of corrupt matter and seed'.[33]

Luther appreciated classical authors, though he did not know them as deeply as distinguished humanists like Melanchthon. Luther preferred Cicero to Aristotle, praised Aesop's fables, admired Virgil and Homer, and was sorry that he did not have more time to read them. Some of the Church fathers were less fortunate. In public writings he was generally respectful, but less so in private. Jerome is useful for history, but not the 'teaching of true religion'. Origen 'I have banned'. Chrysostom is a 'gossip'. Elsewhere Chrysostom is praised for his oratory but not his theology. Basil was only a monk and 'I would not give a penny for him'. Augustine, Ambrose and Hilary are the best.[34]

As well as being a great reformer, Martin Luther was also a man of his time. This paradox may explain why he can be so radical on some points – justification, the Mass, clerical celibacy – yet so conservative on others. He did not question, for example, the perpetual virginity of Mary, and he assumed that Christ's 'brethren' were either His cousins or half-brothers, sons of Joseph.[35]

No man can break completely free from the customs and mores he has grown up in, and it was not until a generation after Luther's death that popular opinions on witchcraft came under the scrutiny of German Protestant divines. Luther believed in witches and sorcery, and that those who practised it deserved their fate because they had effectively made a pact with the devil.[36]

Luther appreciated scientific study and spoke 'not only of the utility, but also the great pleasure in investigating the nature of things'.[37] This, however, was another issue on which he was not as ready as some of his colleagues to listen to new ideas.

The chief scientific authorities of medieval times were Aristotle and Ptolemy. Aristotle we have met already (see Chapters 23–24, 110). Ptolemy was a second-century Greek astronomer, best known for his theory that the earth lay at the centre of the universe while the sun, moon and planets revolved around it. This was a development of the ideas of Aristotle, who had said much the same. This view remained a virtually unchallenged consensus in the medieval world, until the arrival of a contemporary of Luther, a young cathedral canon in Frauenburg with an enquiring mind called Nicholas Copernicus.

Few were willing to listen to Copernicus at first. The earth-centred cosmos suited the Renaissance idea of man at the centre of everything. The medieval Church was also strongly wedded to Aristotle, even though some of his theories were then going out of fashion. The dogma of transubstantiation was based significantly on Aristotle's theories of substance and accidents. (The substance of bread is what bread essentially is – the food made from flour, yeast or meal – while its accidents are its non-essential aspects, like whether it is white or brown.) The Church also accepted the Ptolemaic system and made the unfortunate mistake of granting it Scriptural support.

In fact, contrary to popular belief, the Bible never says that the sun goes round the earth. It talks of the sun rising and setting; but so do our weather forecasters. Joshua says that the sun stood still, but he does not say it was going round the earth *before* it stood still (Joshua 10:12–14). Job 26:7 – 'He hangs the earth upon nothing' – is very poetic, but it seems to suggest a moveable earth, possibly even an earth *in* motion rather than stationary in space. Psalm 104:5 – 'He set the earth on its foundations' – can hardly be sensibly pressed against Job. The Psalmist's subject is the Creation of the earth and its durability, which no power can destroy. Besides, the language in the verses is also highly figurative; God does not literally 'wrap himself in light' (verse 2) or make a physical chariot out of the clouds (verse 3).

The problem, however, was that the Church *decided* that the Bible said the sun moved round the earth, and Luther seems to have followed this because he brusquely dismissed 'this fellow' Copernicus as if he was some kind of a nut.[38]

Most people in the late 1530s took the same view as Luther did, so pervasive was the influence of Aristotelian philosophy and Ptolemaic astronomy. Nor was there much really convincing evidence for Copernican theory until it was developed by Galileo and Kepler in the early seventeenth century. Notable exceptions included some of Luther's friends, including his ministerial colleague Caspar Cruciger, Andreas Osiander, chief Lutheran pastor of Nuremberg, and also George Rheticus, lecturer in mathematics and astronomy at the University of Wittenberg, all of whom were sympathetic or supportive of the new scientific thinking. Copernicus did not convince Melanchthon, though Philip enjoyed discussing the subject, and he wrote about it fairly amicably.[39]

The story of Galileo's condemnation by the Church authorities is too well known to need rehearsing here. Less familiar is the fact that, like Copernicus, Galileo was a good Catholic who knew his Bible well, and he was able to quote Job 9:6 – 'He shakes the earth from its place' (NIV) – as proof that the 'mobility of the earth is not contrary to Scripture'. He also had little difficulty in showing that, whilst Joshua's miracle of the sun standing still was impossible according to the Ptolemaic system, it harmonised easily with the Copernican one.[40]

All this availed him nothing, sadly, but the peculiar modern idea that the medieval Church was 'anti-science' is nonsense. The Church's mistake was that it backed the wrong scientific horse. The authorities in Rome would have fared better had they dumped the pagans, Aristotle and Ptolemy, and listened to their own loyal sons, Copernicus and Galileo. It is, however, noteworthy that Lutherans, though not Luther personally, can be counted among the few supporters of Copernicus during his lifetime. Due to his innate conservatism, Luther may have missed an opportunity here.

Conversely, Jaroslav Pelikan has noted that Luther was a good judge of character, and some of his thoughts on friends and colleagues make for interesting reading.[41]

Philip Melanchthon was the prince among doctors of the Church, in Luther's view. Anyone who wants to be a theologian should read his Bible and Philip's *Loci Communes*, a work surpassing all others in quality and next only to the Scriptures themselves. Philip is 'richly endowed by God's special grace to a greater extent than I am'. Luther understood Philip's conciliatory spirit, even though he felt it was frequently wasted on the papists. 'The little fellow is a godly man' with good intentions, but his judgement sometimes lets him down. (Among other things, Philip had dedicated his *Loci Communes* of 1535 to Henry VIII in the mistaken hope that Henry could be won for the Reformation.) But Luther adds, 'if Philip were not so afflicted he would have curious ideas'. The meaning of this intriguing little quote is not certain. Melanchthon was prone to anxiety, and maybe Luther thought that this was a necessary trial to prevent him from getting too absorbed in philosophy or humanism.[42]

It seems that Katy was also fond of Philip. 'My lord Katy greets you reverently', wrote Luther to Philip, when on a visit to Jena. 'Take care not to provoke me to jealousy, since you too have a wife for my revenge.'[43]

John Bugenhagen, parish pastor at Wittenberg, was a fine man, but known for long-windedness. 'Every high priest should have his private sacrifices', said Luther after a lengthy address one Sunday. 'Accordingly Bugenhagen sacrifices his hearers with his long sermons, for we are his victims; and today he sacrificed us in a singular manner.'[44]

Bugenhagen, said Luther to Katy one day, 'preaches the way you women talk – he says whatever comes to mind'. Such preachers reminded Luther of a talkative maid going to market. On the way she meets another maid and stops for a chat, then another, then another. It takes an age to get to market.[45] At least Bugenhagen was spared the indignity suffered by another talkative reformer, Martin Bucer, whom Luther called a *Klappermaul* (blabbermouth).[46]

'Many sects will arise and Osiander will start one of them, for that fellow can do nothing but criticise others.' Luther's judgement on Andreas Osiander, chief pastor in Nuremberg, may seem harsh, but it contained some truth. Osiander may not have formed a sect exactly, but after Luther's death he departed from Lutheran orthodoxy with some highly individual ideas on the 'essential' rather than the imputed righteousness of Christians. The details need not concern us here, but he succeeded in uniting almost all mainstream Protestant Europe against him.[47]

Among Luther's dislikes were servants and the way they behaved. They are 'like lords and ladies compared with slaves in Roman times'. Luther thought a schoolmaster was as important for a city as a minister, and if he hadn't been a preacher he would have been a schoolmaster himself. All his life he respected secular government and professions, but he was not especially fond of lawyers. 'If I had 100 sons I wouldn't bring up one of them to be a lawyer.' Far too many lawyers are 'greedy … and they rob their clients blind'. He was particularly irked by their habit of spinning out cases to increase fees.[48]

Luther had an even lower opinion of riches – 'the smallest gift that God can give a man', and He usually gives it only to 'crude asses' who get nothing else from Him.[49]

Luther hated profiteering and speculating. When a bachelor in Wittenberg wanted to sell a house for 400 florins that had cost him only 30, Luther threatened him with excommunication. He condemned a nobleman, a speculator and usurer, who charged 30 per cent interest per annum: such a man 'should not be given the Sacrament'. If he repents he should do as Zacchaeus did and 'return what he stole' (Luke 19:2–10). If he remained unrepentant, Luther would not even eat with him. The need for trade Luther accepted; Christians may trade freely, though he opposed importing goods from abroad on the grounds that money should be kept within Germany. But sharp business practices, including bargaining and haggling for the best price, violated Christian charity and the command to love thy neighbour. Speculation and exploitation he attacked for the same reason.[50]

If the rise in capitalism paralleled that of Protestantism, as some historians have suggested, then it did not do so with the blessing of the most famous Protestant of all.

Predictably, papists and monks came in for a good deal of ribbing. When Luther heard a nightingale and the sound of frogs croaking at the same time he could not resist a theological meaning: 'The nightingale is Christ, who proclaims the Gospel', but he is 'drowned out' by frogs like Eck, Cochlaeus and other papists.[51]

Stories abounded of monks 'stealing' from the dying. In one case that Luther claimed to know of and enjoyed telling his friends, a monk visited a nobleman on his deathbed and asked if he would give his goods to the monastery. The dying man was too weak to speak, but he appeared to nod his consent. So the monk claimed the possessions as his from the son and heir, also present. The quick-witted son then asked his father if he could throw the monk downstairs. Again came the same barely perceptible nod. The monk was summarily dispatched, to Luther's great delight.[52]

12

Progress and Setbacks of the Reformation

The Preacher and his Congregation

A family friend, Conrad Cordatus, once asked Luther how preaching should best be done. Luther replied: first you go up to the pulpit; second, you stay there for a while; then you come down again. Cordatus was not amused at first, but he quickly got the message. Preaching should be simple, clear and to the point. This was Luther's way, and if clever people don't want to listen to his sermons 'they can leave'.[1]

Luther's relations with his congregations were not always cordial. Originally he favoured the right of congregations to choose their own pastor. The universal priesthood demanded it. Unfortunately, the spread of radical ideas by Karlstadt and others forced him to modify his early opinions about the spiritual capacity of congregations to judge true teaching and select the right minister. One consequence of the Peasants' War was, to quote Brecht, a 'retreat to the institution of the ministerial office'. Another was closer links with, and dependence on, the civil power in matters of Church administration. An example of this occurred in May 1535, when Elector John Frederick issued an order authorising the Wittenberg theologians to ordain men to the ministry. The purpose was not to abolish episcopal ordination, but to provide another authority when the bishops of the old faith refused to do it.[2]

Luther did not appreciate it when congregations were demanding and hard to please. One Conrad Claudius was fully qualified for the ministry, but parishioners in Lissen objected to him on the grounds that they did not like his voice – they said it was not strong enough. If 'these peasants', said Luther testily, are to choose as they please, and insist on a pastor who is learned, pious, handsome, young, eloquent, who does not shout, who carouses and plays games with them when they want him to, then where are we going to get suitable men from?[3]

In January 1530, he threatened to quit preaching and devote his time to classroom lectures because evangelical freedom was being abused, church attendance was poor, morality had declined and the grace of the Gospel was being treated with contempt. He was back in the pulpit again after a few weeks, but these tensions continued off and on throughout his life. Frequently his anger was roused by the congregation's allegedly bad treatment of pastors, including stinginess in paying for their upkeep, and Luther blamed sheer ingratitude. In 1545, on a trip to Zeitz and Meresburg, he told Katy that he did not want to return to Wittenberg because the people despised the Word; and it took the combined persuasions of the elector, Melanchthon and other leading figures to persuade Luther to change his mind.[4]

The University of Wittenberg

The University of Wittenberg was founded in 1502 by Elector Frederick the Wise, with the permission of the emperor, and was modelled on the universities of Paris and Bologna. Later Frederick asked for, and received, papal confirmation. Initially the main subjects to be studied were the liberal arts (or philosophy), theology, law and medicine. The liberal arts curriculum was dominated by Aristotle. For theology students, Peter Lombard's 'Sentences' was the standard work. The governing body of the university was the Senate, composed of the rector (the head of the university), the masters of theology and liberal arts, professors of law and medicine, the dean and the five canons of the Wittenberg All Saints Castle church. The church benefited from a substantial papal endowment that had been granted in the fourteenth century, placing it directly under Rome, and additional income from more than thirty villages. The costs of the university were met mainly from the elector's reserves until 1507, when Frederick successfully petitioned Pope Julius II to incorporate the university with the Castle church in a joint endowment. After this, the Castle church increased significantly in importance, having other churches under its care, and consequently gained more funds.[5] Without realising it, the pope had provided a secure financial foundation for the Reformation, because during the next ten years or so, Luther and Melanchthon transformed the university from a medieval institution to the principal evangelical seat of learning in Germany.

The Lutherans had no master plan for spreading the Word far and wide beyond the boundaries of Wittenberg. The tendency was to react to opportunities and contacts; in the early days usually by letters and tracts. Initiatives

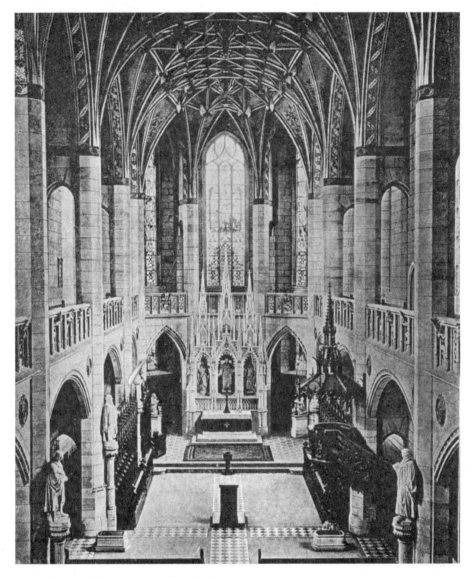

Castle church at Wittenberg. (*Author's Collection*)

generally came from outside. In 1524, for example, Bugenhagen was invited to Hamburg to help establish the Reformation there, and a year later Luther recommended Michael Stifel as preacher to the Jörger family in Tolleth, Upper Austria. But no organised strategic plan was drawn up and approved in Wittenberg for exporting the Gospel.[6]

The need to educate ministers and theologians for the future was being addressed in earnest in the early 1520s, and the university was crucial in providing such men. The names of Luther and Melanchthon acted like a magnet, drawing increasing numbers of students to Wittenberg from all over Germany and beyond. Study of Scripture based on the sacred languages took priority, with the Augsburg Confession and Melanchthon's *Loci* as the chief doctrinal guides.[7] Professor Schwiebert has described the Reformation as a 'University Movement'.[8] At Wittenberg, the future Lutheran missionaries and leaders received their classical Lutheran education; here they could eat, sleep and breathe the new Gospel before taking it back to their own parishes and lands. Luther called the university the 'great ornament' of the town, where the 'assembly of learned men ... are engaged in the study of heavenly doctrine and liberal arts'. He also had some quite zealous young students, some of them 'so full of knowledge after they have been in Wittenberg half a year that they suppose they are more learned than I am'.[9]

Besides the university, Luther encouraged improvements in education at all levels. He appealed to evangelical noblemen to help establish Christian schools and do all they could to overcome the severe educational crisis in Germany. Far too many preferred commerce and trade to learning, which was badly misguided. Society, Luther urged, needs education for the benefit of church and state. He commended the study of law, medicine, liberal arts and particularly languages, without which 'we will not long preserve the Gospel'.[10]

The Reformation in Germany and Europe

The attitude of the German princes to Luther varied considerably. Duke George in Albertine Saxony and William of Bavaria were hostile, but they failed to prevent Luther's message from finding supporters in their domains. Joachim of Brandenburg, Christopher of Bremen-Verden and Henry of Wolfenbüttel were mainly concerned with avoiding civil unrest, while Casimir in Brandenburg-Kulmbach, Ludwig of the Palatinate and Philip of Baden allowed the Gospel to take its course. In Saxony, when Elector John succeeded Frederick the Wise in 1525, the creation of a state church began. Pastors were appointed, opponents of the Gospel dismissed, churches and monasteries were closed or brought under the control of the state, and visitations were arranged to reach the rural areas. Other reformist princes soon followed this example. Albertine Saxony became Lutheran when the Catholic Duke George died in 1539 and was succeeded by his brother Henry. A high-powered delegation, including Luther, Melanchthon and Jonas, went to see Duke Henry and advised him on various matters ranging from abolishing the Mass in the monasteries to pastoral visitations. Also at the end of 1539, Joachim II sanctioned the Reformation in electoral Brandenburg, and liaised with Luther and others regarding a church ordinance. In the process, princes enriched their treasuries with income from the Church and especially monastic lands.[11]

In 1536 the divines of Wittenberg reached an agreement on the Eucharist with Martin Bucer, leader of the evangelicals in Strasbourg. This was quite an achievement as the southern Germans had been leaning towards the views of Zwingli. The Wittenberg Accord was drafted by Melanchthon and hopes were high that Henry Bullinger, Zwingli's successor in Zürich, might be persuaded to accept it as well as Bucer. For a brief period, Luther corresponded with Bullinger fairly cordially. In the event, the Swiss could not bring themselves to sign it and the dream of a single, united evangelical church was not to be realised.[12]

⁓━╬━⁓

In Denmark, King Christian II quickly perceived that Luther's anti-papacy and universal priesthood could be useful in curbing the power of his bishops, and perhaps his nobility too. In 1520 he obtained the services of a Lutheran preacher called Martin Reinhard, and even though he turned out to be a disappointment, some reform soon followed, mainly in the monasteries, in restricting ecclesiastical influence and allowing priests to marry. Then opposition to Christian grew; he was deposed in 1523 and succeeded by his uncle Frederick I, who showed sympathy rather than enthusiasm for the new faith.

The country's most prominent early Lutherans were Hans Tausen and Jørgen Jensen Sadolin. Both were former Wittenberg students. In 1526 Frederick made Tausen his royal chaplain. The king's protection enabled these men and their supporters to continue their missionary work, and Lutheranism soon gained ground and increased in influence.

In Schleswig-Holstein, Lutheran activity began in Husum in 1522 when Hermann Tast, another Wittenberg-trained divine, started preaching with strong support from Frederick's elder son, Duke Christian, himself a committed Lutheran. Christian was further aided by two German ministers, Eberhardt Weidensee and Johann Wenth, who later became an author of the Church Orders of Schleswig-Holstein and Denmark. In Haderslev, Wenth converted the collegiate chapter-school into a theological academy designed to educate students to become Scandinavian Lutheran ministers. Similar schools were soon set up in Malmø and Viborg. New ministers were instructed to preach the Lutheran Gospel and also encouraged to follow Luther's *Kirchenpostille*. Annual visitations, similar to those Luther and Melanchthon had devised for Saxony, were arranged. The Lutheran faith was jealously guarded, and ministers had to renounce on oath Zwinglism and Anabaptism. In all these developments, Duke Christian played an active and supportive role.

When Frederick died in 1533, Christian won the support of the Danish nobility, but the bishops preferred his younger brother Hans. Following a civil war, Christian emerged as the victor in 1536. The Roman Church of Denmark was then effectively abolished, and the bishops' estates were handed over to the Crown to be used for the king and the common good. Next year, Bugenhagen came to Denmark to crown the new king, ordain bishops and reform the University of Copenhagen along the lines of the one in Wittenberg. That same year the Danish Church Order was prepared, and Christian obtained the approval of the Wittenberg theologians for it. Among other things, it made Luther's *Kirchenpostille* and Melanchthon's *Apology* and *Loci Communes* required reading for ministers. The Reformation then proceeded gradually and steadily. King Christian continued to take a personal interest in theology and kept up a regular and cordial correspondence with Luther, Melanchthon and Bugenhagen. Thus Denmark became a Lutheran kingdom, and eventually Norway, a separate kingdom but under Danish rule, followed. By the time Christian died in 1559 and his son Frederick II succeeded him, the new faith was well established.[13]

Among the earliest Swedish Lutheran evangelists were the Petersson brothers, Olaf and Lars (also known as Olaus and Laurentius Petri). Like their Danish counterparts, both had received their theological education at Wittenberg University. King Gustav Vasa, who came to the throne in 1523, gave them and their allies political rather than whole-hearted religious support, but that was enough for the Lutherans to make reasonable progress, and a Swedish New Testament was produced in 1526. In the same year, Gustav closed down the Catholic printing press in Linköping and transferred it to Stockholm, one of the few parts of the country where support for the Reformation was fairly strong. The next year Gustav began to act against the Church, demanding the surrender of property and land to enrich the Crown. But he also faced a peasants' revolt (the Daljunkeren's revolt), partly against the new teaching and preaching. A national synod of Örebro in 1529 failed to reach a religious settlement, resulting in further unrest in Stockholm and rural areas of the south-west.

Progress continued sporadically, though not without resistance from the clergy, the nobility and the country as a whole. In 1531 Lars Petersson was appointed Archbishop of Uppsala, though authority over the other bishops rested with the king. In 1536 Gustav gave tacit support for the Lutheran Mass and for abolishing clerical celibacy. But whereas Denmark was accepted into the Schmalkaldic League in 1538, Sweden had two applications – in 1538 and 1541 – turned down. Then disagreements developed between Swedish Lutherans, including Olaf Petersson, who wanted an independent church, and the king, who sought to bring it under royal control. In 1539 Olaf Petersson and Lars Andersson, the king's Lutheran chancellor, were tried for treason, though soon reprieved. Displeased with his own nationals, Gustav invited the Pomeranian and Wittenberg-educated Georg Norman, a man recommended by Luther and Melanchthon as a tutor for his son, to advise him on Church affairs. Soon after this Gustav brought the Church fully under royal sway. Progress in Sweden was slower than in Denmark, but eventually Lutheranism became the official national religion.

Meanwhile in Finland, a reformist Dominican, Mårten Skytte, was appointed to the see of Turku in 1527. Soon he was arranging for students to go to Wittenberg for their theological education. During the 1530s and after, these men were evangelising in Finland. One of the most prominent was Mikael Agricola, who studied in Wittenberg from 1536–9, then succeeded Mårten Skytte in Turku, and translated the New Testament and some of the Old into Finnish. Virtually all the leading Swedish and Finnish reformers had studied in Wittenberg and had met Luther and Melanchthon personally.[14]

❦

Elsewhere Lutheranism was less successful. In the early 1530s the French king, Francis I, after listening to his evangelically minded sister, Marguerite de Navarre, invited Philip Melanchthon to France with a promise of safe conduct. Melanchthon was willing to go and Luther supported the idea, but Elector John Frederick suspected that the wily Francis was more interested in sowing discord between the Lutheran princes and Charles V, so he refused permission. The elector's judgement was probably sound, though Melanchthon was deeply disappointed. Diplomatically he wrote to Francis saying that he had wanted to go but circumstances did not allow it.[15]

Relations between Luther and England were strained after King Henry's *Assertion of the Seven Sacraments* and Luther's fierce reply (p.60). Luther also disappointed Henry by supporting Catherine of Aragon in the king's Great Matter. However, because Luther was sympathetic to Henry's desire for an heir, he suggested that Henry should have two wives – Anne as well as Catherine. This was preferable to divorcing Catherine, who was innocent of any wrongdoing, and stigmatising Princess Mary with illegitimacy. Polygamy in the Church was a novel idea in an exceptional case and Luther never intended it to become normal, but he could see no other way of providing Henry with a legitimate son and heir without dishonouring Catherine. He reminded Henry that godly patriarchs and kings in the Old Testament, like

Jacob and David, had more than one wife. But his suggestion was not taken up, and he later pitied the woman who had 'lost her cause' all over the world except at Wittenberg, where we would 'gladly have maintained her in royal honour, where she should have stayed'.[16]

Relations with England soon improved. Robert Barnes, a former Augustinian friar and an English exile in Germany, studied at Wittenberg in the late 1520s, and Barnes had a powerful English ally and patron in Thomas Cromwell, Henry's Lutheran chief minister. Thanks mainly to Cromwell, Henry began taking interest in the works of Melanchthon, who obliged by dedicating his *Loci Communes* of 1535 to the king. Cromwell and Luther wrote to each other, and Luther commended the minister's 'earnest and determined will regarding the cause of Christ'; and he prayed God would 'strengthen abundantly His work, begun in Your Lordship, to His glory and the salvation of many'.[17]

Yet, despite the goodwill and all Cromwell's efforts, Lutheranism failed in England. Repeated invitations from Henry to Melanchthon were rejected by John Frederick on the grounds that such a visit was not necessary for Henry to decide whether he wanted to accept the Augsburg Confession and join the Schmalkaldic League. When a Lutheran delegation (without Melanchthon) eventually arrived in England in 1538, differences soon emerged over private Masses, clerical celibacy and communion in one kind. Henry then enforced his own views in the Act of Six Articles, 1539. More seriously, Henry never accepted justification by faith alone, and he failed even to understand the admittedly slightly intricate relationship between saving faith and the good works of fruits of faith that follow. In 1540 Cromwell and Barnes both perished, one by the axe, the other in the flames, and hopes of a Lutheran settlement in England perished with them.[18]

When he heard this news, Luther blasted 'Squire Harry' as a tyrant and praised 'St Robert' as a 'holy martyr'. Luther never liked or trusted Henry, though he kept his feelings in check while religious and political talks were taking place. Biased Luther certainly was, but no one has ever summed up Henry's church policy better: this king just wants 'to be pope in his own land'.[19]

The Landgrave and Bigamy

The time will come, said Luther to Katy after dinner one day, when men will be allowed more than one wife. This was only fair, 'because a woman can bear a child only once a year while a man may beget many'. Katy replied by quoting St Paul – 'let each man have his own wife' (1 Corinthians 7:2). 'Yes', her husband conceded, 'but not *only* his own wife. Paul did not insist on that.' 'In that case', replied Katy, 'I'm going back to the convent and you can look after the children.'[20]

Landgrave Philip of Hesse, after the portrait by Müller. (*Author's Collection*)

This was, of course, all part of the husband and wife banter of the Luther household; but it is difficult to be sure whether Luther was *completely* joking. He enjoyed making fun of the canon lawyers who opposed bigamy. He spoke glowingly of Solomon, a king famed far and wide for his wisdom, who had nearly a thousand wives, and he 'wrote a better book than all the lawyers'.[21] Then, as if to prove that the advice given to Henry VIII was not entirely an aberration, it was repeated in the infamous case of the Landgrave Philip of Hesse in 1540.

The landgrave, host of the Marburg conference of 1529, had had a string of extramarital affairs, and was undergoing treatment for syphilis. Though his wife Christina had borne him seven children, the marriage was not a happy one. A guilty conscience kept him away from the Sacrament, but failed to curb his voracious sexual appetite. Recently he had met and fallen for the 17-year-old Margaret von der Sale, of a Saxon noble family; but her mother Anna, a lady-in-waiting to Philip's sister Elizabeth, would not allow any relationship between Philip and Margaret other than a marriage (echoes of Henry VIII and Anne Boleyn). Because Christina had been a faithful wife, the landgrave realised that he had no Scriptural grounds for a divorce. He therefore sought the consent of Luther and Melanchthon for a second marriage – in plain language, bigamy – though he promised that his children by Christina would be his lawful successors. Martin Bucer acted as intermediary, a role in which he was decidedly unhappy. Landgrave Philip's request was accompanied by a veiled threat that if Luther and Melanchthon refused, he might have to turn to Charles V, an option that could require a dispensation from the pope, which would compromise his role as a member and pillar of the Schmalkaldic League. Princes who supported the Reformation were rare, so after listening to all the intimate details, Luther, Melanchthon and Bucer reluctantly agreed to a secret second marriage out of necessity, emphasising what an exceptional case this was, which should neither be made public nor taken as a blessing on polygamy. A grateful landgrave sent generous supplies of fine wine to Wittenberg.[22]

But the affair did not remain a secret for long. Melanchthon was in Weimar when the story leaked out, and the ensuing scandal made him sorely depressed and seriously ill. By contrast, Luther was almost wholly unperturbed. 'Why does the good man torture himself over this affair?' Luther cried, far more worried about Philip's health than any bigamy controversy or attacks from opponents. 'I have a thick skin and I'm a tough Saxon ... Let the Papists yell if they want to!' Luther was satisfied that he and Melanchthon had given the only advice they could in the circumstances, and if they had done wrong, then they had a gracious God who would be merciful to them for the sake of Christ. He could not see why polygamy should be something so dreadful when the godly Old Testament patriarchs and kings had more than one wife, and he cheerfully decided that he would not 'do the devil and all the Papists a favour by worrying about it'.[23]

Melanchthon was incapable of such jolly defiance in times of trouble, and his illness quickly worsened. Luther went to see him in Weimar and found him near to death, with sunken eyes, his senses almost gone, his face fallen and hollow, unable to eat or drink. The scene that follows is taken from the description of a witness, Solomon Glass.

'God forbid!' Luther exclaimed. 'How has the devil smitten this man?' Luther then prayed for Philip with all the fervour he could muster before turning once more to the patient, still prostrate on the bed. 'Be of good courage Philip, you shall not die. Trust in the Lord, who can slay and make alive again.' Philip drew breath, but only to beg Luther to let him go, for he 'was on a good journey, and to be with Christ is far better'.

'No Philip', insisted Luther. 'You must serve our Lord God yet longer.' When Philip showed faint signs of recovery, Luther demanded that he eat something. Still the patient was reluctant. 'Hark Philip', commanded Luther. 'Eat, or I'll excommunicate you.' This threat worked; Philip ate, and his strength gradually returned. Hugely relieved, Luther dashed off a letter to 'my dear maid and gracious lady Katy'. 'I'm fine', he assured her. 'I eat like a Bohemian and drink like a German. Thanks be to God that Master Philip, who was dead, like Lazarus has returned to life again.'

Luther had no doubt that his own appeals to heaven by Melanchthon's bedside had prevailed. 'Our God could not refuse me', he later recalled. 'I threw my sack before His door and wearied Him with all His promises of hearing prayers; I told Him He *had* to hear me, else I'd never trust Him again.'[24]

So Luther's prayers for Melanchthon were answered. As for his indulgence to the landgrave, that continues to excite comment, much of it disapproving. But it is necessary to understand that what motivated him was more than just a wish to gratify a supportive prince. As with Henry VIII, Luther, in his own highly original way, was simply trying to be helpful, to make the best of a bad job. Luther was, by nature, sympathetic to people, especially Christians, caught in life's dilemmas: hence, as noted in Chapter 9, he is one of the few interpreters of Scripture to spring to the defence of the patriarchs, Rebecca and even Lot. He could not see how a second wife, in an exceptional case, could be so terribly wrong, given the precedents in Scripture, albeit the Old Testament rather than the New. However, this Professor of Theology was a political innocent who could not foresee what seems so obvious, that nothing but trouble could come of it. His devil-may-care reaction to the furore he caused – he seemed almost to be enjoying it – is also typical Luther, and one of the many reasons why he is such an entertaining and intriguing, if sometimes difficult, character. With Luther there is rarely a dull moment.

13

Controversial Last Years

Lord, keep us steadfast in thy Word
And curb the Turk's and Papists' sword.[1]

The Turks

*L*uther's hymn was written shortly after the Turkish force defeated King Ferdinand of Austria at Budapest in August 1541. Fears abounded that the Turk would now advance up the Danube into Germany. Rome and some Catholic princes were also hoping that they could crush Lutheranism by force. Evangelicals felt besieged by enemies.

Luther had mixed feelings about the Turkish Islamic power. In one sense, it was the 'hereditary foe' of Christianity, but Luther acknowledged that the Turk allowed the nations he had conquered to practise their own religion. The pope was far more hostile and 'has done more harm to the kingdom of Christ'. The Turk 'thinks highly of Christ and concedes that He was a great prophet ... but he does not confess that Christ is His God and Lord'.[2]

To crusades Luther had always been opposed. He agreed, however, that Western Europe had to be defended against the Turk, but the emperor, not the pope, should be their leader.[3] Shortly after Budapest, and urged by Elector John Frederick, Luther issued his *Appeal for Prayer Against the Turks*, in which he donned the mantle of an Old Testament prophet calling a sinful nation to repentance.[4]

Luther saw the Turk as a manifestation of God's wrath against Germany for its coldness to the Gospel. Sects had arisen; too many were worshipping the 'great god mammon'; dishonesty was rank in all levels of society; money lending and speculating, despite Luther's pulpit rebukes, was rife, and Luther did not take kindly to being told by merchants that he knew nothing about commerce or finance. Pastors were neglected and despised. Things were worse than in the days just before the Flood. The Turk is our 'schoolmaster' sent to impose discipline and drive us to repent, pray and trust in God. Only through prayer could the danger be averted, even if Germany had competent generals and noblemen, which Luther doubted.

Luther faced up to the possibility that the Turk would overrun Germany. If so, all true Christians who died would be 'martyrs for God'; but through prayer the Turk, and the pope as well, could yet be defeated. As a measure of how seriously he took the threat from the East, Luther urged all parents to teach their children the Catechisms more diligently than ever, so that any who were taken captive would take the Christian faith with them, as Joseph did to Egypt. If pious women were carried away and 'forced to share bed and board' with Turkish men, Luther 'would counsel them to submit in patience and endure'; no blame would attach to them. Though Luther's tract is a grim one, he could still end on a hopeful note of confidence in God: 'We commit all to Him.'

The Turkish advance into Germany was thwarted rather than defeated, and Luther continued his appeal for prayer for help from danger into 1543 and after.

Jews

Hitherto, Luther's main work on the Jews was *That Jesus Christ was Born a Jew*, 1523–4. He wrote it following wild allegations in Nuremberg that he had not only denied the real presence in the Eucharist, but had claimed that Joseph was the natural father of Jesus.[5]

In it, Luther seemed full of goodwill to the Jews, hoping to win them for the Gospel. Jews were the chosen people from whom the Christ came. He went over Old Testament passages prophesying that the Christ would be born of a woman, beginning with Genesis 3:15. At this stage he was trying to convince the Jews that Jesus was their Messiah, but he knew the belief that Jesus was God's Son offended many, so he did not labour the point. He was critical of the way Christendom had treated converted Jews.

But Luther's hopes in the Jews were disappointed. In his commentary on Psalm 109 in 1526, Luther notes how the Jews call Jesus *Thola*, 'the hanged one'; it appears he heard about this after discussions with two rabbis.[6]

During his lectures on the Old Testament he is frequently critical of Jewish commentators, though his sharpest critiques are directed at medieval theologians and papists. Generally he saw the Jewish Pharisees as types of Romanists with their work-righteousness, their traditions and their rejection of the saving grace of Christ.

He had limited personal contact with Jews, though sometime in 1536 three rabbis visited him because they knew of his interest in the Hebrew language. They discussed the Old Testament and, predictably, the rabbis did not agree with him that it prophesied of Christ. At the end of the meeting Luther gave them a letter asking for safe passage for them 'for the sake of Christ'. When the rabbis saw the name of Christ they would not accept the letter.[7]

Luther never lost hope that at least some Jews might be won for the Gospel.[8] However, a crisis point arrived sometime in 1542 when he heard a report that Jews in Lutheran territories were ritually blaspheming Christ and Mary in their synagogues. In summer or autumn that year, Luther told dinner guests that he was going to write against the Jews once again, 'because I hear that some of our lords are befriending them'. He would advise them to 'chase all the Jews out of their land'. Jews had no right to 'slander and insult the dear Virgin Mary ... they call her a stinkpot, a hag, a monstrosity ... The Jews put their own flesh and blood to shame when they defame Christ. They bear a grudge against us, who believe in Him who was born from their blood.'[9]

The result was *On the Jews and their Lies*, completed in December and published early in 1543.[10] The work was divided into four parts.

In Part I, Luther attacks the false boasts of the Jews and their work-righteousness, which makes them incorrigible and their conversion impossible. They are no longer the people of God. Since the Romans suppressed the Jewish revolt and destroyed their temple in AD 70, they have been scattered and dispersed, but they cannot learn the lesson of history. Yet they boast they are the descendants of the patriarchs, like the Pharisee in the Gospel – 'I am not like other men' (Luke 18:11). But the advantage of birth avails nothing spiritually, because Isaac was preferred to Ishmael and Jacob to Esau. Besides, the Scriptures say that all have sinned, Jew and Gentile alike. Nor can the Jews boast in circumcision, because other nations have that rite as well, and uncircumcised men like Job were commended by God. The Jews should weigh the evidence against them from their own Scriptures. God has promised to hear the prayers of His own people who are afflicted, but He has not listened to the Jews (e.g. Psalm 34:17); they still have no homeland.

Part II is the longest part, but it can be covered here quickly, because the argument is not new (see Chapter 9). Luther sets out to show that Old Testament texts promising the Messiah were fulfilled in Christ. His main texts are Jacob's blessing to Judah (Genesis 49:10), the covenant with David (2 Samuel 23:1–5), Daniel's seventy weeks (Daniel 9:24) and Haggai 2. This is Luther's Christological understanding of the Old Testament, which the Jews rejected. Luther seems to have selected these texts because they foretell, not only Christ, but the casting off of the religion of Judaism.

Thomas More, by Hans Holbein. Some of his comments on Luther are not printable. (*THP Archive*)

In Parts I and II, Luther does not preach to the Jews on the Trinity or the Incarnation, which he knows will have little effect. Instead, in his typically hard-hitting way, he tries to convince his opponents from their own Scriptures. Luther can get a bit rough at times, but sixteenth-century polemic can be quite vitriolic, and it is not difficult to find worse than this, for example, in the writings of 'Saint' Thomas More.

In Part III, Luther deals with these Jewish calumnies against Christ and Mary in the synagogues. His sources are historical records and, more recently and significantly, the testimony of Jews he knows who have converted to Christianity. The Jews allegedly say that Jesus was possessed by the devil and they call Mary a 'whore' and a 'dung heap'. Why, asks Luther, do the Jews curse a man who has been dead for 1,500 years? Even if Jesus was not the Messiah as Christians claim, even if He was a criminal and a false teacher as the Jews say, He has paid for His crimes and is gone. The Jews must be smitten with madness and hatred against Christ and Christians. Now Luther repeats some popular (though unproven) charges against the Jews common in the medieval age: poisoning wells, kidnapping and killing children etc. He denies Jewish claims that they were held captive in the West; far from holding them captive, many countries have banished them. The Jews are now accused of living idly and in luxury in Germany.

Luther has now built up a picture of the Jews, who are not only in great error on religion, but are also a troublesome immigrant community, abusing the host country, especially with their ritual cursing of Jesus and Mary. In Part IV he calls for drastic action.

'We dare not tolerate their conduct, now that we are aware of their lying and reviling and blaspheming. If we do, we become sharers in their lies, cursing and blasphemy.' Therefore, their synagogues and schools should be burned, 'so that God might see that we are Christians, and do not condone or knowingly tolerate such public lying, cursing and blaspheming of His Son'. What we tolerated in the past – and Luther insists he was unaware of it – God will overlook. Jews' houses should likewise be destroyed, and their prayer books and literature. Rabbis should be 'forbidden to teach henceforth on pain of loss of life and limb'. Free travel and the right to practise usury should be denied them, their silver and gold taken from them and 'put in safe keeping'. Young Jews should be made to work for their living.

At this point Luther realises that the princes and his fellow countrymen might balk at what he is saying. In that case the Jews should be expelled. Luther then admits this may be better. A Christian state cannot tolerate overt blasphemy of Christ and Mary. Pastors should warn their flocks to avoid having dealings with Jews. Luther knows no one can be forced to become a Christian, but by vilifying Christ and Mary, the Jews have forfeited the right to the protection of the Saxon state or the tolerance of the Church.

A short recapitulation follows. Luther will let it pass if the Jews do not wish to accept the doctrine of the Trinity, but he charges them with accusing the Christians of worshipping three gods, and this enrages Luther because they know it is false. Luther would summon Jewish rabbis to an assembly and demand them to substantiate this charge or withdraw it. Luther detests the idea of a Jewish political Messiah, which offers no salvation, no eternal life and no rest for the conscience.

Before discussing the contemporary reaction to this work, a word may be timely on the modern one. As always, Brecht's discussion is balanced and mature, but elsewhere there has been a great deal of affected outrage from persons who fancy they can trace a long chain of German anti-Semitism, stretching from Luther to Wagner and the Third Reich, which is fantastically overblown. There is some strong stuff in *On the Jews*, but it is not the racial anti-Semitism of the kind seen in Germany and elsewhere in the previous 100 years or so.

A modern Christian who wants to debate theology with a Jew is likely to use guarded language when doing so, because they cannot put out of their mind what happened to the Jews in the twentieth century in a historically Christian country, albeit one ruled by a very anti-Christian regime. But Luther was under no such inhibitions, so he felt free to deal with the Jews just as he dealt with Henry VIII, Erasmus, Eck, Zwingli and all his other opponents, in his usual combative style. Horrors on the scale of the Holocaust were unimaginable to Luther and his age. Just as inconceivable as was the evolutionary ideology that helped fuel it. Twentieth-century Germany was particularly receptive to Darwinian ideas, to the development of 'biological racism', and the concept of races (plural) and the superiority of the European or Aryan 'race' over all others.[11] All this was alien to the sixteenth-century mind. Luther knew of only one race – the human race – descended from Adam and then Noah; now divided by language, nationality and custom, but not genetically, ethnically or racially. Luther did not think in terms of races (plural again) the way we do; consequently, his polemic is theological, not racial. Luther is not anti-Italian for attacking the Roman papacy, or anti-English for calling Henry VIII an apostate and an idiot. And besides, the typical modern anti-Semite cares not a jot about the Trinity and the Christology of the Old Testament, which were the subjects in contention between Luther and the rabbis of his time.

Luther was anti-Judaism, but not anti-Jewish *in toto*. He stressed the Jewishness of Jesus (in *That Jesus Christ was Born a Jew*). Elsewhere he called the Jews the 'chosen people', and no one held the Jewish patriarchs, prophets and apostles in higher honour than he did. He was enthralled by the Hebrew language, calling it a 'sacred language', and 'we Gentiles are in no way equal to the Jews' because the Scriptures were written by Jews.[12] Strange anti-Semite, this!

Possibly because he was aware of Luther's interest in the Jewish language and history, Rabbi Josel of Rosheim, a contemporary of Luther, regretted that 'never before has a *Gelehrter*, a scholar, advocated such tyrannical and outrageous treatment of our poor people'. The key word here is 'scholar': what is unusual about *On the Jews* is not the demand for the expulsion of religious dissidents, which was hardly unheard of in those times;[13] what startled the rabbi was the fact that he was hearing this sort of thing from a scholar like Luther – it seemed so out of character. Was this the same man who, twenty years earlier, had said this:

> Heresy can never be restrained by force ... God's Word must do the fighting. If it does not succeed, certainly the temporal power will not succeed either, even if it were to drench the world in blood. Heresy is a spiritual matter which you cannot hack to pieces with iron, consume with fire or drown in water.

Or this:

> My friend, if you wish to drive out heresy, you must find some way to tear it first of all from the heart and turn men's will away from it. With force you will not stop it, but only strengthen it.[14]

It was never in Luther's nature to want to crush all opposition and dissent. As the rabbi probably knew, Luther habitually encouraged the printing of his opponents' works, because that way it was easier for him to refute them. Partly for that reason, in 1542 Luther agreed to the printing of the Koran in Germany.[15]

Although Luther opposed persecution for the sake of conscience, like everyone else of his age he did not support religious pluralism either, which left him with the problem of how to treat religious dissidents. In his lectures on the Psalms in 1530 he says that rulers should not allow false teaching in their territories. Here he exempts the Jews, because they 'are outside Christendom and cannot hold any public office'.[16] Why, therefore, is the exemption withdrawn in 1542?

It is not true to say that he has grown more hostile or intolerant to the Jews than he once was. His opinions on the Jewish religion, on their reading of the Old Testament, on their work-righteousness and their different Messianic hopes, are the same in 1542 as they had ever been. And even in *On the Jews*, when he is at his most vehement, Luther insists that no one should be forced to accept the Christian faith. He will not compel the Jews to believe the Trinity. 'We accord everyone the right not to believe ... this we leave to everyone's conscience. But to parade such unbelief so freely ... to revile and curse the true faith ... that is a far different story.'[17]

This blaspheming of Christ and Mary, which Luther insists he did not know about before, is the main reason for his change of heart, as he says more than once in the last part of his book.[18]

Luther expected Jews, Anabaptists and anyone else who did not accept Reformation Christianity, to disbelieve quietly and deferentially, and if they did that they would come to no harm. Harsh penalties would be meted out only to radicals who preached sedition and stirred up strife, and others who brazenly abused the state Church and its faith. For religious dissidents in the sixteenth century this was actually quite reasonable, and in this respect Luther was marked more by the spirit of Elizabeth I than of Thomas More or 'Bloody Mary'.

Shortly after Luther's death, some German cities expelled English and French Calvinists from their lands, despite Melanchthon's attempts to intercede for them. Their offence was not that they had reviled or cursed the Augsburg Confession: they simply had not accepted one article in it, one out of twenty-eight, the one on the real presence in the Eucharist.[19]

So despite the fire and fury in *On the Jews*, Luther was really more forbearing than many of his time. His problem was his famously short fuse, now shorter than ever in old age and with failing health. He might, for instance, have asked the elector for a formal enquiry to substantiate these blasphemy allegations before demanding severe reprisals. He might have preferred to deliver a strong private warning to the Jews, backed up by the threat of action if it went unheeded. He could also have investigated more critically these medieval stories about Jews poisoning wells and kidnapping Christian children, as some of his fellow reformers were beginning to do. In the event, he did none of these things. But even if these Jewish blasphemies were openly proven, there still remains, as Brecht says, an inherent inconsistency in using the power of the *state* to defend the *spiritual* kingdom of Christ. As Luther notes even in the most controversial part of *On the Jews*, though the irony seems to pass him by, the apostles 'used no spear or sword, but only their tongues'.[20]

Meanwhile, Protestant Europe did not respond warmly to Luther's demand for the expulsion of the Jews. Melanchthon and Osiander were distinctly unhappy, while Bullinger and the Zürichers likened it to the methods of the Inquisition. The reaction of the princes was generally half-hearted. Some quietly ignored it. Even when Jews were expelled by Margrave Hans of Brandenburg-Küstrin, they were soon received by his brother, Joachim II, in whose lands they settled mostly contentedly. *On the Jews* has done more harm to Luther's reputation than it ever did to the Jews.[21]

Zwinglians: The Eucharistic Controversy Renewed

'Our Pericles', wrote Melanchthon gloomily, in the summer of 1544, is about to 'thunder violently and go to war' once more over the Eucharist.[22]

The reasons for renewing this controversy were complicated, but were chiefly these: though Luther was heartened to hear that the Gospel was spreading beyond Germany into Hungary and even to parts of Italy, it dampened his joy to learn that many evangelicals, including former students of his, were drawn towards Zwinglian views on the Eucharist. Then, in August 1543, a Zürich printer sent Luther a Latin Bible produced by Zwinglian theologians. This rankled with Luther, and he told them to send him no more works from Zürich because he did not consider himself as being in communion with them. The Zürichers were livid, including Henry Bullinger, Zwingli's successor as chief pastor in Zürich. Luther was also furious with Martin Bucer, because he suspected that Bucer, even though he had signed the Wittenberg Accord, was now compromising on the real presence. Urged on by Amsdorf, he decided he would write on the subject one last time.[23]

Luther's *Brief Confession concerning the Holy Sacrament* appeared in September 1544. Luther directed it against Karlstadt, Zwingli, Oecolampadius, Schwenckfeld 'and their disciples at Zürich', which would presumably include Bullinger, although he is not mentioned in the book by name.[24]

Luther goes over the old arguments and condemns those who tried to make Zwingli a saint after his death on the battlefield. Luther wants no fellowship with anyone who denies the real presence. Though Luther does not mention ubiquity, he asks how anyone who does not believe in the Lord's Supper can believe in the humanity and divinity of Christ or in the Incarnation. Zwingli's followers were 'lying' when they claimed to believe these things. 'Whoever does not believe one article of faith cannot truly believe in others … Everything is to be believed completely and without exception, or nothing is to be believed', except in the case of young or new Christians, who are willing to be taught and do not 'stubbornly oppose the truth'. Arius said he believed in the Creation, in salvation and the Sacraments, but by his denial of Christ's deity, Arius stands condemned (1 John 2:23), and his claims to believe other articles are in vain. Similarly, the 'babbling' of fanatics about spiritual eating in the Lord's Supper is nothing but 'fig leaves … it is useless for them to believe in God the Father, Son and Holy Spirit and in Christ the Saviour'.

Taken in its historical context, this is far more provocative than his call to expel Jews for blasphemy. Luther was implicitly calling Henry Bullinger unchristian because of differences over the Eucharist.

Melanchthon was aghast when the work was printed. He dashed off a letter to Bullinger regretting this 'most harsh book' in which strife over the Lord's Supper had flared up again.[25] He and Bucer were making frantic efforts to calm things down, though with only partial success. Bullinger wrote a lengthy defence, to which Luther thought of replying but did not do so. Instead, he kept up his polemic against the Swiss in his lectures and in the pulpit. He adapted Psalm 1 against them: 'Blessed is the man who walks not in the way of the sacramentarians, nor stands in the way of the Zwinglians, nor sits in the seat of the Zürichers.' They were 'heretics and estranged from the holy Christian church'; they had 'disgraced the Sacrament'.[26]

For anyone who held the Zwinglian teaching on this issue, there was nothing in the *Brief Confession* likely to dissuade him. It merely restated well-known opinions with a gruff 'take it or leave it' attitude. The gap between Luther and the Swiss was more marked than ever. It may also have had wider repercussions. Jasper Ridley has plausibly suggested that the renewed dispute prompted English reformers like Nicholas Ridley and Thomas Cranmer to reconsider their hitherto more or less Lutheran views, and to move over to a neo-Swiss position.[27]

Against the Roman Papacy

At the diet of Speyer in 1544, Charles V took quite a conciliatory attitude to his Protestant subjects, chiefly because he needed all the support he could get to withstand the threat from the Turk. Rome did not approve of this, and was pressing Charles to crush heresy in his dominions, by force if necessary. Rome also insisted that a General Council, not an imperial diet, should settle the religious divisions in Germany. In September, Charles and Francis I of France agreed with the plan to convene a council at Trent.[28]

Rome's involvement in Germany's affairs goaded Luther into writing one of his harshest tracts ever, entitled *Against the Roman Papacy, an Institution of the Devil.*[29] Before discussing the work, it should be noted that here and in other anti-papal works, Luther is attacking specifically the *Renaissance* papacy of his times.

Luther was enraged with the pope for urging Charles to act ruthlessly against the Lutherans. In that case, what sort of a council is Trent likely to be? For his duplicity the pope should be called 'your hellishness'. Besides, a council must be above the pope, not vice versa. Evangelical German princes had been calling for twenty years for a free, Christian German council, where all issues outstanding should be put to the test of Scripture; but the pope will never agree to such a council. Now the pope was interfering with the rights of princes and the emperor, manipulating them for his own ends. The princes should let the 'damned scum of Satan in Rome just go to the devil'.

The rest of the work is divided into three parts. The subject of Part I is whether the pope is head of Christendom and above councils, princes and angels; Luther's unsurprising answer is no. Luther appeals to Church history and the writings of the fathers, according to which the first popes were bishops of Rome and nothing more. He dates the rise of the papacy as he knew

Thomas Cranmer, by Gerlach Flicke. He married the niece of Andreas Osiander, Lutheran pastor of Nuremberg. (*THP Archive*)

it from Boniface III in the seventh century. The rock in Matthew 16 is Christ, not the pope, as all ancient authorities accepted. Then Luther rehearses familiar arguments against the papacy – its corruption, vices, the popes who exalt themselves over the princes and the denial of the Gospel. The papacy has no basis in Scripture and it was never instituted at the request of the kings of Europe, so it can come only from the devil. The papacy teaches false doctrine, and the pope has 'grabbed the keys of St Peter for himself'. Christ is Head of the universal Church, and it is common knowledge that Christian churches in the East have never acknowledged papal supremacy. Luther knows the story of Peter's martyrdom in Rome, though he is unsure how reliable it is; but, even if it were true, it would not make him pope or even bishop, because there were many martyrs in Rome besides Peter. The false teaching of the papacy marks it out as the Antichrist sitting in the temple of God (2 Thessalonians 2:4). The Turk is an enemy of Christianity too, but he does not sit in the temple of God or claim to be Christ's vicar or Peter's successor.

Now for Part II: whether no one may sentence, judge or depose the pope. Luther admits the question is a bit theoretical because the pope is the most powerful man in Christendom; yet every baptised Christian is spiritually competent to judge the papacy's false works. The pope will care nothing for such a verdict, but God will judge him. Luther recalls once more how, at Augsburg, the papal theologians had to admit that the Lutherans had Scripture on their side. Thus the papacy stands condemned from Scripture and by its own experts, and is incorrigible.

Part III asks whether the pope has transferred the Roman Empire from the Greeks to the Germans, as he claims. No, says Luther, and here he is unusually brief. The pope never had anything to give to anybody. The German Empire dates from Charles the Great and the emperors in Constantinople. Here Luther ends, hoping he can say more in a second work (which he did not live to write).

The language in this book is more violent than in *On the Jews* (though none of our scholars has claimed to detect anti-Italianism in Luther). To make it even more caustic, it was printed complete with coarsely satirical caricatures of the papacy drawn by Lucas Cranach, with Luther's support.[30]

Review

These last polemical works of Luther's are impassioned by his own standards and those of his age, and various reasons may be suggested to explain why. First, he was never a man to shirk a fight, a fact that even some friends like Melanchthon regretted. This irascible element in Luther's nature was now exacerbated by ill health, old age and the godless ungratefulness of the world. 'Our doctrine', said Luther one day to his students, 'frees all nations from the torture and tyranny of Satan, from sin, from eternal death, from the countless monstrosities of the pope, and from the notoriously heavy burden of conscience; but the thankless world is not aware of these countless kindnesses of God.' Such ingratitude tormented Luther – 'Nothing like it is recorded in any chronicle of the heathen'. The old Luther was bitterly disappointed that his Gospel message, his whole life's work, had yielded far less fruit than he had once hoped for, and it left him sick of the world and tired of life. He would have 'sworn a thousand oaths that man could not be so depraved as wantonly to condemn God's Word and truth'. He was not surprised that the world 'is at loggerheads with the Ten Commandments'; but the rejection of the Gospel is 'nothing else than devilish wickedness'.[31]

All the while his *Anfechtung* continued to vex and wear out his spirit. Frustrations with his Wittenberg congregation made his mood worse. In his lectures he complained of the impiety 'among our citizens and peasants, whose taverns resound far and wide with shouts and yelling even during our sermons'. The picture was not all gloom, and he could rejoice to see how some congregations 'flourish in pure and sound teaching, and they grow day by day through many excellent and most sincere pastors'.[32] Over against this, as seen in Chapter 12, in February 1545 he felt so estranged from his own townsfolk that he threatened to leave Wittenberg for good, because the preaching of faith had failed to produce satisfying results.

Nor did Luther ever lose the unhappy memory of those years he had spent in the monastery. As an old man it saddened him that 'young people are ignorant of these monstrous things' done in monasteries, and neither do they care very much when they are told of them; instead they are 'berserk in their boundless license and arrogance'.[33] Luther felt that youngsters had it far too easy.

Luther did not expect the world to last for more than a generation or two. Events seemed to him to be rushing towards an apocalyptic climax, and this may have convinced him that the need of the hour was a spirit of defiance against enemies, rather than one that would persevere in labouring for a reconciliation that looked increasingly unlikely. Though this was a personal view and never a dogma, he divided the world into six ages: of Adam, Noah, Abraham, David, Christ and the pope, a thousand years each from the Creation; and he did not think the pope would 'complete his thousand years'. (Here, unfortunately, he has made the same slip as he did with Copernicus; because just as the Bible never says that the sun moves round the earth, neither does it say that the world will endure for only six thousand years.)[34]

One other point may be suggested. In the early 1520s, Luther was the great reformer of the Church. Then, *having* reformed it, he became its chief pastor and guide. This transition from reformer to shepherd is not an easy one. The qualities vital for the first – the zeal, the passion, the uncompromising bold-ness, even the rage at abuses and corruption in the old order – do not always suit the second. Though the new evangelical Church needed a stout defender, there was no real need to reignite the Eucharistic controversy: discretion may have been the better part of valour. Some response to Rome's call for a council was in order, but in *Against the Roman Papacy* old Luther is so pent up at the thought of his opponents that he is often reduced to spluttering, and does not deliver anything really effective.

But it is not necessary to spend much time musing on Luther's psyche. The writer of these last works was, quite simply, a tired, troubled and angry old man, fed up with the world, weary of life, and his spiritual and physical powers were fading. Anyone wishing to can verify this for themselves by reading them alongside the *Babylonian Captivity* or the *Freedom of a Christian*. It is a pity he could not bow out with a *tour de force* more worthy of him.

14

Gone is the Charioteer of Israel

Charles V was now at peace with France, and was, for the time being, unthreatened by the Turks, so this lull gave him the opportunity to try once more to settle Germany's religious division. This time he would use military force. It was a crisis that Melanchthon would live through, but not Luther. In January 1546, Luther had gone to Eisleben, his hometown, to try to settle certain largely secular disputes there. For some time he had been troubled by Count Albrecht's oppressive rule and the greed of the nobility. Luther made the journey safely despite the river Saale flooding, but it was never going to be a comfortable mission for him. As negotiations dragged on, the inevitable happened: never the most patient of men, Luther quickly became irritated with the greedy rulers and merchants. To make matters worse, lawyers were involved. Luther hated their long, drawn-out arguments and hair-splitting, and after a particularly irksome and protracted session he nearly punched the nose of one of the jurists.[1]

While he was away Luther kept up a regular correspondence with Wittenberg. Tensions between him and Melanchthon over the Eucharistic controversy had apparently eased, and relations were harmonious once again. Luther addressed his letters to 'the man of outstanding learning, Philip Melanchthon, theologian and servant of God, my dearest brother in the Lord'. Philip replied to the 'Reverend man, Restorer of the pure doctrine of the Gospel, my most dear father'. Luther wrote to Katy, 'my gracious mistress and most holy Doctoress', telling her roughly, but affectionately, to stop fretting about his health. 'Since you started worrying about me, the fire nearly burned me, and a great stone almost crushed me. Therefore be at peace. Amen.'

On 14 February Luther told Katy and Philip that he was coming home, and was glad of it. He asked Katy to get some medicine ready that he was wont to take for his ailments, which included high blood pressure. Philip wrote back on the 18th wishing him a safe journey, looking forward to seeing him again. Katy had prepared the medicine he asked for.[2]

Next day, 19 February 1546, Melanchthon's students in Wittenberg assembled for the morning lecture on Romans. Philip appeared sombre and shocked; he had just heard news which 'troubles me so much that I doubt whether I can continue my duties at the university'. Two days ago, he explained to the hushed assembly before him, after the evening meal, our 'venerable father and dear teacher Dr Martin Luther' was seized by sudden, severe stomach and chest pains (Brecht calls this *angina pectoris*). Through the night, attempts of friends to heal him failed. Early next morning, while commending his soul to Christ, he was 'taken by God into everlasting life ... to the heavenly university ... into the fellowship of the Father, the Son and the Holy Ghost, and all the company of the apostles and prophets'. There had been no ceremonial, no last confession, no last Sacrament, no priestly ministrations; only a clear, resounding 'yes' when witnesses asked him, chiefly for their own consolation and that of the faithful, whether he was ready to die in the evangelical faith that he had taught and defended. Melanchthon appealed to God for strength and grace. 'Gone is the Charioteer of Israel', the one to whom God had revealed the 'true Gospel of the forgiveness of sin and faith in Christ ... I beseech thee, O Son of God, Emmanuel, who was crucified for us and rose again, rule and protect thy church'.[3]

It is not clear who broke the news to Katy, but arrangements for the burial were made quickly. The funeral oration was delivered by Melanchthon.[4]

Philip came not merely to speak well of the dead. 'The Reverend Dr Martin Luther, our most dear father and Preceptor', was a minister of the Gospel, raised up by God. Philip traced briefly the history of the 'church of all ages', from the patriarchs to the prophets and apostles, followed by the fathers and eminent men since. 'To that splendid list' the name of Martin Luther must now be added, and Philip ranked him alongside Isaiah, John the Baptist, Paul and Augustine. It was in the midst of the 'densest darkness' that Luther brought to light 'true and necessary doctrine', on justification, the Law and the Gospel, the righteousness of faith and the Sacraments. He showed what true worship is, he translated the Scriptures and left many worthy writings. He was a man taught of God, and 'throughout all eternity pious souls will magnify the benefits which God has bestowed on the church through Luther'.

Philip admitted that some 'by no means evil minded persons' feared that Luther could be harsh in his judgements. Philip would not deny it, but because of the great disorders in the Church 'God gave the age a violent physician'. (This is a quote from Erasmus.) It is natural, Philip went on, for 'mediocre and inferior minds to dislike those of more ardent character'. No man is perfect, but it may be said of Luther, as the ancients did of Hercules and others: 'rough indeed, but worthy of all praise.'

Philip paid tribute to Luther's personal qualities, which all who knew him attested: his kindness, affability and graciousness, his lack of personal ambition, his love of good religion and the liberal arts. 'Brave, lofty, ardent souls, such as Luther had, must be divinely guided.' His companions are left feeling like orphans, but Luther is a spectator of heavenly and eternal things; 'we do not doubt that Luther is eternally happy'. Let us, therefore, remember the man and the doctrine he taught and hold fast to it. The oration ended with a prayer for the protection of the Church and an exhortation to keep the faith.

Luther left no official last testimony, but the following note was jotted down by him in Eisleben a day or two before his death:[5]

Nobody can understand Virgil in his *Bucolics* and *Georgics* unless he has been a shepherd or a farmer for five years.

Nobody understands Cicero in his letters unless he has been engaged in public affairs of some consequence for twenty years.

Let nobody suppose that he has tasted the Holy Scriptures sufficiently unless he has ruled over churches with the prophets for a hundred years ... Lay not your hand on this Divine *Aeneid*, but bow before it, adore its every trace.

Notes

Abbreviations used in the Notes

AC   Augsburg Confession★
Apology   Philip Melanchthon's *Apology of the Augsburg Confession*
Brecht   Martin Brecht's biography of Luther
CR   *Corpus Reformatorum*
LCC   *Library of Christian Classics*
LW   *Luther's Works: American edn*
KJV   King James Version
NIV   New International Version
Pelikan, *Creeds*   Pelikan and Hotchkiss, *Creeds and Confessions ... vol. 2: Part 4:*
                    Creeds and Confessions of the Reformation Era
UP   University Press
WA   *Dr Martin Luthers Werke* (Weimar edn, 61 vols)
WA, TR   *Dr Martin Luthers Werke: Tischreden* (6 vols)

★ The Augsburg Confession and other Lutheran Confessional Documents are
  printed in Pelikan, *Creeds* (see above). Students may also wish to use the
  Internet to search for 'Book of Concord'.

1. The Late Medieval World
  1. Cameron, *European Reformation*, p. 16; Duffy, *Stripping of the Altars*, pp. 91–130;
     MacCulloch, *Reformation*, pp. 10–16.
  2. Cameron, *European Reformation*, pp. 79–83; Duffy, *Stripping of the Altars*,
     pp. 60–2, 191.
  3. Cameron, *European Reformation*, pp. 79–80; Duffy, *Stripping of the Altars*,
     pp. 341–48; MacCulloch, *Reformation*, pp. 11–12.
  4. The above is a very general picture taken from Duffy's *Stripping of the Altars*; see
     especially pp. 11–77, 234–8.
  5. Cameron, *European Reformation*, pp. 10–11, 16–17; Duffy, *Stripping of the Altars*,
     pp. 155–205; MacCulloch, *Reformation*, pp. 19–22.

6. Walker, *History of the Christian Church*, pp. 376, 388, 390–1, 395–6; Cameron, *European Reformation*, p. 23; Duffy, *Saints and Sinners*, p. 146; Swanson, 'The Pre–Reformation Church' in *Reformation World*, ed. Pettegree, pp. 10–13.

7. Cameron, *European Reformation*, pp. 49–51; Thomson, *Popes and Princes, passim*, especially pp. 14–19, 24, 28–37, 53; Gordon, 'Conciliarism in Late Medieval Europe' in *Reformation World*, ed. Pettegree, p. 31; Swanson, 'The Pre–Reformation Church' in *Reformation World*, p. 13; MacCulloch, *Reformation*, pp. 39, 43–52.

8. Swanson, 'The Pre–Reformation Church' in *Reformation World*, ed. Pettegree, p. 15; Cameron, *European Reformation*, pp. 56–61; Duffy, *Saints and Sinners*, pp. 146–69.

9. Schwiebert, *Reformation*, p. 278; Thomson, *Popes and Princes, 1417–1517*, pp. 37–8.

10. Schwiebert, *Reformation*, p. 160; Cameron, *Reformation of the Heretics*, pp. 85, 93; Cameron, *Waldenses*, pp. 2, 298–303.

11. Cameron, *European Reformation*, pp. 83–7; Walker, *History of the Christian Church*, pp. 322–59. For more detailed study of scholastic theology, a good start is Oberman, *Harvest of Medieval Theology*.

12. Pelikan, *Growth of Medieval Theology*, pp. 289–91; Walker, *History of the Christian Church*, pp. 332–4.

13. Pelikan, *Growth of Medieval Theology*, index refs on p. 327; MacCulloch, *Reformation*, pp. 106–15.

14. Rex, 'Humanism' in *Reformation World*, ed. Pettegree, pp. 51–70; MacCulloch, *Reformation*, pp. 76–87.

15. See further discussions on these and related themes in Spitz, *Religious Reformation of the German Humanists*, especially pp. 3–5, 269–74, 279, 290–1.

16. Duffy, *Saints and Sinners*, pp. 137–42; MacCulloch, *Reformation*, p. 81.

2. Brother Martin

1. Exodus 16; Matthew 16:19; Duffy, *Saints and Sinners*, p. 143; Brecht 1, p. 1.

2. *LW* 54, no 5573.

3. Ibid., nos 2888a, 3838, 5573; Brecht 1, pp. 2–3.

4. *LW* 54, no 3566A; Manschreck, *Melanchthon*, p. 31.

5. Brecht 1, pp. 1–50.

6. *LW* 8, p. 182; *LW* 48, p. 331.

7. Brecht 1, pp. 51–2.

8. Ibid., pp. 43, 162–5; *LW* 48, p. 9.

9. Brecht 1, pp. 98–105; *LW* 54, no 3582a.

10. Brecht 1, pp. 98–105, 125–32; *LW* 48, p. 49.

11. Brecht 1, pp. 63–75; *LW* 22, p. 377; *LW* 54, nos 495, 1558, 4422.

12. Brecht 1, pp. 76–82; quote on p. 80. Brecht believes the worst of the *Anfechtung* about election occurred in Luther's first years at Wittenberg.

13. *LW* 12, p. 273; *LW* 54, no 3548, p. 230.

14. Brecht 1, pp. 82–90, 130–5; *LW* 54, nos 116, 4691.

15. Brecht 1, pp. 145–53.

16. Ibid., pp. 166–71; *LW* 48, p. 12.

17. Brecht 1, pp. 175–8; Duffy, *Saints and Sinners*, p. 139; Thomson, *Popes and Princes*, pp. 87–8.

18. Brecht 1, pp. 178–9; Duffy, *Saints and Sinners*, p. 150.

19. Brecht 1, pp. 180–3.

20. Ibid., pp. 183–90.

21. *LW* 31, pp. 17–34; *LW* 48, pp. 43–8; Brecht 1, pp. 190–2. For Luther's subsequent and lengthy explanation of the theses, see *LW* 31, pp. 77–252.

22. Brecht 1, pp. 192–202.

23. See discussion in Brecht 1, pp. 200–1.

24. Brecht 1, pp. 206–11.

3. The Reformation Discovery: Here I Stand

1. Brecht 1, p. 122.

2. *LW* 27, p. 377; *LW* 34, pp. 336–7; *LW* 54, nos 3232c, 4007, 5518; Brecht 1, pp. 221–30.

3. These testimonies are collated and tabulated in Lowell Green, *How Melanchthon Helped Luther Discover the Gospel*, pp. 40–1, 174.

4. *LW* 31, pp. 35–70; Brecht 1, pp. 213–15, 231–5 (this section in Brecht includes a helpful section on the much discussed 'Theology of the Cross').

5. Brecht 1, pp. 242, 246–65; *LW* 31, pp. 253–92; *LW* 48, pp. 90–1.

6. *LW* 14, pp. 281–2. This is a preface to a commentary on Psalm 1, dedicated to the Elector Frederick: it is possible that Luther was being consciously diplomatic, though perhaps unlikely.

7. *LW* 31, pp. 309–25; Brecht 1, pp. 299–348.

8. *LW* 31, pp. 295–306.

9. Brecht 1, p. 229; *LW* 31, p. 295; Lowell Green, *How Melanchthon Helped Luther*, p. 174.

10. *LW* 44, pp. 17–114.

11. *LW* 31, pp. 216, 317; *WA* 2, p. 416 (36) (No *LW*).

12. *LW* 44, pp. 117–217.

13. Brecht 2, p. 70.

14. *LW* 31, p. 330; Brecht 1, pp. 389–422.

15. *LW* 31, pp. 334–43.

16. Ibid., pp. 343–77.

17. *LW* 36, pp. 3–126.

18. Brecht 1, pp. 423–32.

19. Unless otherwise stated, the following account of the diet of Worms is taken from Brecht 1, pp. 433–76; Schwiebert, *Reformation*, pp. 180–1.

20. *LW* 48, pp. 175–9.

21. Ibid., p. 198.

22. Ibid., pp. 199–200.

23. Olivier, *Trial of Luther*, p. 167.

24. *LW* 48, p. 202.

25. Schwiebert, *Reformation*, pp. 29, 46.

4. The Handmaiden of Theology

1. *LW* 48, p. 225.

2. Brecht 2, pp. 1, 4, 6, 47.

3. *LW* 48, pp. 246, 295, 319.

4. Brecht 2, pp. 25–7; *LW* 48, pp. 308–9, 311.

5. *LW* 44, pp. 250–400; see also AC 15, 27.

6. Brecht 2, pp. 29–33.

7. *LW* 45, pp. 53–74; quotes from pp. 62–3.

8. Brecht 2, p. 34.

9. *LW* 48, pp. 365–6; Brecht 2, pp. 34–7, 137–8.

10. Brecht 2, pp. 38–45; *LW* 48, p. 395.

11. *LW* 51, pp. 70–100.

12. Brecht 2, pp. 61, 65.

13. Ibid., pp. 57–8, 65–6, 122–4, 253–8.

14. *LW* 53, pp. 11–25, 55.

15. Ibid., pp. 53–90; Brecht 2, pp. 253–6.

16. *Apology*, 15 (51).

17. *LW* 53, pp. 193, 195, 202.

18. Ibid., pp. 235–6, 283–5.

19. Ibid., pp. 211–16.

20. Ibid., pp. 217–20.

21. Ibid., pp. 223–8.

22. Ibid., pp. 242–4.

23. Ibid., pp. 255–7.

24. Ibid., pp. 268–9.

25. Ibid., pp. 289–91.

26. Ibid., pp. 271–3.

27. Ibid., pp. 306–7.

28. Ibid., pp. 277–9.

29. Ibid., pp. 295–301.

30. Ibid., pp. 249–54.

31. Ibid., pp. 308–9.

32. Quoted in MacCulloch, *Reformation*, p. 589.

33. *LW* 40, pp. 84–91, 99–100; *LW* 53, p. 316.

34. *WA*, TR 2, no 2545; TR 3, no 3815; TR 4, no 4192.

35. *LW* 53, pp. 321–4; *LW* 49, pp. 427–8.

36. *LW* 54, no 1258.

37. Spitta, *Bach* 3, pp. 63–4.

38. *LW* 53, pp. 319–20.

5. Church and State, Princes and Peasants

1. *LW* 37, pp. 367–8; *LW* 41, pp. 143–67; AC 8.

2. *LW* 3, p. 53; *LW* 45, pp. 116, 120.

3. Brecht 2, pp. 85–7, 107–12.

4. Briefly summarised from Luther's *Temporal Authority: To what extent it should be obeyed*, *LW* 45, pp. 75–129; see also discussion in Brecht 2, pp. 117–19.

5. Brecht 2, pp. 261–7.

6. *LW* 46, pp. 95–8; Brecht 2, pp. 357–8; Brecht 3, pp. 199–202.

7. Brecht 2, p. 175; Stayer, *German Peasants' War*, pp. 21–2, 32–3; Scott and Scribner, *German Peasants' War*, pp. 6–14.

8. Brecht 2, p. 174; Baylor, *Radical Reformation*, pp. 231–41; Scott and Scribner, *German Peasants' War*, pp. 32, 251–7.

9. *LW* 46, pp. 5–43.

10. Friesen, *Müntzer*, pp. 244–5; Scott and Scribner, *German Peasants' War*, pp. 145–8.

11. *LW* 46, pp. 47–55.

12. Friesen, *Müntzer*, pp. 259–68; Scott and Scribner, *German Peasants' War*, pp. 290–1.

13. Printed in Scott and Scribner, *German Peasants' War*, pp. 292, 322–4; see also Brecht's discussion in Brecht 2, pp. 185–91.

14. Luther's *Open Letter on the Harsh Book*: *LW* 46, pp. 59–85.

15. This and the next paragraph from Brecht 2, pp. 100, 195–7.

6. Controversies: Anabaptists, Erasmus, Zwingli and the Anfechtung

1. Bagchi, *Luther's Earliest Opponents: Catholic Controversialists, 1518–1525*.

2. Clasen, *Anabaptism*, Chapter 2.

3. Goertz, *The Anabaptists*, pp. 59–67, quote on p. 62.

4. Clasen, *Anabaptism*, pp. 91–2, 95–7, 121–5, 141–3, 175, 180–1; Haude, 'Anabaptism', in *Reformation World*, ed. Pettegree, pp. 237–54.

5. *LW* 40, pp. 227–62.

6. *LW* 49, pp. 218–19; *LW* 50, pp. 73–4.

7. Erasmus's *Diatribe* and Luther's response, the *Bondage of the Will*, are translated and printed in *LCC* 27. The *Bondage* also appears in *LW* 33, pp. 3–295. Fine discussions include Brecht 2, pp. 312–38; *LCC* 17, pp. 1–34.

8. Brecht 2, p. 231.

9. Ibid.

10. Ibid., p. 235.

11. Schofield, *Melanchthon*, pp. 33–7, 52–4, 64–5; Formula of Concord 11 (Pelikan, *Creeds*, pp. 198–200).

12. For Erasmus' religious beliefs, see Pelikan, *Reformation of Church and Dogma*, pp. 261, 270, 308; Spitz, *The Religious Renaissance of the German Humanists*, pp. 226–36; MacCulloch, *Reformation*, pp. 97–105.

13. *LW* 40, p. 216.

14. For Luther on the Eucharist, see Brecht 2, pp. 293–325; Pelikan, *Luther the Expositor*, Chapter 7. Luther's original works are collated in *LW* 37, which has an extremely helpful index. For Zwingli on the Eucharistic presence and his exchanges with Luther, see Potter, *Zwingli*, pp. 156–8, 287–315; Locher, *Zwingli's Thought*, pp. 19–22, 180, 215–28; Stephens, *Theology of Zwingli*, pp. 180–93, 218–59. For Zwingli on the Christological aspect of the Eucharist in particular, see Locher, pp. 173–7; Stephens, pp. 111–18. Locher and Stephens have extensive quotes, with references, from Zwingli's original writings.

15. *LW* 37, pp. 206, 231 (Matthew 12:45).

16. On Marburg and after, see Brecht 2, pp. 325–34; Potter, *Zwingli*, pp. 316–42. For a presentation of the Marburg colloquy, based on earlier reconstructions from primary sources, see Sasse, *This is My Body*, pp. 178–220.

17. *LW* 54, no 1451; Brecht 2, p. 423.

18. One example only is *LW* 24, p. 291. There are hundreds more.

19. *LW* 22, pp. 388–9.
20. *LW* 24, p. 58.
21. Ibid., p. 229.
22. *LW* 54, no 4422.
23. *LW* 8, p. 276.
24. *LW* 54, no 122.
25. Ibid., no 469.

7. *The Bible, Catechisms and the Augsburg Confession*

1. *LW* 35, pp. 228–9; Brecht 3, pp. 98, 107.
2. *LW* 35, pp. 355–411.
3. Ibid., p. 394; *LW* 8, p. 178.
4. *LW* 35, pp. 227–354.
5. Ibid., pp. 294–316.
6. This and more examples in Brecht 2, pp. 49–50.
7. Daniell, *Tyndale*, p. 286.
8. See also *LW* 17, p. 223.
9. *LW* 35, pp. 182–6, 188–9, 192–6.
10. Luther's Catechisms, see Pelikan, *Creeds*, pp. 31–48.
11. Brecht 2, pp. 369–405. The Augsburg Confession is printed in Pelikan, *Creeds*, pp. 49–119.
12. Brecht 2, p. 377. Luther's mother died soon after, on 30 June 1532: see *LW* 50, p. 17, fn. 2.
13. AC 11.
14. AC 5, 14, 28. Also, the proclamation of the Gospel is the 'foundation for all other functions' (such as deacons, helpers, governing the Church and so on): see *LW* 40, p. 36.
15. *LW* 34, pp. 50–1, 92; Brecht 3, pp. 303–4; Smalcald Articles 3.10 (1–3) = Pelikan, *Creeds*, pp. 145–6. On Elizabeth, see discussion in Gibson, *Thirty-Nine Articles*, p. 744.
16. AC 28 (Pelikan, *Creeds*, pp. 109–14 [33, 44, 53, 57–64]).
17. Brecht 2, pp. 402–10; *LW* 13, p. 353.

8. *The Bible Teacher: The New Testament*

1. *LW* 54, nos 3493, 4462.
2. Brecht 3, p. 136 and Pelikan's Introduction to *LW* 1.
3. *LW* 21, pp. 298, 314, 321.
4. Ibid., pp. 322–3, 329.
5. Ibid., p. 344.
6. Ibid., pp. 352, 355.
7. Ibid., pp. 3–5.
8. Ibid., pp. 10–16, 34–5.
9. Ibid., pp. 39–41.
10. Ibid., pp. 85–8, 96–7.
11. Ibid., pp. 101–2, 105–6, 109.

12. Ibid., pp. 142–3, 157–62.
13. Ibid., pp. 167, 172, 195–200.
14. Ibid., pp. 210–13, 225–7, 244–6, 252–61.
15. Ibid., p. 281. The words in quotes may sound more like Melanchthon than Luther, but there is no editorial note to suggest any subsequent additions at this point, so I have used the text freely.
16. *LW* 22, p. 7.
17. Ibid., pp. 5, 8.
18. Ibid., pp. 17–18, 20–2, 74.
19. Ibid., pp. 80–1.
20. Ibid., pp. 111–13.
21. Ibid., pp. 51, 129–34.
22. Ibid., p. 166.
23. Ibid., p. 3. Luther takes it that John 1:32 refers to the baptism of Jesus described in Matthew and Luke.
24. Ibid., pp. 218–19.
25. Ibid., pp. 277–362.
26. Ibid., pp. 393–4. This is another passage that may sound more like Melanchthon than Luther, but as before there is no suggestion in *Luther's Works* that any editing has been done here.
27. Ibid., pp. 394, 399–401.
28. *LW* 23, pp. 43, 49, 116, 118, 154, 165–6.
29. Ibid., pp. 84–7. This sermon was delivered sometime during 1530–31; see pp. x, 197 (fn).
30. Ibid., p. 61.
31. Ibid., pp. 299–305.
32. *LW* 24, pp. 8, 57, 91, 104.
33. Ibid., pp. 187–90.
34. Ibid., pp. 290, 373.
35. Ibid., pp. 313, 320, 414, 422.
36. See discussion in Brecht 1, pp. 129–37; *LW* 25, pp. x–xii; quote on humility from *LW* 25, p. 441.
37. *LW* 26, pp. 252–3, 272–3, 313–14.
38. Ibid., pp. 4–12, and *passim*.
39. Ibid., pp. 133, 232–3.
40. Ibid., pp. 181, 199–200, 301; *LW* 27, p. 93.
41. Ibid., pp. 45, 283, 300, 312; *LW* 54, no 146; Brecht 2, p. 455.
42. *LW* 28, pp. 21, 36–7, 80.
43. Ibid., pp. 276, 310–18.
44. *LW* 30, pp. 52–5, 63–4.
45. Ibid., pp. 112–15.
46. Ibid., pp. 219, 221, 257–8, 285–8, 295.

9. The Bible Teacher: The Patriarchs

1. *LW* 1, p. 22; *LW* 20, p. 125; *LW* 37, p. 321; *LW* 35, p. 362. See also Pelikan, *Luther the Expositor*, especially Chapter 5.

2. *LW* 1, p. 1.
3. Ibid., pp. 1–4.
4. Ibid., pp. 9, 12, 16–17; *LW* 8, pp. 163–4.
5. *LW* 1, pp. 11, 14.
6. Ibid., pp. 30–2.
7. Ibid., p. 45. See also *LW* 54, no 5573.
8. *LW* 1, pp. 56, 62–3.
9. Ibid., pp. 69, 83.
10. Ibid., pp. 93–7.
11. Ibid., pp. 97–100.
12. Ibid., pp. 111.
13. Ibid., pp. 123–4.
14. Ibid., pp. 125–8.
15. Ibid., pp. 129–30.
16. Ibid., pp. 1, 147–9, 162.
17. Ibid., pp. 114, 142–3, 165–6.
18. Ibid., pp. 170–9.
19. Ibid., pp. 195–6, 220, 229.
20. Ibid., p. 233.
21. Ibid., pp. 237–42.
22. Ibid., pp. 251–8, 280.
23. Ibid., pp. 282, 299–301, 309, 312.
24. Ibid., p. 325.
25. Ibid., pp. 330–1.
26. *LW* 2, pp. 10–12.
27. Ibid., pp. 32–9, 56–7, 71.
28. *LW* 54, no 3476; *LW* 2, p. 173.
29. *LW* 2, pp. 175–6.
30. Ibid., pp. 178–9.
31. Ibid., pp. 178–81.
32. Ibid., pp. 187–209.
33. Ibid., pp. 246–8, 252–5, 261, 280. For the promise to Abraham see Genesis 12:1–3; 15:1–4; 17:1–22; 18:18; 22:17–18; Galatians 3:16.
34. *LW* 2, pp. 294, 305–12, 321–3.
35. Ibid., pp. 286, 363–96.
36. *LW* 3, pp. 20–3.
37. Ibid., pp. 43–4.
38. Ibid., pp. 70, 95, 111.
39. Ibid., pp. 226–39, 247, 252–7.
40. Ibid., pp. 259–60, 308–13.
41. Ibid., pp. 316, 326.
42. *LW* 4, pp. 20–3, 37–9, 46–51, 71.
43. Ibid., pp. 84–5.
44. Ibid., pp. 93–6, 103–17.
45. Ibid., pp. 247–304.
46. Ibid., pp. 300–403; *LW* 5, p. 101.

47. *LW* 5, pp. 28–41.
48. Ibid., pp. 113–27, 200.
49. Ibid., p. 148.
50. Ibid., pp. 179–202.
51. Ibid., pp. 209–10.
52. Ibid., pp. 218–20, 260–1.
53. Ibid., pp. 282–92.
54. Ibid., pp. 296–315.
55. Ibid., pp. 288, 330–1.
56. Ibid., pp. 324–43.
57. Ibid., pp. 325, 350–1.
58. *LW* 6, pp. 25–60.
59. Ibid., pp. 125–44, 158–70.
60. Ibid., pp. 192–212.
61. Ibid., pp. 279, 312, 362–3, 397–401.
62. *LW* 7, pp. 10–14. Luther reckons that the events in the first part of Chapter 38 – Judah's marriage and the birth of his sons – occurred before the crime against Joseph, and the defilement of Tamar some time after: see *LW* 7, p. 51.
63. Ibid., pp. 59–100.
64. Ibid., pp. 104–5.
65. Ibid., pp. 105–35.
66. Ibid., pp. 163–6, 191–224.
67. *LW* 6, pp. 288–9; *LW* 8, pp. 7–8.
68. *LW* 7, pp. 225–7, 271–7, 368–77.
69. Ibid., pp. 340; *LW* 8, pp. 1–4, 16.
70. *LW* 8, p. 319.

10. *The Bible Teacher: Psalms and the Prophets*

1. *LW* 14, p. 286. The following sections on the Psalms are taken from *LW* vols 12–13 and occasionally vol. 14. For the dates of these lectures and sermons, see the introductions to these volumes. Volumes 10 and 11 also contain lectures on the Psalms, but these were mostly given before the Reformation breakthrough, so they are not discussed here.
2. *LW* 12, pp. 44–5, 63–70, 85–6, 90–3; *LW* 14, pp. 321, 332–3.
3. *LW* 12, pp. 97, 110–14, 127–33.
4. Ibid., pp. 139–43.
5. Ibid., pp. 147, 164–5.
6. Ibid., pp. 201–4, 230–1, 259.
7. Ibid., pp. 304–9, 332, 347–8, 359–71, 396–400.
8. *LW* 13, pp. 44–50, 61–3.
9. Ibid., pp. 77, 134.
10. Ibid., pp. 146–7, 166–8, 198–201.
11. Ibid., pp. 232–43.
12. Ibid., pp. 271–3, 304–23.
13. Ibid., pp. 345–8.
14. Ibid., pp. 351–63.

15. *LW* 14, pp. xi, 8.
16. Ibid., pp. x, 45–8, 55, 73–4.
17. Ibid., pp. 45, 96, 105.
18. *LW* 16, pp. 3–4.
19. Ibid., pp. 5–9, 28–30; *LW* 18, pp. 237–8.
20. *LW* 16, pp. 31–3; *LW* 18, p. 239.
21. *LW* 16, pp. 122–3, 299; AC 17.
22. *LW* 16, pp. 72–5.
23. Ibid., p. 84.
24. Ibid., pp. 100–2.
25. Ibid., pp. 200, 273, 280.
26. Ibid., pp. 305–30.
27. Ibid., p. 331.
28. Ibid., pp. 346–7.
29. *LW* 17, p. 3.
30. Ibid., pp. 3–7.
31. Ibid., pp. 18–32.
32. According to Luther, Cyrus comes in at 44:24 – *LW* 17, p. 117. Unlike some exegetes, he applies 43:14 to Christ, not Cyrus, because this is 'too grand and Christian; it cannot fit the times of Cyrus' – *LW* 17, p. 95.
33. Ibid., pp. 122–45.
34. Ibid., p. 169.
35. Ibid., pp. 221–5.
36. Ibid., p. 260.
37. Ibid., pp. 255–6, 265–8, 331.
38. Ibid., pp. 325, 389–90.
39. Ibid., pp. 388–9, 399, 404–16.
40. *LW* 18, p. 79.
41. Ibid., pp. 3–4.
42. Ibid., pp. 79, 208.
43. Ibid., pp. 129–30.
44. *LW* 19, pp. 36–7.
45. Ibid., pp. 151, 197.
46. *LW* 20, pp. 155–7.
47. Ibid., pp. 181–2, 204–17, 225, 315.
48. Ibid., pp. 337–47.
49. *LW* 18, pp. 418–19.

11. *Dinner with the Luthers*

1. On the compilation, see the Introduction to *LW* 54.
2. Brecht 1, pp. 297, 313–14; Brecht 3, p. 175.
3. Quotes from Brecht 1, p. 297; Brecht 2, p. 57.
4. *LW* 8, pp. 271; *LW* 22, p. 500; *LW* 24, p. 207; *LW* 54, nos 452, 5537.
5. Brecht 2, pp. 204–11.
6. Ibid., pp. 429–30; Brecht 3, pp. 22–3, 185–8. The Smalcald Articles of 1537 were written by Luther in expectation of a council. In substance they are as the

Augsburg Confession, though the tone is somewhat more belligerent. They are printed in Pelikan, *Creeds*, pp. 119–49.

7. Brecht 3, pp. 229–33.
8. *LW* 3, p. 354.
9. *LW* 2, pp. 327–8; *LW* 54, no 250.
10. *LW* 49, pp. 154, 238, 312, 321, 316; *LW* 50, p. 80.
11. *LW* 54, no 5441.
12. *LW* 2, p. 301; *WA*, TR 6, no 6910.
13. *LW* 54, nos 3528, 3530, 4625.
14. *WA*, TR 2, no 2034; *LW* 54, no 3755.
15. *WA*, TR 3, nos 3787–9.
16. *LW* 1, p. 202; *LW* 15, p. 131.
17. *LW* 2, p. 311; *LW* 4, pp. 291, 293.
18. *LW* 54, no 4105.
19. Brecht 2, pp. 203–4, 432, 439; Brecht 3, pp. 21, 237.
20. Brecht 2, p. 204; Brecht 3, p. 238.
21. *LW* 54, nos 148, 1559, 3566a.
22. Ibid., nos 81, 4367.
23. Ibid., nos 5498–9.
24. Brecht 3, p. 22; *LW* 54, nos 274, 2849b.
25. Brecht 3, p. 20.
26. *LW* 54, no 3390b.
27. Ibid., no 3811.
28. Ibid., nos 217, 222, 273, 5381.
29. Ibid., no 3477.
30. Ibid., no 5207; Althaus, *Ethics of Martin Luther*, pp. 96–7, fn. 82.
31. *LW* 54, nos 1329, 2931, 3574, 3799, 3814.
32. Ibid., no 3476.
33. *LW* 54, nos 5229–30.
34. *LW* 49, p. 34; *LW* 54, nos 252, 3490, 3975, 5440.
35. *LW* 22, pp. 214–15; *LW* 54, no 4435.
36. *LW* 54, no 2982b; see also discussion in Brecht 3, p. 255.
37. *LW* 15, p. 9.
38. *LW* 54, no 4638.
39. Kolbe, 'Copernicus and Martin Luther': p. 194; Brecht 3, p. 118.
40. Drake, *Galileo*, pp. 203, 211–15.
41. Pelikan, *Luther the Expositor*, p. 233.
42. *LW* 49, p. 75; *LW* 54, nos 5017, 5089, 5511.
43. *LW* 50, p. 117.
44. *LW* 54, no 2898.
45. Ibid., no 5489.
46. Brecht 3, p. 327.
47. *LW* 54, no 5047; Cameron, *European Reformation*, p. 365.
48. *LW* 23, p. 403; *LW* 54, nos 3575, 3622, 3771, 5427, 5663.
49. *LW* 54, no 5559.
50. Ibid., nos 2958b, 4073b (p. 316, last para), 5216. See also Luther's *On Trade and*

Usury, LW 45, pp. 231–310.
51. *LW* 54, no 4543.
52. Ibid., no 3826.

12. *Progress and Setbacks of the Reformation*

1. *LW* 54, nos 3573, 5047 (p. 384), 5171b.
2. Brecht 2, pp. 67–72, 447; Brecht 3, pp. 124–5.
3. Brecht 3, p. 276.
4. *LW* 17, p. 128, fn. 6; Brecht 2, pp. 287–9; Brecht 3, pp. 5–6, 262–71.
5. Schwiebert, *Reformation*, pp. 185, 220–31, 319–24.
6. Brecht 2, pp. 77, 345–47.
7. Ibid., pp. 127–9, 241–3; Brecht 3, pp. 115–24; Schwiebert, *Reformation*, p. 484.
8. Schwiebert, *Reformation*, Part 2, pp. 184ff.
9. *LW* 6, p. 93; *LW* 12, p. 189.
10. *LW* 45, pp. 339–78.
11. Brecht 3, pp. 287–318; C. Scott Dixon, 'The Princely Reformation in Germany' in *Reformation World*, ed. Pettegree, pp. 146–62.
12. Brecht 3, pp. 39–58.
13. Ibid., pp. 318–19; Grell, 'Scandinavia' in *Reformation World*, ed. Pettegree, pp. 257–71; Grell (ed.) *Scandinavian Reformation*, pp. 12–41, 179–80.
14. On the Reformation in Sweden and Finland, see Brecht 3, p. 319; Grell, 'Scandinavia' in *Reformation World*, ed. Pettegree, pp. 271–4; Grell (ed.) *Scandinavian Reformation*, pp. 42–69, 100–13, 144–78.
15. Manschreck, *Melanchthon*, pp. 222–5.
16. *LW* 50, pp. 27–40, 127.
17. Ibid., pp. 136–8.
18. On the diplomatic negotiations between England and the Lutherans, see McEntegert, *Henry VIII, passim*. On the theological discussions: Schofield, *Melanchthon*, Chapters 5–8. On the fall of Cromwell: Schofield, *Cromwell*, Chapters 16–17.
19. *WA* 51, pp. 445–51 (no *LW*).
20. *LW* 54, no 1461.
21. Ibid., no 3609b.
22. Brecht 3, pp. 205–15.
23. *LW* 54, no 5096.
24. *CR* 3, pp. xvii–xviii (the account of Solomon Glas in the Appendix at the end of *CR* 3); *LW* 50, pp. 207–9, 218.

13. *Controversial Last Years*

1. *LW* 53, pp. 304–5.
2. *LW* 8, p. 187; *LW* 22, pp. 81, 333.
3. *LW* 22, p. 83.
4. *LW* 43, pp. 213–41.
5. *LW* 45, pp. 195–229.
6. *LW* 14, pp. x, 210, 269.

7. Brecht 3, pp. 336–7.
8. *LW* 3, pp. 338–40.
9. *LW* 54, no 5462.
10. *LW* 47, pp. 123–306.
11. Weikart, *Darwin to Hitler*, pp. 10–17, 103–26, 232–3.
12. *LW* 12, p. 199; *LW* 54, no 4425.
13. *LW* 47, p. 135.
14. *LW* 45, pp. 114–15.
15. Brecht 3, p. 355.
16. *LW* 13, pp. 60–1, 67.
17. *LW* 47, pp. 279, 291.
18. Ibid., pp. 268, 291–5.
19. Schofield, *Melanchthon*, pp. 181–2.
20. Brecht 3, p. 346; *LW* 47, p. 297.
21. *LW* 47, p. 123; Brecht 3, p. 349.
22. Schofield, *Melanchthon*, p. 146.
23. See full discussion in Brecht 3, pp. 323–32.
24. *LW* 38, pp. 279–319.
25. Schofield, *Melanchthon*, p. 147.
26. Quotes in Brecht 3, pp. 330–1.
27. Ridley, *Nicholas Ridley*, pp. 95–6.
28. Brecht 3, p. 358; *LW* 41, pp. 259–60.
29. *LW* 41, pp. 257–376.
30. Brecht 3, p. 362.
31. *LW* 3, p. 342; *LW* 24, pp. 286–7.
32. *LW* 8, p. 260; *LW* 50, p. 242.
33. *LW* 8, p. 173.
34. *LW* 54, no 5300; Brecht 2, p. 366; Brecht 3, pp. 138, 333. For the Bible on the end times, see Matthew 24:36, 44.

14. *Gone is the Charioteer of Israel*

1. Brecht 3, pp. 369–82.
2. *LW* 50, pp. 292–315; Schofield, *Melanchthon*, p. 147.
3. Brecht 3, p. 376; Manschreck, *Melanchthon*, p. 274.
4. A full English translation of the oration is printed in Richard, *Melanchthon*, pp. 381–92.
5. *LW* 54, no 5677.

Bibliography

Primary Sources

Eusebius, *The Ecclesiastical History* (Loeb Classical Library, 2 vols, London: Heinemann, 1926–32)

Library of Christian Classics, ed. J. Baillie *et al.* (26 vols, London: SCM, 1969)

Luther, M., *Dr Martin Luthers Werke: Kritische Gesamtausgabe* (61 vols, Weimar: Hermann Böhlaus, 1883–1983)

———, *Luthers Werke, Tischreden* (6 vols, Weimar: Hermann Böhlaus, 1920–21)

———, *Luther's Works: American edn*, ed. J. Pelikan (55 vols, Philadelphia and St Louis: Fortress Press and Concordia, 1955–86)

Pelikan, J. and Hotchkiss, V. (eds), *Creeds and Confessions of Faith in the Christian Tradition*, vol 2: Part 4: 'Creeds and Confessions of the Reformation Era' (New Haven: Yale UP, 2003)

Secondary Sources

Althaus, P., *The Ethics of Martin Luther*, trans. R. Schultz (Philadelphia: Fortress Press, 1972)

Bagchi, D., *Luther's Earliest Opponents: Catholic Controversialists, 1518–1525* (Minneapolis: Fortress Press, 1991)

Baylor, M.G. (ed.), *The Radical Reformation* (Cambridge: Cambridge UP, 1991)

Brecht, M., *Martin Luther*, trans. J.L. Schaff (3 vols, Philadelphia and Minneapolis: Fortress Press, 1985, 1990, 1993 …)

———, 1: *His Road to Reformation, 1485–1521*

———, 2: *Shaping and Defining the Reformation, 1521–1532*

———, 3: *The Preservation of the Church, 1532–1545*

Cameron, E., *The Reformation of the Heretics: The Waldenses of the Alps, 1480–1580* (Oxford: Clarendon, 1984)

———, *The European Reformation* (Oxford: Clarendon, 1991)

———, 'Philip Melanchthon: Image and Substance', *JEH* 48 (1997): 705–22

———, *Waldenses: Rejections of the Holy Church in Medieval Europe* (Oxford: Blackwell, 2000)

Clasen, C.P., *Anabaptism: A Social History, 1526–1618* (Ithaca: Cornell UP, 1972)

Daniell, D., *William Tyndale: A Biography* (New Haven and London: Yale UP, 1994)

Drake, S., *Discoveries and Opinions of Galileo* (New York: Doubleday, 1957)

Duffy, E., *The Stripping of the Altars: Traditional Religion in England 1400–1580* (New Haven and London: Yale UP, 1992)

———, *Saints and Sinners: A History of the Popes* (New Haven: Yale UP, 1997)

Friesen, A., *Thomas Müntzer, a Destroyer of the Godless: The Making of a Sixteenth-Century Religious Revolutionary* (Berkeley: California UP, 1990)

Gibson, E.C.S., *The Thirty-Nine Articles of the Church of England* (2nd edn, London: Methuen, 1898)

Goertz, H-J., *The Anabaptists* (London: Routledge, 1996)

Green, C. Lowell, *How Melanchthon helped Luther discover the Gospel: The Doctrine of Justification in the Reformation* (Fallbrook, California: Verdict, 1980)

Grell, O. (ed.), *The Scandinavian Reformation: From Evangelical Movement to the Institutionalisation of Reform* (Cambridge: Cambridge UP, 1995)

Kobe, D., 'Copernicus and Martin Luther: An Encounter between Science and Religion', *American Journal of Physics*, 66/3, March 1998: 190–96

Locher, G.W., *Zwingli's Thought: New Perspectives* (Leiden: Brill, 1981)

MacCulloch, D., *Reformation: Europe's House Divided, 1490–1700* (London: Allen Lane, 2003)

Manschreck, C.L., *Melanchthon, The Quiet Reformer* (reprint Westport, Connecticut: Greenwood, 1975)

McEntegart, R., *Henry VIII, The League of Schmalkalden and the English Reformation* (Woodbridge: Boydell Press, 2002)

Oberman, H.A., *The Harvest of Medieval Theology: Gabriel Biel and Late Medieval Nominalism* (Cambridge, Mass.: Harvard UP, 1963)

Olivier, D., *The Trial of Luther* (London: Mowbrays, 1978)

Pelikan, J., *Luther the Expositor: Introduction to the Reformer's Exegetical Writings* (St Louis: Concordia, 1959)

———, *The Emergence of the Catholic Tradition (100–600)* (Chicago: Chicago UP, 1971)

———, *The Growth of Medieval Theology (600–1300)* (Chicago: Chicago UP, 1978)

———, *Reformation of Church and Dogma (1300–1700)* (Chicago: Chicago UP, 1984)

Pettegree, A. (ed.), *The Reformation World* (London: Routledge, 2000)

Potter, G.R., *Zwingli* (Cambridge: Cambridge UP, 1976)

Richard, J.W., *Philip Melanchthon: The Protestant Preceptor of Germany, 1497–1560* (reprint New York: Burt Franklin, 1974)

Ridley, J.G., *Nicholas Ridley: A Biography* (London: Longmans Green, 1957)

———, *Thomas Cranmer* (Oxford: Clarendon, 1962)

Sasse, H., *This is My Body: Luther's Contention for the Real Presence in the Sacrament of the Altar* (revised Australian edn, Adelaide: Lutheran Publishing House, 1977)

Schofield, J., *Philip Melanchthon and the English Reformation* (Aldershot: Ashgate, 2006)

———, *The Rise and Fall of Thomas Cromwell: Henry VIII's Most Faithful Servant* (Stroud: The History Press, 2008)

Schwiebert, E.G., *The Reformation* (Minneapolis: Fortress Press, 1996)

Scott, T. and Scribner, R. (eds), *The German Peasants' War: A History in Documents* (New Jersey: Humanities Press, 1994)

Scribner, R.W., *Popular Culture and Popular Movements in Reformation Germany* (London: Hambledon, 1988)

Spitta, P., *The Life of Bach* (3 vols, trans. Clara Bell and J. Fuller Maitland, London: Novello, 1899)

Spitz, L.P., *The Religious Renaissance of the German Humanists* (Cambridge, Mass.: Harvard UP, 1963)

Stayer, J., *The German Peasants' War and Anabaptist Community of Goods* (Montreal: McGill-Queen's UP, 1991)

Stephens, W., *The Theology of Huldrych Zwingli* (Oxford: Clarendon, 1986)

Thomson, J.A.F., *Popes and Princes, 1417–1517: Politics and Polity in the Late Medieval Church* (London: George Allen and Unwin, 1980)

Walker, W., *A History of the Christian Church* (4th edn, Edinburgh: T. and T. Clark, 1986)

Weikart, R., *From Darwin to Hitler: Evolutionary Ethics, Eugenics and Racism in Germany* (New York: Palgrave, 2004)

Index